DATE DUE

		WITHDRAWN	
			PRINTED IN U.S.A.

FAST AND
FABULOUS
DINNER
PARTIES

· · · · · ·

BOOKS BY MICHELE BRADEN

Fast and Flashy Hors d'Oeuvres
Fast and Fabulous Dinner Parties

FAST AND FABULOUS DINNER PARTIES

Michele Braden

Macmillan Publishing Company • *New York*

Maxwell Macmillan Canada • *Toronto*

Maxwell Macmillan International
New York • *Oxford* • *Singapore* • *Sydney*

Macmillan Publishing Company
866 Third Avenue, New York, NY 10022

Maxwell Macmillan Canada, Inc.
1200 Eglinton Avenue East, Suite 200
Don Mills, Ontario M3C 3N1

Macmillan Publishing Company is part of the
Maxwell Communication Group of Companies.

Library of Congress Cataloging-in-Publication Data
Braden, Michele.
    Fast and fabulous dinner parties / Michele Braden.
      p. cm.
    ISBN 0-02-514370-0
    1. Dinners and dining. 2. Entertaining. I. Title.
  TX737.B73 1991
  642'.4—dc20   90-49506   CIP

Macmillan books are available at special discounts for bulk purchases for sales
promotions, premiums, fund-raising, or educational use. For details, contact:

Special Sales Director
Macmillan Publishing Company
866 Third Avenue
New York, NY 10022

10 9 8 7 6 5 4 3 2 1
Printed in the United States of America

DEDICATION

. . . .

This labor of love is dedicated to my husband, Alan. His support, encouragement, and patience have been invaluable to me. Besides all of that, he has been a willing taste-tester. My parents, brother, and daughter have instilled in me a special sense of self and strength. As a child, my mother gave me free reign in the kitchen, teaching me that cooking and entertaining were fun, nurturing, and a place for unrestrained creativity, an expression of one's uniqueness. Also, when I was a child, my aunt opened up horizons, exposing me to new and exciting foods and the techniques for handling them. My father provided me with wonderful business ideas and an enthusiasm for life. I also dedicate this book to my grandmother, Anne Levy, who passed her gift for cooking on to me. And finally, I want to give special thanks to my agent, Hal Lockwood, who believed in me and my book.

Thank you!

CONTENTS

. . . .

ACKNOWLEDGMENTS

This book has been greatly enriched by the contributions, efforts, and talents of many. It was a joy to have worked with all of them.

The Wineries:
 Dry Creek Vineyard
 Freixenet Sparkling Wines
 R & J Cook Winery

The Flower, Vegetable, Cheese, Herb, and Wine People:
Dana McVey—a very talented landscape designer from Carmel, California. He was responsible for molding my material on flowers;
Rose Parr—a dedicated flower lover who provided me with a great deal of assistance;
TuttoBella—of Sand City, California, provided beautiful flowers and props for the photography;
Lavender & Thyme Nursery—of Aptos, California, provided magnificent herbs and edible flowers, as well as beautiful blooms;
Roth's Gourmet—of Carmel Valley, California, provided luscious cheeses and deli items for the photography;
Dalgety Produce, Inc.—of Salinas, California, provided an abundance of fresh vegetables and mountains of peeled garlic; and
Steve Schleusener—wine consultant, Creme Carmel Restaurant (Carmel, California), provided the wine recommendations.

Fabulous tablecloths for photography: Party Tables (Durham, North Carolina)
Props for photography: Macy's of California (Monterey, California)
The wonderful friends who provided me with invaluable assistance and/or loaned me their treasures for the photo sessions:
 Janet Gendelman
 Louise LaGue Punzi

Linda Weil

Sue Pius

Carolyn Crist

Jeanne Cooperrider

The Computer Guru: Sarge Furman

The Master Photographer: Grant Huntington (Monterey, California)

The Amazing Editor: Pam Hoenig—who made it all work!

INTRODUCTION

Dinner parties provide us with the ultimate opportunity to bring a bit of fantasy into our lives. They are a vehicle for pampering ourselves and those we care about. I think of them as fabulous escapes from our hectic, everyday existence. With all the pressures in today's world, the role of dinner parties is more vital than ever.

Fast and Fabulous Dinner Parties is for people who love to cook, entertain, dine, and just plain party! It is designed to charge your batteries and get your creative juices flowing. The intent is for these recipes and menus to build your confidence and inspire you to create variations of your own. That, after all, is what cooking is all about. Never again will you be stumped for a creative menu, an imaginative tablescape, or an attractive garnish. This book is especially for busy people who must be time-efficient. You will see how you can have and do it all, with flair!

Fast & Fabulous refers to my method of fearless and flamboyant cooking and entertaining. Viewed as a blueprint, it liberates Culinary Clones and Kitchen Martyrs. Culinary Clones follow recipes as if they were heaven-sent. They forget to use their own judgment and the rule that there are no absolutes in cooking. After all, we are dealing with an art form involving organic ingredients that are impossible to standardize. Have you ever seen two identical cloves of garlic or smelled onions of the exact same strength? *Fast and Fabulous* cooks involve every sense in the cooking process. Appearance, aroma, texture, sound, and taste are all essentials in the cooking process. Often I'm confronted with resistance when it comes to taste. People are afraid of ruining their appetites or waistlines. Wrong! I am talking about developing and sensitizing your palettes. Only a tiny taste, $1/4$ to $1/2$ teaspoon, is required. Kitchen Martyrs simply leave their organizational skills outside of the kitchen. Consequently, they end up being servants rather than star performers at their parties.

My *Fast & Fabulous* methodology is based on the simple principles of organization and advanced preparation. Intelligent and successful people rely on these two basic principles in every area of their professional lives, but for some unknown reason, discard them when it comes to cooking or entertaining. Why would you take time away from your guests to slice bread, unwrap a stick of butter, or make a sauce? Most of these tasks can be taken care of several hours in advance. Let's look at a simple detail such as bread. Slice it earlier in the day and wrap it in foil to keep it fresh, then warm before serving. If this is done while guests are there, not only have you taken time away from your primary role as host or hostess, but you've also created a needless mess in your kitchen. Setting the table and selecting serving pieces and wine glasses are vital to a fabulous dinner party and should be given great consideration. Take care of these items when there isn't much cooking to be done. For example, if there is time two days in advance, do it then, leaving only the flowers for the day of the party. This is the time to think of every possible detail. We have all been in the position of frantically scrounging for dessert plates or a serving spoon, trying to remain outwardly calm in front of guests, while the food is getting cold.

To further illustrate this point, consider whipping cream. How many times have you been enjoying good conversation and food, when you realize that you must race into the kitchen to whip cream for dessert? This task can easily be done a day in advance and refrigerated. Wine selections and your bar should be taken care of as soon as your menu is set. Racing to the liquor store the day of your party robs you of valuable time. The point is, there are precious few items that require last-minute attention.

Fast and Fabulous Dinner Parties is carefully designed to reinforce this methodology. Each menu is followed by a *Faster & Flashier Menu* or how to create magic in minutes. It is designed for all those times when you are faced with an extreme time-crunch, but still want to retain style. Next comes the party plan, a *Fast & Fabulous Timetable,* which gives a breakdown of all the major menu tasks and when they can be done, without sacrificing quality. Also, every recipe is followed by invaluable tips that may include:

Fast: How far in advance the dish can be prepared and refrigerated or frozen without sacrificing taste or quality.

Flashy: What to serve the dish with, and ideas for garnishing and presentation.

Fabulous: Alternatives and variations that will serve as stimulus to spur you on to your own creations.

Further: Innovative ways for handling leftovers.

My *Fast & Fabulous* methodology goes further. It is concerned with excellence and style in both food and ambiance. It views cooking and entertaining as valuable forms of personal expression, a living, three-dimensional art form, and an essential ingredient for a full life-style.

Fast and Fabulous Dinner Parties provides ideas for creating wonderful ambiance to surround your menus. It gives valuable tips for transforming your home into a magical setting. Each chapter covers one season and begins with an outline, *At a Glance,* providing an overview of that season. This introduces the entertaining style and covers everything from the food to ideas for creating the appropriate seasonal ambiance.

Speaking of flowers, they are not only a passion with me, but an essential ingredient for any successful party. Therefore, you will find a listing of some of my seasonal favorites starting on page 11. This will make it easier for you, whether you intend to plant or order from a florist.

Which brings me to another essential ingredient . . . fresh herbs. They are invaluable to any cook. If you have never grown herbs, you will be delighted by how cooperative they are. Whether you just have a sunny windowsill, a small patio, or a full-size garden, growing herbs brings pleasure and adds a wonderful dimension to your cooking. Besides flavoring food, there is no better way to garnish than with fresh herbs. In addition, you will save money.

Fast and Fabulous Dinner Parties is organized by the season. Food, cooking, and entertaining styles should reflect and celebrate the season. To fully understand this point, visualize a rich, hearty stew served on a hot summer night. Or worse yet, an icy cold slice of watermelon eaten in the rain or a saucy pot roast at a picnic.

When you fall in love with a menu for the "wrong" season, don't despair, adapt it. I call this process "seasonizing." For instance, the Spring Salmon Menu, starting on page 44, with some minor variation, makes a sensational summer menu. The hors d'oeuvre already works well for summer. The salad, however, requires some changes. Because asparagus is not a very good buy during the summer months, substitute blanched zucchini spears. Celery root may also be difficult—try grated daikon radish, jicama, and/or turnips. As for the entree, salmon is a great choice for summer, while the risotto needs "seasonizing." Fennel is scarce during summer, so I used chopped tomatillos along with minced red jalapeño chiles. The result: a fabulous new risotto that provides a wonderful contrast to the rich and delicately prepared salmon. Neither the vegetable nor dessert require any change. You can see how "seasonizing" creates exciting new dishes and innovative menus.

You will note that the chapters are further broken down into *Casual* and *Formal* menus within each season. This will assist you in rapidly locating the perfect menu to fit your needs. **All of the menus are designed for parties of eight.** I have found this number to be a good middle-ground. It is not too large a group for the average home to accommodate and is small enough to maintain intimacy. When you need to entertain a larger group, simply adjust the recipes as needed. Of course, for smaller parties the recipes can be reduced.

Now that you know what *Fast and Fabulous Dinner Parties* is, I want you to know what it is not. First of all, it is not "fast & tacky." It does not rely on gimmicks, or packaged or convenience items. It stresses high-quality, fresh ingredients. You will notice that the *Faster & Flashier* menus use some prepared items. I naturally assume that when shopping for these items you will be discriminating enough to select only the highest quality products. For example, when buying butter cookies, look for ones that are prepared with real butter, without colorings, preservatives, or artificial flavorings. This standard should be applied to any prepared item.

This book does not for a minute mean to insinuate that you will be able to throw a fabulous party without investing any effort. The old adage that anything worthwhile requires work is true. The complete party process should be a pleasure, from planning, to preparation, to party. What this book is about is how to approach a dinner party intelligently and with confidence, without wasting time or leaving tasks for the last minute, thereby sabotaging your efforts.

You will notice that I rely heavily on the food processor and utilize it whenever possible. It is one of the best ways to cut cooking time. I also view freezers as a real necessity. They cut chilling time in half. There is no greater convenience than to be able to pull out a scrumptious soup, sauce, entree, dessert, or hors d'oeuvre from the freezer.

I hope *Fast and Fabulous Dinner Parties* will serve as inspiration for many wonderful celebrations and bring much joy and happiness into your lives.

Explore and enjoy!

FAST AND FABULOUS DINNER PARTIES

• • • • • •

CHAPTER ONE

. . . .

Planning Your Dinner Party

Before we try to unravel the strategy for staging a successful dinner party, it is important to consider the role dinner parties play in today's society. There has always been great importance given to breaking bread with people, but in the 90s this activity has taken on a new meaning. In today's fast-paced, often impersonal world, it becomes necessary to exhibit only one side of our personalities, the serious, controlled adult. The stresses of everday family life can easily perpetuate this behavior at home. Also, in our big cities, filled with big companies, the individual can easily get lost. These conditions make it more important than ever to distinguish ourselves and express our individuality and for this the dinner party is a perfect vehicle.

Now, let's deal with strategy. Once you make the decision to give a party, you need to create a guest list. This is a challenge and could be considered an art in and of itself. It is essential not simply to repay social obligations—your party will lack effervescence. A guest list must balance personalities and professions. A group consisting of all introverts or brain surgeons is deadly. One of the most successful parties I have ever given stemmed from the fact that one of my guests was an introvert. I tried very hard to balance that and the results were electric. In terms of professions that were represented, they ranged from a psychic to a TV anchorman.

Next comes the menu selection. *Fast and Fabulous Dinner Parties* solves this problem for you. Designing a menu involves considering a great many factors. The season should shape the menu. Then pay close attention to drama and balance. By drama, I mean the sparkle, power, or impact of your dishes. When giving a party, we naturally want to dress up our food, homes, and ourselves for the occasion. Balance refers to the composition of the menu. It is important to compose all the elements, from the colors to the textures. Richness also plays a very important role. You do not want every dish to have cream or butter in it. If such attention to detail is difficult for you, hopefully after studying several of the menus you will develop a feel for creating your own. The last factors influencing your menu are your kitchen and home and the limitations they pose. It will be necessary to adjust the menu to suit your needs. For example, if your dining room comfortably seats six and you have almost no kitchen counter space, it is important to stay simple. Pare the menu down and invite only as many guests as can be comfortably entertained.

Now it is time to create a battle plan. *Fast and Fabulous Dinner Parties* to the rescue once again. Following each menu, you will find the *Fast & Fabulous Timetable,* which breaks the menu into manageable steps.

The *Fast & Fabulous Timetable* attempts to leave you with very little to do on the day of the party. It is amazing how much time last-minute details take. If possible, set the tables, arrange the flowers and seating, and set the serving pieces out the day before. On the day of the party, schedule time for rest and relaxation. A tired and haggard kitchen martyr cannot be a vivacious host or hostess.

The *Fast & Fabulous* entertainer makes everything appear easy and ensures that everyone has fun! This is the critical organization. Too many of us just do not know what can be done when. Most recipes leave you guessing by saying that the dish can be prepared in advance. How far in advance is critical. Many of you will be amazed to realize how easy this becomes when you give yourself the necessary advance time. If, for instance, you decide to have a party in three weeks, use each weekend to partially prepare and freeze several dishes. By the time of the party, the menu will have come together comfortably, allowing you the necessary time and energy to devote to all areas, including the ambiance and look of the table. If you follow the *Fast & Fabulous* suggestions, you will find that the entire process is pleasurable.

After all, when tackling any major project professionally, you would not begin to think you should be able to finish it in one day. Why then do we feel that we should be able to awaken on Saturday morning, shop, cook, clean, and be prepared to entertain guests? What an overwhelming task! By the time your guests arrive, you're ready to faint, not party!

I'm convinced that the fear factor associated with entertaining all stems from something so simple as not having necessary organizational skills. Once you put those skills into practice, you will find that staging a dinner party no longer seems like the impossible dream. Automatically, your confidence level is raised and no matter how busy you are, you see that there is still time for celebration.

It is important to consider your home and its role in a successful party. It is essential to pay close attention to comfort and ambiance. Realistically, fun becomes almost impossible when comfort is not considered. Seating and lighting are essential to comfort. If you have ever been packed into a dinner table with the elbows of those on either side jabbing you all evening, you know what I am talking about. Good seating facilitates the free flow of conversation.

Lighting is every bit as important. Bad lighting, whether it is too dim or bright, destroys the ambiance you have worked so hard to create. You can transform a cold, stark space into a warm, dramatic, or romantic room. Candles are an inexpensive but effective way to create lighting magic. It is amazing to see how good lighting sparks personality changes and social interaction.

Flowers and arrangements of fresh greens are invaluable props for creating ambiance. They symbolize the celebration of nature and provide a festive aura. If budget is a concern, relax, flowers need not be costly. Most of us have greens or flowers in the garden or on the patio that we can pick. In the fall and winter it's fun to take walks and collect interesting dried weeds and greenery for arrangements. As for flowers, if your garden is not in bloom, ask a friend. Sharing flowers is something most gardeners take delight in. Purchasing exotic flowers and using them individually to create stark and dramatic arrangements is another approach.

Be sure to include the entrance to your home when decorating for a party. This instantly welcomes your guests and establishes a tone. When decorating, I also give as much attention to my kitchen and bathrooms as to my living and dining rooms.

Keep in mind that the rooms in which you stage a party play an important role in establishing the desired mood. For example, the family room has a relaxed warmth, whereas a living room projects greater formality and elegance. If you need to use a certain room, but don't want the party to take on the feeling of that particular room, work with your props to create the mood you want. Dress up family rooms with candles and flowers, and try using tinted bulbs in the lights. Living rooms can be given a more casual feel by placing pillows on the floor and arranging the furniture in a more intimate manner. Formal pieces can be removed. And don't forget your yard—outdoor parties can be either casual or elegant and offer the opportunity to turn an open space into a wonderful party set.

THE CHEF'S PALATE

• •

Before you proceed to the first dinner party, it is absolutely crucial for you to understand some of my flavor prejudices. This is just as important as knowing the personal bias of a movie critic or restaurant reviewer.

OK, let's start with the hors d'oeuvres. It is a natural starting point. This is the crucial point of a party. Its role is awesome! This is when you make your first impressions on your guests. It is also an ice breaker. Most of us are all too aware of those first few awkward minutes when the party momentum needs to be jump-started. Interesting and impressive hors d'oeuvres are called for. Those adorable little cubes of cheese speared with colored frilled toothpicks do not exactly fit the bill. Delicate miniature pastry tartlets, pâtés, magnificently marinated seafood, exotically flavored dipping sauces with crisp, garlicky melbas, or pita chips, not generic chips, do rise to the occasion. I always lean toward offering my guests choices. This means instead of preparing one hors d'oeuvre, often I will do three. Remember, the perfect hors d'oeuvre teases the palate, never satisfying, always arousing the appetite—they are "palate pleasers and teasers." I am definitely of the opinion that this can be a party maker or breaker. Be flamboyant; set the tone for the evening.

As for the rest of the meal, all of the dishes should make strong and exciting statements. Unusual, luxurious, and enticing is the goal. As for the pacing, it should be leisurely, allowing everyone the opportunity to truly enjoy the food and company. Speaking of food, I only have one rule. Any discussion of calories, fat, and/or diets is forbidden. End of subject, case closed. There is an appropriate time and place for everything. Guilt has no place at a party.

Another prejudice of mine is against hosts and hostesses who are unable to be at the table. You know the types. They are locked away in the kitchen madly trying to keep up with the dishes. The remedy is simple—hire help. This is a necessity and need not be out of reach for anyone's budget. If yours happens to be limited, use your kids, their friends, and/or neighborhood teenagers. However, you must let anyone whom you employ know what is expected. I have been to many parties where the hostess had plenty of professional help, but still was busy doing God-only-knows-what! Don't fall into this trap.

Moving right along, I like desserts that are not very sweet. If you enjoy yours sweeter, simply adjust the sugar.

Now for portion size, my culinary style values abundance. That does not mean that I am waging a one-woman war on anorexia. I want my food to look gracious and generous. I do not want it to appear as if each lettuce leaf is counted. It is a terrible feeling to be at a party and be afraid to take a decent serving. It is always better to have too much than not enough, which is that old adage most of us have heard from our mothers and grandmothers. What wisdom!

You will rapidly notice that I gravitate toward big flavors. I would be the first to categorize myself as a flavor junky. Please adjust the seasoning to your own palate.

Texture is vital to good food. I balance the textures in each dish I prepare, as well as in the entire menu. The perfect example of poor textural composition is the standard Thanksgiving dinner. Almost everything is mashed or pureed. How boring! Now you are ready to go forth and create parties.

THE COOK'S SHELF

• •

Just as a painter needs a full palette, so does the home cook and entertainer need a well-stocked pantry. These are the items that will help create gastronomical ecstasy for your family and friends, whether preparing for a fabulous party or a midweek dinner.

Don't panic over cost; it's not necessary to purchase everything at once. Collect these items gradually and be a smart shopper. Don't go to the priciest food boutique. Hunt around at discount and import stores and take advantage of sales.

Assorted Dried Herbs and Spices
- apple pie spice
- bay leaves
- basil
- cardamon (ground)
- caraway seeds
- celery seeds
- chili powder
- chilies (whole, red)
- cinnamon (ground and stick)
- cumin (ground and seeds)
- curry powder
- dillweed
- fennel seeds
- fines herbes
- Italian herbs
- mace
- marjoram
- mint leaves
- mustard (prepared—Dijon and coarse ground—and seeds)
- nutmeg (whole)
- oregano
- paprika, sweet Hungarian
- peppercorns (Szechuan, white, pink, green, and black)
- poultry seasoning
- pumpkin pie spice
- rosemary

- sage leaves
- tarragon
- thyme (leaves and ground)

Assorted Oils
- avocado oil
- canola oil
- grapeseed oil
- olive oil (extra virgin and pure)
- peanut oil
- sesame oil
- walnut oil

Assorted Olives
- Spanish olives
- black olives
- Greek (calamata) or Italian olives

Toasted Nuts and Seeds
To toast nuts and seeds, preheat the oven to 350°F. Place the nuts or seeds on an ungreased cookie sheet in a single layer and set them in the oven until they are fragrant and taste toasty, about 15 to 20 minutes. Store them in an airtight container in the freezer to prevent them from becoming rancid.

- almonds
- pecans
- pine nuts
- pistachios
- poppy seeds
- pumpkin seeds
- sesame seeds
- sunflower seeds
- walnuts

Assorted Marinated or Pickled Items
- capers
- marinated artichoke hearts
- pickled ginger
- pickled mango
- Greek pepperoncini

Assorted Rices, Grains, and Beans
- arborio rice
- basmati rice
- long grain white rice
- short grain white rice
- wild rice
- bulgur
- couscous
- pastas (assorted, dried)
- polenta (regular and/or instant)
- black beans (dried)
- garbanzo beans (canned or dried)
- great northern beans (dried)

Assorted Sauces

- barbecue, Chinese-style (canned or in jars)
- hoisin sauce, Chinese-style (canned or in jars)
- mango chutney
- mayonnaise
- plum sauce, Chinese-style (canned or in jars)
- soy sauce
- tonkatsu sauce (Japanese-style Worcestershire)
- Worcestershire

Assorted Staples

- all-purpose flour
- baking powder
- baking soda
- brown sugar, light and dark
- cake flour
- cornmeal
- granulated sugar
- powdered (confectioners') sugar
- unflavored gelatin

Assorted Vinegars

- balsamic
- cider
- raspberry
- rice
- sherry wine
- tarragon
- white and red wine

Wines for Cooking

- dry vermouth
- marsala
- Madeira
- merlot and/or dry red
- port
- sherry (cream, dry, and regular)
- white wine

Cheeses
(Stored in freezer)

- feta
- mizithra (a Greek grating cheese that can be used in place of Parmesan or Romano)
- Parmesan
- Romano
- teleme

Miscellaneous

- anchovies (tinned and paste)
- black fungus (dried)
- garlic (fresh)
- green chilies (whole, canned)
- onions (fresh)
- pancetta (stored in freezer)
- porcini mushrooms (dried)
- potatoes (fresh)
- prosciutto (stored in freezer)
- shiitake mushrooms (dried)

- sun-dried tomatoes
- tomatoes (canned or fresh)
- tuna, canned

THE COOK'S HERB GARDEN

. . . .

Fresh herbs add a lovely dimension to cooking and food presentation. Herbs provide an excellent way to keep in touch with the seasons and celebrate them. I can't imagine not having an herb garden. Trust me, you don't need a green thumb. Herbs grow like weeds. If you're still not convinced that you can do it alone, visit a library or bookstore, they're loaded with good books on growing and preserving herbs. As for the required space, it can be a sunny window, an apartment patio, or an entire garden.

Once your herbs start to thrive, the fun begins. It's time for you to start experimenting. You'll be thrilled by the limitless possibilities for matching herbs with different foods. In terms of garnishing, the results are just as exciting. Use fresh herbs in three different ways for garnishing: minced, sprigs, and blossoms.

You can also preserve your surpluses. The most common method is to dry them by hanging a bunch, tied with string, upside-down in a warm, dry room, out of direct sunlight. Placed in olive oil, wines, and vinegars, they infuse the liquid with their essence. The liquid then becomes a delicious way to season food. When bottled attractively, they make lovely gifts and are decorative when displayed in the kitchen. Fresh herbs can also be frozen either chopped or straight from the garden.

The following is a list of popular herbs to grow:

Perennials

Anise—A dill-like plant with a licorice scent and taste. The seeds are used in cooking. The leaves are very delicate and resemble dill; they are used raw in salads and for garnishing.

Bay laurel—An evergreen tree with small yellowish flowers. Use the dried leaves to flavor foods, to garnish, and for medicine. Add cut branches to floral arrangements.

Chervil—A part of the herb combo that we purchase dried called *fines herbes*; but not yet a superstar herb. Looks like parsley but much more delicate and lacelike. Has an aniselike fragrance and its flavor is aniselike with a hint of pepper. Easy to grow. Delicious in salads, vinaigrettes, compound butter, and butter sauces, and to season fish.

Chives—A cluster of narrow green hollow leaves, about 8 inches high, with pink to purplish flowers that resemble balls. The taste and smell is a combination of onions and leeks. Use blooms for garnishes and in bouquets. Minced leaves can be used, fresh or dried, to season and garnish.

Garlic—What our grandparents knew, we rediscovered, and now revere garlic for its healthful properties in combatting high blood pressure. A member of the lily family, garlic has dark green foliage and pink flowers. When the leaves are dry, the garlic is ready to be harvested. Use leaves as you would use sorrel or spinach. Use blossoms as a garnish and the cloves, fresh or dried, as a seasoning.

Lavender—A beautiful shrub used in landscaping. Has spikelike flowers with long narrow lavender flowers. Used in floral arrangements, as well as fragrance and beauty products. Use flowers sparingly in soups, sorbets, jellies, ice creams, or with fowl.

Leeks—A member of the lily family with a mild, onionlike flavor. Once were known as "the poor man's asparagus," but have become expensive. The leaves grow about two feet tall and are flat and solid, not hollow, like an onion. Use both leaves and bulb in cooked dishes. Has a very ornamental white or lavender bloom.

Lemon verbena—Grows up to ten feet tall and is deciduous. Use lemon-scented leaves fresh in teas, fruit drinks, and perfumes.

Mint—A lush, low, spreading plant available in orange, apple, spearmint, and peppermint varieties. Use leaves, fresh or dried, to flavor both sweet and savory dishes and to garnish.

Onions—A very easy-to-grow shallow-rooted bulb. Use both the bulb and green tops raw and/or cooked in a wide variety of dishes. Use the blossoms as a garnish or in floral arrangements.

Oregano—A small shrub about two feet tall that has tiny oblong leaves and purple blossoms. Use leaves fresh or dried as a seasoning and cuttings in floral arrangements.

Rosemary—A small woody shrub with tiny spiky leaves and purple flowers. Works well in landscaping. Use leaves, fresh or dried, as seasoning and cuttings in floral arrangements and as a garnish. Has a sweet smell and a pleasantly bitter flavor.

Sage—An aromatic and hardy plant with a woody stem and thick, soft, velvety leaves. Usually blooms after the second year, in June, with blue, spiky flowers. Attains a height of about two feet. Leaves change color with the season. Use leaves, fresh or dried, to season and garnish.

Shallot—A member of the lily family with a mild, onionlike flavor. Use the bulb, fresh or dried, as with garlic. Has green foliage similar to chives and green onions. They rarely flower, but grow to a height of about eight inches.

Tarragon—An airy plant with delicate white flowers. Use narrow, lance-shaped leaves fresh or dried. Has a flavor slightly reminiscent of anise. Use cuttings in arrangements.

Thyme—A slender, woody stemmed plant that grows about eight inches tall. Makes a good ground cover or border in landscaping. Has lavender blooms in early summer. Use the very small leaves, fresh or dried. Has a pleasant, earthy flavor. Use cuttings and flowers to garnish. Lemon thyme is a variety with, naturally, a marvelous lemony flavor.

Winter savory—A dainty, elegant herb with beauty, fragrance, and flavor. Has a white or purplish blossom. Use leaves fresh or dried to season anything from soups to pork.

Yarrow—A pleasant-looking, leafy plant with one of the longest flowering seasons (June to November). Even though it is often thought of as a weed, it makes a lovely addition to the garden, and in floral arrangements. Depending on growing conditions, flowers are grayish white to pink.

Annuals

Dill—A delicate, airy plant with clusters of tiny yellow flowers at the end of a slender, three-foot stem. Use cuttings in floral arrangements; use the threadlike leaves fresh or dried to season anything from salads to fish. Every part of the plant, except the roots, can be used for seasoning.

Fennel—An exquisite fernlike plant, the bulb is used raw or cooked, and is similar to celery, except that it has a slight anise flavor. Use the flowers and leaves as a garnish and in floral arrangements. Use the seeds, dried, in a wide variety of dishes, from sweet to savory.

French sorrel—A very hardy plant with bittersweet leaves that have a lemonlike flavor. Use leaves fresh, either raw or cooked, to season soups or sauces, or in place of spinach or chard.

Nasturtium—Often thought of simply as a flowering plant. Has a joyful look, with smooth, round leaves and flowers ranging in color from yellow to dark red. Grows like a weed, reseeds itself, and produces more flowers when not fertilized. Every part, except the root, can be used fresh. Leaves, stems, and flowers can be tossed into salads, Chopped leaves and stems can be substituted for watercress. The peppery flavor is reminiscent of that of a radish. Use the flowers for garnishing.

Parsley—One of the most common herbs, it has a fresh, clean flavor. There are two varieties, one with curly and one with flat leaves. The latter has more flavor and vitamins. Can be used raw or cooked to season anything from salads to soups.

Summer savory—A dainty, pink-flowered, elegant herb with beauty, fragrance, and flavor. Use tiny leaves fresh or dried as a flavor enhancer. Will not mask other flavors.

Sweet basil—One of the most popular herbs. It is a compact, bushy plant with white blossoms, that grows to a height of about eighteen inches. Use leaves fresh or dried to impart a very pronounced flavor to sauces, vinaigrettes, soups, fish, meat, poultry, seafood, and vegetables.

Sweet marjoram—A member of the mint family, it has a pleasant aromatic bitterness. Very attractive plant with a dainty quality. Has a smooth texture and blooms are a pinkish white. Use leaves fresh or dried (the flavor is milder when dried) to season soups, sauces, poultry, and vegetables.

Tarragon—Buy only the French variety. An airy plant with delicate flowers that makes a good winter potted plant. Use the leaves both fresh and dried. Used to season soups, vinaigrettes, cream sauces, fish, poultry, lamb, or vegetable dishes.

THE COOK'S FLOWERS

· · · · · · · · · · · · · · · · · · · ·

Flowers are an essential ingredient of any party. They, almost magically, transform a home into a festive environment. I use them everywhere, even as garnishes. Whenever flowers come directly in contact with food, it is important that you be certain they are nontoxic. This section is designed to assist you in planning your flower arrangements, garnishes, and even your garden. It is an absolute joy to be able to grow your own flowers.

Flowers for Arrangements

Amaryllis (Amaryllis belladonna)
SEASON: Late summer through fall

Available in many colors. It has six to twelve blossoms at the head of a leafless stalk. Usually forced indoors in winter. The amaryllis arranges nicely with poppies and irises.

Anthurium (Anthurium andraeanum)
SEASON: All year

A deep red, waxy, heart-shaped flower with a whitish tail coming from its center on a leafless stalk. A long-lasting exotic flower.

Aster (Aster novi-belgii)
SEASON: Summer and fall

Available in vibrant pink, purple, and lavender. Their petals surround a bright yellow center. A long-lasting flower that arranges well with zinnias, dahlias, lilies, and irises. A wire may be needed to hold the stem.

Baby's breath (Gypsophila paniculata)
SEASON: Summer

A twiggy-looking plant that is covered with tiny white blossoms. An excellent filler plant, also good for drying. Nontoxic; can be in direct contact with food.

Bird-of-paradise (Strelitzia reginae)
SEASON: All year (best in cool season)

A long-lasting exotic flower. A tall straight stalk with a purple and orange bloom resembling a bird's head.

Camellia (Camellia japonica)
SEASON: Fall to winter

Nontoxic; can be in direct contact with food. Available in wide range of colors. Leaves are dark, glossy green.

Carnation (*Dianthus caryophyllus* hybrids)
SEASON: All year

Come in miniature and standard sizes in a range of colors. They are long-lasting, always available, and inexpensive.

Celosia (*Celosia argentea*)
SEASON: Summer through fall

Available in red, yellow, and orange. A long-lasting flower that is feathery and oval in shape.

Chrysanthemum (*Chrysanthemum morifolium*)
SEASON: Fall

Like the carnation, they are available in many, many colors and inexpensively priced. Their sizes range from one inch across to the large pompoms that are five to six inches across.

Cornflower (*Centaurea cyanus*)
SEASON: Spring through fall

Available in pink, white, and blue with a thin, delicate stem. The leaves are gray-green in color. They are not a long-lasting flower. Nontoxic; can be in direct contact with food.

Cosmos (*Cosmos bipinnatus*)
SEASON: Summer through fall

Available in red, yellow, orange, white, and rose. It has large petals that surround a yellow center. Not a long-lasting flower.

Cymbidium orchids (*Cymbidium orchis*)
SEASON: Late winter to late spring

Available in a variety of colors. It will have many blossoms on a long stem.

Daffodil (*Narcissus*)
SEASON: Late winter through spring

They are a fragrant flower, available in yellow and white. The trumpet-shaped flower is on a firm stem with long, upright, slender leaves.

Dahlia (*Dahlia* hybrids)
SEASON: Summer through fall

Available in a variety of colors except for blue. They are long-lasting and look lovely alone or mixed with gladiolus, asters, and chrysanthemums.

Feverfew (*Chrysanthemum parthenium*)
SEASON: All year
  They come in white and are very fragrant.

Forsythia (*Forsythia intermedia*)
SEASON: Late winter through spring
  Holds a cluster of little yellow flowers on a stem. Mixes well with your spring-blooming flowers.

Freesia (*Freesia* hybrids)
SEASON: Spring
  They have a beautiful scent and are available in many colors.

Gerbera daisy (*Gerbera jamesonii*)
SEASON: All year
  Available in a variety of colors, except for blue. They are, as their name suggests, a daisylike flower that lasts four to five days.

Gladiolus (*Gladiolus* hybrids)
SEASON: Spring through fall
  Available in a variety of colors. They are a long-lasting flower. The flowers open one at a time on a strong extending spike.

Hibiscus (*Hibiscus moscheutos*)
SEASON: Spring to summer
  A shrub with deep green leaves and large single or double tropical flowers in pink, red, or white. Nontoxic; can come into direct contact with food.

Iris (*Iris reticulata*)
SEASON: All year
  Available in shades of white, lavender, and blue. They are very short-lived.

Johnny-jump-up (*Viola tricolor*)
SEASON: Spring
  Look like mini-pansies. Available in blue, or in mix of colors, including lavender, yellow, mauve, apricot, and red. Resows itself profusely. Nontoxic; can come into direct contact with food.

Larkspur (*Consolida ambigus*)
SEASON: Spring through summer
  Available in white, dark blue, and lavender, it bears a stalk that is covered with flowers. It arranges well with lilies, daisies, and snapdragons for a country garden look.

Lilac *(Syringa vulgaris)*

SEASON: All year

Available in blue, lavender, purple, and white. Masses of tiny blossoms on a woody stem with heart-shaped leaves. Nontoxic; can be in direct contact with food.

Lily *(Lilium)*

SEASON: All year (peaks in spring)

Available in every color except purple and blue. They have a royal look to them. Beware of its pollen; it can damage clothing.

Lily-of-the-Nile *(Agapanthus africanus)*

SEASON: Midsummer to early fall

Available in blue and white. There are no leaves on this long stalk. The flower is dramatic and bold, nice for a contemporary setting.

Marguerite daisy *(Chrysanthemum frutescens)*

SEASON: All year

Available in yellow and white. Before arranging, remove foliage.

Marigold *(Tagetes)*

SEASON: Summer through fall

Available in pale yellow through gold. Hardy, trouble-free plants with dense, round flowers with tall or short stems. Many have strong scents; make sure to get the odorless varieties. Nontoxic; can come into direct contact with food.

Pansy *(Viola cornuta)*

SEASON: Spring through summer

A five-petal flat flower in white, blue, yellow, pink, and purple with dark centers. Have sweet scents.

Peruvian lily *(Alstroemeria)*

SEASON: May to midsummer

Available in pink, yellow, red, apricot, rose, and rust. A long-lasting flower.

Poppy *(Papaver rhoeas)*

SEASON: Spring through summer

Blossoms are 2 inches or more across, held on slender stems with short leaves, and come in red, pink, salmon, orange, white, or scarlet, or bicolored. Nontoxic; can come in direct contact with food.

Protea (*Protea*)
SEASON: All year

The flower sets on a woody stalk with petals that resemble a pinecone and are prickly at the ends like an artichoke. They come in many colors.

Rose (*Rosa* hybrids)
SEASON: All year

Available in a variety of colors. Fragrant, beautiful alone or as mixers. It is a good idea to cut their stems under water for longer life. Nontoxic; can be in direct contact with food.

Snapdragon (*Antirrhinum majus*)
SEASON: Spring through early summer

Bell-shaped blooms held on a tall, narrow stem, in the full range of colors. Provides an excellent vertical accent in flower arrangements.

Statice (*Limonium*)
SEASON: All year

Available in yellow, lavender, pink, white, and purple. They hold their color and are good for drying.

Stock (*Matthiola incana*)
SEASON: Spring through summer

A very fragrant flower, available in many colors with long, thin gray-green leaves. Flowers are vertical clusters. They are fairly long-lasting and great alone in arrangements or mixed with almost any other flower.

Tuberose (*Polianthes tuberosa*)
SEASON: Summer through fall

These have a very sweet odor. Their white, waxy flower looks like a cluster of stars.

Tulip (*Tulipa*)
SEASON: Winter through spring

They come in a variety of colors. Purchase them as buds for a flower lasting five to eight days.

Windflower (*Anemone coronaria*)
SEASON: Early spring to early fall

Available in vibrant colors of red, purple, pink, lavender, and white. Enjoy these while you can as they are not long-lived. They are on a leafless stem.

Zinnia (*Zinnia elegans*)

SEASON: Late summer to early fall

Various colors are available and they will last up to a week. They combine nicely with asters, chrysanthemums, irises, or statice for an informal country bouquet.

Green Foliage for Arrangements

Coast redwood (*Sequoia sempervirens*)

SEASON: All year

Flat, green, featherlike leaves that grow out from the stem.

Evergreen huckleberry (*Vaccinium ovatum*)

SEASON: All year

Dark lush green leaves with white or pinkish flowers in March to May. Berries are black and edible.

Galax (*Galax urceolata*)

SEASON: All year

A shiny heart-shaped leaf that turns a beautiful bronze color in the fall.

Ivy (*Hedera*)

SEASON: All year

Thick, leathery, heart-shaped leaves that grow on a woody vine.

Japanese aralia (*Fatsia japonica*)

SEASON: All year

Dark green, fanlike leaves that give a tropical appearance. They have a very large leaf, are nontoxic, and are very effective to use with food.

Leatherleaf fern (*Rumohra adiantiformis*)

SEASON: All year

Triangular, leafy, and glossy green. Lasts a long time in arrangements.

Lemon (*Gaultheria shallon*)

SEASON: All year

The leaves are long and a bright glossy green.

Ruscus (*Ruscus aculeatus*)

SEASON: All year

Deep, dark, waxy green foliage. Leaves are small.

Silver dollar *(Eucalyptus polyanthemos)*
SEASON: All year
   Leaves are green or gray and round or oval. The leaves cover a woody, barklike stem.

Silver tree *(Leucodendron argenteum)*
SEASON: All year
   Silvery white, silky leaves that densely cover the branches.

Umbrella pine *(Sciadopitys verticillata)*
SEASON: All year
   Glossy, dark green needles grow along branch ends and spoke out like on the wheel of a bicycle.

Decorating with Flowering Potted Plants

Azalea *(Rhododendron)*
SEASON: Winter through spring
   Small dark green leaf covered with delicate red, pink, orange, or salmon blossoms. Can also be cut and used in arrangements.

Chrysanthemum *(Chrysanthemum morifolium)*
SEASON: All year
   A sturdy upright plant with large blooms in many colors. Will last three to four weeks indoors. Keep soil moist. Can also be cut and used in arrangements.

Coleus *(Coleus hybridus)*
SEASON: Winter
   Colorful foliage. Has a tropical look.

Cyclamen *(Cyclamen persicum)*
SEASON: All year
   Available in crimson, red, salmon, purple, or white. Their bloom is on a leafless stem with green kidney-shaped leaves at the base. They like cool nighttime temperatures.

Hydrangea *(Hydrangea macrophylla)*
SEASON: Winter to spring
   Large green leaf. Flowers come in white, pink, or blue. Long-lasting. Flowers can also be cut and used in arrangements, fresh or dried.

Kalanchoe *(Kalanchoe blossfeldiana)*

SEASON: All year

Available in many colors. Their leaves come from the stem and are thick, dark green. The flower blooms above the leaves in a thick cluster.

Narcissus *(Narcissus)*

SEASON: Winter through spring

Small white, yellow, or orange flowers on an upright stem.

Poinsettia *(Euphorbia pulcherrima)*

SEASON: Winter

Large green leaves with inconspicuous yellow flowers surrounded by colorful red, yellow, white, or pink petallike bracts.

Snapweed or touch-me-not *(Impatiens balsamina)*

SEASON: Summer

Colorful flowers in white, pink, rose, lilac, and red. An erect plant. Nontoxic; can be in direct contact with food.

Tulip *(Tulipa)*

SEASON: Winter through spring

Delicate stem in a variety of bright colors. Short-lived indoors. Purchase with the buds tight.

CHAPTER TWO

. . . .

Terms and Techniques

ACIDULATED WATER
Water that has vinegar or lemon juice added to it. This is done to prevent certain fruits and vegetables from discoloring when placed in it.

ANCHO CHILES
Sometimes called *poblano* or *pasilla.* They can be found fresh or dried, and have a rich, herbal, earthy, usually mild flavor. When fresh, they are glossy green and resemble a somewhat flattened bell pepper. When dried they are dark red, almost black.

ARBORIO RICE
Italian short grain rice used for making risotto; can substitute short grain pearl rice.

BALSAMIC VINEGAR
A mild, mellow Italian vinegar with a slightly sweet flavor. Can be found in gourmet specialty shops or markets that carry imported items.

BARBECUE SAUCE (CHINESE)
A thick, full-flavored sauce found in the Asian section of supermarkets. Use as a seasoning in marinades and sauces, or brush directly on foods and barbecue or bake. Refrigerate indefinitely.

BLANCHING VEGETABLES
Use this process to cook fully, partially, or just to soften vegetables; the cooking times varying with the state of doneness desired. For instance, to loosen the skin of a tomato, blanch it for only a few seconds. To blanch them, vegetables are placed a large pot of boiling salted water. Then they

are removed from the pot and either used immediately or placed in ice water or under cold running water. This is referred to as *refreshing vegetables.* It stops the cooking process and locks in the vegetable's color and nutrients. This is a very practical technique that allows you to prepare in advance without overcooking. Restaurants commonly use this technique.

BULGUR
Cracked toasted wheat found in supermarkets or health food stores. Cook like rice or just soak in water until it softens, and use in salads.

CALAMATA OLIVES
Cured Greek black olives. Fabulous but salty flavor.

CAPERS
The unopened flavor buds of the prickly caperbush plant. It grows on the mountain slopes bordering the Mediterranean Sea in Italy, Spain, and southern Greece. They are purchased in brine and are found in the pickle or import section of most supermarkets. I recommend rinsing them before using, for best results.

CARAMELIZING SUGAR
Place the sugar in a heavy saucepan over medium-low heat until the sugar is completely dissolved, while holding the handle and swirling frequently. Increase the heat to medium-high and cover with a tight-fitting lid for 1 to 2 minutes, until the mixture boils and has thick bubbles, then uncover and cook until it turns a light golden caramel color, swirling the pan frequently. Remove the pan from the heat and continue to swirl until the syrup turns a rich, deep caramel color. Place the saucepan over a pan of cold water until the caramel cools slightly; this will prevent it from turning too dark. Do not let it harden. At this point, if necessary, the pan can be placed over very low heat to maintain a liquid consistency. A word of caution: never let your skin come in contact with hot caramel—it burns instantly.

CHÈVRE CHEESE
A rich, herbal French-style goat cheese. It is very expensive. Often, feta cheese can be substituted.

CHINESE BLACK FUNGUS
Also known as *wood ears*. Until very recently it was only available in dried form. When rehydrated it has almost no flavor, but it provides a crunchy texture and black color. To rehydrate black fungus, place it in a small bowl and let it sit, covered with water, until it softens and expands. This will take about 30 minutes. To speed up this process, soften it in a pot of boiling water. When used fresh, it has a delicate, earthy flavor. In folklore, it is prized for its healthful properties, expecially in preventing heart disease. I like to use it in rich menus to help balance the fats. It is my insurance policy against cholesterol and falls into the category of "it couldn't hurt."

CITRUS ZEST
The flavorful colored part of the citrus rind, not the bitter white portion. To remove the zest, use a vegetable peeler or a zester that can be found anyplace that handles gourmet gadgets.

CORNICHONS
Small French sour pickles.

COUSCOUS
Moroccan pasta (medium-grain semolina).

DEGLAZE
Refers to adding liquid to a hot, degreased cooking pan after sautéing or roasting food in it. The liquid is brought to a boil to capture all the flavor from the remaining brown bits and juices, which should be vigorously scraped. Use this liquid as a sauce or add to a final sauce.

DEGREASE
Degreasing removes the fat from cooked liquids. One of the easiest methods is to refrigerate the item overnight. The next morning you will find a layer of solidified fat that you can easily remove. To remove fat immediately, put ice cubes in the pan or pot with the liquid. The fat will cling to the ice and rise to the top. It is easier if you are able to transfer the liquid to a smaller bowl and then add the ice cubes.

Eggs

It seems as if there's always a new food villain. Currently the focus has been on eggs contaminated by the salmonella bacteria. This is of greater concern to pregnant women (because of the risk to the fetus), the elderly, and people already weakened by serious illness or whose immune systems are suppressed. According the United States Department of Agriculture, the chances of a healthy person being affected are extremely small. They do, however, recommend not eating homemade foods containing raw or lightly cooked eggs. These foods range from mayonnaise to ice cream. The same items are risk-free when commercially prepared because they are pasteurized, which kills the bacteria.

It is very important to follow the safe food handling practices listed below when using eggs:

- Buy only Grade A or AA eggs from a reputable market that keeps them under refrigeration. Open the carton to make sure the eggs are clean and crack free. Do not purchase them if the expiration date has passed.
- Make sure you store your eggs in the refrigerator at a temperature no higher than 40°F. Use them before the expiration date. Once they are hard-cooked, they should be used within one week. Leftover yolks and whites should be used within four days.
- When cooking, eggs should not be left at room temperature for more than two hours.
- Always wash your hands, utensils, and work surfaces with hot, soapy water when working with raw eggs.

You will find that some of my recipes could pose the risk of salmonella. However, the recipes are so delicious and the risk so small that I could not eliminate them. Harold McGee, the author of *The Curious Cook*, provides a microwave method for eliminating salmonella that you might want to look into. The bottom line is that the decision to make any of these dishes is yours, but it is important to be informed and to take into consideration the health of the people who will be enjoying your food.

Escarole

Also known as *Batavia endive*. A delightful green that can be used any way spinach is used. Has a fibrous texture and a slightly bitter flavor.

Flash freeze

A technique for freezing delicate foods and for conserving space. It allows you to store foods in plastic bags, rather than on trays. Place the item unwrapped on a cookie sheet or tray and freeze until firm. Then transfer them to plastic bags or containers and store in the freezer.

Fermented black beans

These have an intense salty flavor and contribute a rich, earthy flavor when used as a seasoning. Also referred to as *salted black beans* or *Chinese black beans*. Can be found in Asian markets or in the Asian section of supermarkets. Refrigerate indefinitely.

Fresh ginger

A pungent root used as a seasoning. It is also recognized as having many healthful properties, ranging from a digestive aid to an anticarcinogen. Can be refrigerated only for about a week before it begins to mold. To preserve it in the freezer, store whole or chopped in a plastic bag or container. To store in the refrigerator, put it in a jar of sherry or rice vinegar, whole or chopped. It can be stored this way for at least six months.

Green peppercorns

Immature pepper berries with less power and a more herbal flavor than mature black peppercorns. Purchase packed in brine or freeze-dried. Rinsing the brine-packed peppercorns in water before use is optional.

Gruyère cheese

A rich and nutty-flavored Swiss cheese.

Handling chiles

It is advisable to wear plastic gloves when working with chiles to prevent them from burning your skin. It is important not to touch any part of your body, especially your eyes, after touching chiles. Always wash your hands after handling them.

Hoisin sauce

A prepared Chinese sauce with a very thick consistency. Refer to *barbecue sauce* as it is used in the same manner. A great way to achieve bold flavors without adding fats or lots of calories.

Instant-read meat thermometer

A small, thin thermometer that is inserted into meat or poultry to check for doneness and almost instantly provides the temperature. It is not left in like the more common thicker variety that leaves a larger hole and conducts heat, causing whatever you are cooking to cook at two different rates.

INSTANTIZED FLOUR

This processed flour offers hope to all those afflicted with lumpy sauces. It can be whisked into any liquid or sauce and it never fails to dissolve and thicken.

KIRSCH

A cherry liqueur.

LEMON GRASS

An Asian seasoning that has the appearance of a grass. It is gray-green with stalks about two feet long. Use the fibrous portion to flavor liquids, in the cavity of poultry, or to put under roasting meat. Mince or slice the tender inner portion and use in cooking.

MELTING CHOCOLATE

Chocolate burns easily, which destroys its texture by making it stiffer. The safest method for up to 8 ounces is to melt chocolate pieces in the top of a double boiler set over several inches of water that has been brought to a boil and removed from the heat. Cover the saucepan and let it sit for about 5 minutes. Then stir until the chocolate is smooth. If the chocolate still has not melted, return the double boiler to the burner over medium-low heat for several minutes more. Chocolate can also be melted in the microwave. I always use low power and usually start with 3 minutes, increasing the time if needed.

One thing I've discovered about melting chocolate—when you run into a snag and are having a problem getting the chocolate to melt, stir in some Simple Syrup (see page 91). It works beautifully.

MIZITHRA CHEESE

A very tasty white Greek grating cheese that is difficult to find. Substitute Romano or Parmesan.

ORZO

A rice-shaped pasta.

Pancetta

An Italian cured bacon often coated with coarsely ground black pepper. Can be found at good delicatessens or butcher shops. Store in the freezer for up to a year and cut off what you need while still frozen. Use as a seasoning in small amounts.

Peeling carrots faster

If you are going to cook carrots, do not bother to peel them. After they have been blanched or fully cooked, wipe off the peel while refreshing them. Sometimes it is necessary to use a knife to lightly scrape the skin off.

Peeling garlic faster

Just recently raw garlic has been made available already peeled in plastic jars (without preservatives). What a convenience! If this is not available to you, place heads of garlic in a paper or plastic bag. Hit it with a meat pounder or the bottom of a pan. This will separate it into cloves. Then put the cloves in boiling water for a few seconds. Remove with a strainer and place in the sink under cold running water. When cool enough to handle, the garlic will squeeze out of its skin.

Peeling tomatoes

Place tomatoes in boiling water for about 30 seconds or until the skin can be removed easily. Immediately plunge into cold water, then peel.

Pickled ginger

Sliced ginger that is pickled in a solution of salt, sugar, and vinegar, which mellows it. Also referred to as *sushi ginger.* Can be found in Asian markets, or in the produce or Asian section of supermarkets. You may want to rinse it to remove some of the salt.

Pink peppercorns

These have a milder flavor than black peppercorns and a beautiful color. Use whole, ground, or crushed. Purchase freeze-dried or in brine. Rinsing the brine-packed variety is optional. Popular in French cooking.

Plum sauce

A prepared sauce that can best be described as a plum jam with ginger and chiles. For information on its usage and storage, refer to *barbecue sauce.* A great way to achieve bold flavors without adding fats or lots of calories. Can be found in Asian markets or in the Asian section of many supermarkets.

PORCINI MUSHROOMS
Also known as *bolete* or *cèpe.* Very meaty texture when fresh. They resemble domestic mushrooms but are much larger. The caps are tan- to brown-colored but the flesh is creamy white. Available fresh or dried; more commonly available dried. Fabulous earthy flavor. To rehydrate the dried variety, simply place them in a bowl and cover them with any liquid, from water to broth. Let sit at room temperature for about 1 hour or until soft. To speed up with process, place in a saucepan and boil until tender.

PROSCIUTTO
Specially cured Italian ham found at good delicatessens or butcher shops. Use in small amounts as a seasoning.

RED JALAPEÑO CHILES
Small peppers with thick flesh. They are very hot with a slight sweetness that makes them intriguing.

REDUCE (OR REDUCTION)
This refers to the process of boiling down cooking liquids to intensify their flavors and/or thicken them.

RICE VINEGAR
A delightfully mellow and refreshing vinegar with a slightly sweet flavor. A great way to achieve bold flavors without adding fats or cholesterol. Found in Asian markets or the Asian section of many supermarkets.

ROASTING GARLIC
To roast garlic, cut the top one third from each head of garlic to expose the cloves. Using your hands, peel away some of the excess skin from around the garlic. Place the heads in a baking pan or heavy skillet and toss with a small amount of olive oil. Cover with a lid and bake in a preheated 250°F oven until the cloves are soft and buttery, about 2 hours. If you are lucky enough to be able to purchase prepeeled garlic cloves,

simply toss them in olive oil and bake as directed above. Roasted garlic can be frozen for up to six months or refrigerated for at least 5 days.

ROASTING PEPPERS

Cut the peppers in half and remove the seeds and veins. Place them on an aluminum foil–lined cookie sheet cut-side down in a preheated 350° to 450°F oven until the skin is charred. This will take between 30 to 60 minutes. When cool enough to handle, remove and discard the skin. Use or store, wrapped, in the freezer for up to one year.

Roasted red peppers are one of the most wonderful ingredients. I suggest your keeping them on hand in your freezer. They will add instant magic to salads, dressings, sauces, and soups. One of my favorite hors d'oeuvres is chèvre, feta, or Brie placed in a skillet or ovenproof baking dish, topped with chopped roasted red peppers, pine nuts, and chopped fresh basil. This is warmed in a preheated 350°F oven for about 10 minutes and served with Garlic Crouton Rounds (see page 192) or thinly sliced pieces of baguette.

ROASTING SHALLOTS

Simply cut a small portion of the tip off of the shallot and proceed as directed in roasting garlic (see page 27)

SAFFRON

The most precious and costly spice. It is the stigma of autumn crocus and must be harvested by hand. It gives food a yellow/golden color and an exotic/earthy flavor. Always purchase saffron threads; the powdered form is not as flavorful and often not pure.

SESAME OIL

Use very sparingly as a seasoning, not as a cooking oil. It has a rich and intensely nutty flavor and aroma. Store in the refrigerator to prevent it from becoming rancid; it will last for over a year. Can be found in Asian markets or in the Asian section of many supermarkets.

SHIITAKE MUSHROOMS

Also known as *Black Forest mushrooms* or *Chinese mushrooms*. Can be purchased fresh, but their flavor is more intense when used dried. They have a rich, earthy flavor. They are always soaked in liquid to rehydrate before using. This will take about one hour. To speed up the process, place the mushrooms in a saucepan and boil for several minutes, until tender. Never discard the soaking liquid. Strain it to remove any grit, reduce it, and use in soups, stocks, and/or sauces.

Storing seeds or nuts
These items will get rancid if they are not stored in the freezer. They can be stored for at least 6 months this way.

Sun-dried tomatoes
Italian pear-shaped tomatoes that are salted and dried. They can be very expensive, especially if purchased marinated. I recommend buying them in bulk, just dry and marinate them yourself. To soften them for immediate use, place in a plastic or glass jar with a few tablespoons of vinegar, wine, or water. Cover with a lid and place in a microwave for a few minutes, until softened. To do this on the stove, place the tomatoes in a saucepan and add an equal amount of the liquid of your choice. Bring to a boil, then gently simmer until tender, about ten minutes. Use as is or cover them with olive oil. Add garlic cloves, bay leaves, peppercorns, and/or fresh or dried herbs of your choice and store in the refrigerator for up to one year. The oil becomes infused with the pungent tomato-herb essence and is wonderful used on bread or in cooking.

Szechuan peppercorns
Peppercorns with an intriguing flavor that is a combination of menthol and heat. Use whole or crushed to flavor both Asian and non-Asian foods. Can be found in Asian markets, gourmet stores, or in the spice section of many supermarkets.

Teleme cheese
An aged jack cheese with a softer texture and a more complex flavor.

Toasting seeds or nuts
Place on an aluminum foil–lined cookie sheet in a preheated 350°F oven until toasted. Watch carefully, shaking the pan from time to time, to avoid burning; it should take 15 to 20 minutes.

TOMATILLOS

Also referred to as *Mexican green tomatoes*. They resemble a small green tomato and are covered with a greenish husk that is not eaten. Use raw or cooked. They have a tart, lemonlike herbal flavor. When used raw, it is more acid; when cooked it adds some gelatinous texture.

TONKATSU SAUCE

Japanese-style Worcestershire sauce. Refer to *barbecue sauce* for information on its usage and storage. A great way to achieve bold flavors without adding fats or cholesterol. Can be found in Asian markets or in the Asian section of many supermarkets.

UNMOLDING FORMED ITEMS

Dip a knife into hot water and run it around the perimeter of the mold or container; then place the mold in warm water for a few seconds, until the formed mixture can be jiggled away from the edge. Place a platter or plate on top of the mold and invert it. Sometimes it needs a tap to loosen it. For guaranteed, worry-free results, always oil the inside of the mold and line it with plastic wrap or cheesecloth. To unmold, simply pull it out.

WHITE PEPPERCORNS

Milder, richer flavor than black peppercorns. Widely used in delicate light-colored sauces since it does not add black flakes.

For further assistance with cooking terms or techniques, I recommend Julia Child's *The Way to Cook*.

CHAPTER THREE

$\cdot \quad \cdot$

Spring Dinner Parties

SPRING AT A GLANCE

The Setting

ELEGANT
- Begin to focus on the outdoors, but primarily staged indoors
- Should have a fresh and revitalized look

CASUAL
- Stylishly casual, often outdoors
- Country charm
- Primitive, rustic and/or exotic with a playful fresh spirit

Party Props

ELEGANT
- Colors—refined and subdued pastels: gray, pink, mauve, light green, peach, lilac
- Silver, china, crystal serving pieces—all your best!
- Simple, bold floral arrangements with an Oriental feel or lush country bouquets
- Champagne flutes, glass bowls, or traditional vases
- Candelabra, glass candlesticks, or masses of votive candles in clear glass holders

CASUAL
- Bright colors: red, green, yellow, orange, purple, blue
- Cast-iron skillets, pottery, clear or colored glass, and/or vivid contemporary plastic for serving pieces

---

- Boldly patterned, checkered picnic cloths or brightly colored solid tablecloths
- Solid or patterned sheets or cotton bedspreads used as tablecloths
- Oversized napkins or fresh and brightly colored kitchen towels
- Unstructured country bouquets mixing flowers with fresh herb cuttings
- Jelly-jar glasses, French canning jars, baskets, tin pails, wine carafes, pottery crocks, terra-cotta pots, and/or ceramic pitchers as vases
- Simple heavy glassware
- Votive candles in terra-cotta pots or in terra-cotta saucers filled with sand, or mini tin pails, or imported tin candle holders

Foods for Decorating

- Fresh fruits: grapes, strawberries, lemons
- Fresh vegetables: asparagus, eggplant, peppers, peas, pea pods

ELEGANT SPRING MENUS

Roast Lamb Dinner

Spring and lamb are traditional teammates. At this dinner party they join forces to create a menu of classic elegance. This is definitely a menu with an important feel to it.

Garlic and Feta Tartlets are a wonderful way to introduce a lamb dinner. Both garlic and feta are naturals with lamb. Here, they are used to create a fantastic filling for delicate pastry tartlets. If you are not already accustomed to preparing pastry in the food processor, you will be amazed and delighted by the ease of preparation and the resulting quality.

The salad that follows not only arouses the palate but also acts as a digestive aid. Trust me, this is a winner! As a matter of fact, it is so good that you will probably want to transform it into a luncheon entree by adding chicken or seafood.

Instead of the traditional approach to leg of lamb, I have the butcher bone and butterfly it, producing a moister, more flavorful cut. The lamb absorbs more marinade since there is more surface to come into direct contact with it. You will also find the cooking time reduced significantly.

Pilaf is a common accompaniment for lamb; however, we use orzo and bulgur rather than rice for a delicious variation. Bulgur, which is cracked, toasted wheat, provides a nutty flavor. The orzo, a rice-shaped pasta, adds a delightful surprise, but the zing in this dish comes from the marinated artichoke hearts.

Asparagus with hollandaise would be the predictable vegetable choice to serve with this lovely menu. However, instead of the standard garden variety hollandaise, I transformed it into a Dill Caper Sauce. Both of these flavorings complement the asparagus as well as the lamb. Again, we utilize the miracle machine, which transforms the tedious task of preparing a hollandaise-type sauce into child's play.

Our menu finishes with a light, cold Zabaglione Mousse with Strawberries and Almonds. Both the texture and flavor of this dessert provide a perfect ending for this dinner. It too is whipped together in the food processor.

For some unexplainable and mystical reason, purple iris seem to be a must for this party. I like to arrange them in three elongated, crystal vases on a tablecloth in a very pale shade of purple with matching candles. Dark purple napkins provide a bit of contrast, drama, and an added touch of elegance.

MENU

Garlic and Feta Tartlets

Pea Pod, Prosciutto, and Papaya Salad

Sliced Baguettes with Sweet Butter

Butterflied Leg of Lamb with Red Wine-Rosemary Sauce

Orzo and Bulgur with Artichoke Hearts

Asparagus with Dill-Caper Sauce

Zabaglione Mousse with Strawberries and Almonds

Lemon-Butter Thins

FASTER & FLASHIER MENU

Warm Goat Cheese with Walnuts

Pea Pod, Proscuitto, and Papaya Salad

Butterflied Leg of Lamb with Red Wine-Rosemary Butter

Orzo Tossed with Artichoke Hearts

Blanched Asparagus with Lemon

Vanilla Ice Cream with Strawberries Marinated in Champagne

WINES

Chardonnay or Champagne

Merlot

Rosé Champagne

Fast & Fabulous Timetable

Up to 6 Months in Advance and Frozen
Lamb Stock • Marinade • Red Wine-Rosemary Sauce

Up to 3 Months in Advance and Frozen
Garlic and Feta Tartlets

Up to 1 Month in Advance and Frozen
Zabaglione

5 Days in Advance and Refrigerated
Vinaigrette for salad

4 Days in Advance and Refrigerated
Lamb Stock

3 Days in Advance and Refrigerated
Marinate the lamb • Red Wine-Rosemary Sauce

2 Days in Advance and Refrigerated
Garlic and Feta Tartlets • Dill-Caper Sauce • Zabaglione • Lemon
Butter Thins • Thaw frozen prepared-ahead foods

1 Day in Advance and Refrigerated
Start Orzo and Bulgur with Artichoke Hearts • Mascerate strawberries
• Blanch asparagus • Wash salad greens

Party Day!
Bake tartlets • Pea Pod, Prosciutto, and Papaya Salad • Roast lamb •
Finish orzo and asparagus • Assemble dessert • Warm bread

GARLIC AND FETA TARTLETS

FILLING

6 to 8 cloves garlic

1/2 cup medium-dry sherry

1/4 cup heavy cream

2 large eggs, plus 1 large
  yolk

1 cup crumbled feta cheese

Freshly ground black pepper
  to taste

1/2 cup minced sun-dried
  tomatoes

Tartlet Shells (recipe follows)

Yield: enough to fill about 36 tartlets

This is an hors d'oeuvre with world-class flavor!

1. Preheat the oven to 350°F.
2. Put the garlic in a small saucepan with the sherry. Simmer over medium heat, covered, until the garlic is tender, about 15 to 20 minutes, adding more sherry if needed.
3. Stir in the cream, increase the heat, and bring to a boil. Cook until the mixture thickens and reduces by one half. Stir frequently.
4. Meanwhile, combine the eggs, egg yolk, and feta in a bowl or food processor fitted with a metal blade. While mixing or while the machine is running, slowly add the garlic-sherry mixture. Season with the pepper.
5. Place several pieces of sun-dried tomato in each prebaked tartlet shell, then top with the feta mixture. Bake for about 30 minutes or until a toothpick comes out clean.

Fast: Can prepare filling up to 2 days in advance and refrigerate. Can flash-freeze assembled tartlet for up to 3 months. Cook frozen, adding about 10 minutes to the baking time.

Fabulous: Seasoned with minced fresh basil, oregano, dill, rosemary, green chiles, or crushed Szechuan peppercorns.

TARTLET SHELLS

2 cups all-purpose flour
10 2/3 tablespoons (1 1/3
   sticks) unsalted butter,
   frozen and cut into small
   pieces
1/4 teaspoon salt
1/4 cup ice water
1 large egg white, lightly
   beaten

Yield: about 36

Using the food processor makes this unbelievably easy!

1. Combine the flour, butter, and salt in a food processor fitted a with metal blade until it resembles coarse cornmeal.
2. Slowly add the ice water through the feed tube while the machine is running. Process until the pastry begins to form a ball.
3. Wrap the pastry with plastic wrap and chill in the freezer for about 10 to 15 minutes.
4. Preheat the oven to 450°F.
5. Roll out the dough onto a lightly floured surface to a thickness of about 1/4 inch and cut into circles using a wine glass or 1 1/2 to 2-inch cookie cutter. Fit the circles into ungreased mini-muffin cups.
6. Brush with the beaten egg white and bake for about 8 minutes or until almost fully baked and lightly browned.

Fast: Can prepare up to 2 days in advance and refrigerate, or freeze for up to 3 months. No thawing necessary.

Fabulous: Filled with anything.

PEA POD, PROSCIUTTO, AND PAPAYA SALAD

VINAIGRETTE

1 cup extra virgin olive oil

1/3 cup red wine vinegar

1/2 to 1 teaspoon Dijon
    mustard

1 to 2 cloves garlic

Salt and freshly ground white
    pepper to taste

ASSEMBLY

1 pound pea pods, strings
    removed

1 to 2 papayas, peeled,
    seeded, and thinly sliced

1/4 pound prosciutto, thinly
    sliced and minced

Watercress leaves

Yield: 6 to 8 servings

A wonderful combination of flavors, colors, and textures.

1. Combine all the ingredients for the vinaigrette in a food processor fitted with a metal blade, or in a blender. Taste and adjust the seasonings.
2. Bring a large pot of salted water to a boil. Add the pea pods and blanch for just a few seconds, until they turn a deeper shade of green. Remove them to a colander and place under cold running water to stop the cooking process and preserve their color. Drain them when they are cool to the touch.
3. On individual salad plates, arrange pea pods and papaya slices.
4. Sprinkle prosciutto and watercress leaves on top and drizzle with the vinaigrette.

Fast: Can prepare salad up to 4 hours in advance and refrigerate. Can prepare dressing up to 5 days in advance and refrigerate.

Fabulous: With minced fresh herbs added to dressing. With sliced cooked red potatoes and grilled meats, chicken, or seafood to create an entree salad.

ASPARAGUS WITH DILL-CAPER SAUCE

1 1/2 to 2 pounds
   asparagus, trimmed
Dill-Caper Sauce (recipe
   follows)

Yield: 6 to 10 servings

This represents a perfect combination of flavors. Believe me . . . it is well worth the calories!

1. Blanch the asparagus in a large pot of boiling water until they reach the desired degree of tenderness, about 4 to 5 minutes for crisp cooked.
2. Remove and serve with the sauce drizzled over top, or serve separately.

Fast: Can prepare through step 1 up to 1 day in advance if you undercook the asparagus and refresh them immediately. To refresh them, plunge them into ice water or place them in a colander set under cold running water until they are cool to the touch. This stops the cooking process and locks in the color. Before serving, finish cooking in boiling water for a few minutes or in the microwave.

DILL-CAPER SAUCE

1/2 pound (2 sticks)
   unsalted butter
6 large egg yolks (see page
   23)
1/4 cup minced fresh dill
1/4 cup capers, rinsed and
   drained
1 teaspoon Dijon mustard
1 shallot, minced
Several drops hot pepper
   sauce
Salt and freshly ground white
   pepper to taste
Fresh lemon juice to taste

This is one of many variations of hollandaise sauce. With the advent of the food processor this type of sauce becomes a snap!

1. Heat the butter in a skillet or the microwave until bubbly.
2. Meanwhile, process the egg yolks with the dill, capers, mustard, and shallot in a food processor fitted with a metal blade until the yolks are lemon-colored.
3. Slowly add the hot, melted butter through the feed tube while the machine is running, then season with salt, pepper, and lemon juice.

Fast: Can prepare up to 1 hour in advance and keep warm in the food processor with the lid on and covered with a thick turkish towel, or in a thermos bottle. Can prepare up to 2 days in advance and refrigerate. To reheat, place in a larger bowl of hot water and warm gently, or on top of a double boiler over simmering water, whisking frequently.

Flashy: On almost any vegetable, fish, veal, scallops, or a chicken breast.

Fabulous: With tarragon, basil, or sorrel instead of the dill.

Further: Reheat leftover sauce in the top of a double boiler, stirring continuously.

BUTTERFLIED LEG OF LAMB WITH RED WINE-ROSEMARY SAUCE

MARINADE
1 1/2 cups olive oil
1/4 cup soy sauce
1 cup minced fresh parsley
1/2 cup dry vermouth
8 green onions, minced
1 onion, chopped
1/4 cup packed fresh mint
   leaves, minced
4 to 6 tablespoons fresh
   lemon or lime juice
10 to 20 cloves garlic,
   pureed
1/4 cup Triple Sec or any
   orange-flavored liqueur
1/4 cup Dijon mustard
Minced fresh or dried
   rosemary to taste

One 8- to 10-pound leg of
   lamb (have the butcher
   butterfly and bone it)
1/2 cup dry red wine
Red Wine-Rosemary Sauce
   (recipe follows)

Yield: 6 to 8 servings

Once you prepare a butterflied leg of lamb, you will never do one any other way. It cooks much faster and the meat is moister and more flavorful. If you aren't in the mood to make a sauce, it is delicious without, or simply served with the deglazed juices.

1. Combine all the ingredients for the marinade in a food processor fitted with the metal blade, in a blender, or in a bowl, then pour over the lamb. Refrigerate and allow to marinate for 24 to 48 hours, turning the lamb from time to time.

2. Bring the lamb to room temperature. Preheat the oven to 400°F. Remove the lamb from the marinade and pat dry with paper towels.

3. Place the lamb in a roasting pan and into the oven. Reduce the oven temperature to 350°F. Cook until an instant-read meat thermometer registers 125° to 130°F for rare, or to the desired doneness. This should take about 10 minutes per pound.

4. Place the lamb on a platter, tent with aluminum foil, and allow the meat to rest for about 20 minutes before carving.

5. In the meantime, set the roasting pan over high heat, after pouring off any fat that may be in pan. Add the red wine and stir to loosen the cooked bits. Let reduce a bit, then stir into the red wine sauce or serve with the lamb.

Fast: Can marinate lamb for up to 3 days in advance and refrigerate. Can freeze the marinade for up to 6 months. Thaw in the refrigerator for 2 days or at room temperature for about 4 hours.

Flashy: Slice lamb and serve on a large platter with sauce drizzled over the top or served separately. Garnish with sprigs of fresh rosemary and/or mint, along with nontoxic flowers of your choice.

Further: Cut leftovers into small bite-size pieces. Heat with the remaining sauce, then toss into freshly cooked hot orzo, couscous, or bulgur. For added moisture, add beef broth or chopped tomatoes to the lamb and sauce when heating. Also delicious with minced fresh rosemary, mint, or parsley added to the sauce while heating.

RED WINE-ROSEMARY SAUCE

2 tablespoons unsalted butter
2 cloves garlic, minced
2 shallots, minced
2 tablespoons all-purpose
 flour
1 tablespoon Dijon mustard
1 cup dry red wine
2 cups Lamb Stock (recipe
 follows) or beef broth,
 homemade or canned
1/2 to 1 teaspoon dried
 thyme
1 tablespoon dried rosemary
Salt and freshly ground white
 pepper to taste

Yield: about 2 cups

1. Melt the butter in a large, heavy saucepan and sauté the garlic and shallots over low heat until tender.
2. Stir in the flour and cook over low heat, whisking, for 1 minute.
3. Whisk in the mustard, wine, and stock, along with the seasonings.
4. Bring the sauce to a boil over high, then reduce the heat to low. Cook until the flavors develop and the sauce thickens enough to coat the back of a spoon. Taste and adjust the flavors.

Fast: Can prepare up to 3 days in advance and refrigerate, or freeze for up to 6 months. Thaw in the refrigerator for 2 days or at room temperature for about 8 hours.

Fabulous: With 2 tablespoons of cold butter stirred in right before serving. With a combination of sliced domestic and imported mushrooms sautéed with the garlic and shallots in step 1.

LAMB STOCK

4 lamb shanks
1/2 to 1 carrot, chopped
1 onion, chopped
Celery leaves from 1/2
   bunch of celery, chopped
2 to 4 cloves garlic, peeled
1 bay leaf
10 black peppercorns
1/2 teaspoon dried thyme
2 cups dry red wine

Yield: 1 1/2 to 2 quarts

1. Preheat the oven to 400°F.
2. Place the lamb and vegetables in a roasting pan and cook until nicely browned, about 1 hour.
3. Transfer the browned mixture to a medium-size stock pot along with the bay leaf, peppercorns, and thyme. Add enough water to cover everything by at least 1 inch. Deglaze the roasting pan with the red wine by bringing to a boil and cooking over high heat while stirring to dissolve any of the brown bits that cling to the bottom of the pan. Add the mixture to the stock pot.
4. Bring the mixture to a boil, then reduce the temperature to its lowest setting and cover the pot. Cook for 4 to 8 hours, or until the flavors develop to your liking. Skim off the scum that will form, using a strainer, from time to time.
5. Strain the stock and transfer it to a metal bowl. Chill in the refrigerator to congeal the fat, then remove and discard.

Fast: Can prepare up to 4 days in advance and refrigerate, or freeze for up to 6 months. Thaw in the refrigerator for 2 days or at room temperature for about 8 hours.

ORZO AND BULGUR WITH ARTICHOKE HEARTS

4 tablespoons (1/2 stick)
  unsalted butter
2 to 3 shallots, minced
One to two 6-ounce jars
  marinated artichoke
  hearts, drained, 2
  tablespoons marinade
  reserved, and hearts
  coarsely chopped
2 cups orzo, cooked
  according to package
  instructions
3/4 cup bulgur, cooked
  according to package
  instructions
1/4 cup minced fresh parsley
Freshly ground white pepper
  to taste
Freshly grated Parmesan
  cheese for garnish

Yield: 8 to 10 servings

Here we use rice-shaped pasta and cracked wheat as if they were rice, to create a flavorful pilaf variation. Fabulous with lamb!

1. Melt the butter and sauté the shallots in a large skillet over medium-high heat until tender.
2. Stir in the artichoke hearts, along with the reserved marinade, the orzo, bulgur, and toss well.
3. Stir in the parsley, white pepper, and Parmesan.

Fast: Can prepare up to 1 day in advance and refrigerate. Reheat in the oven, microwave, or on top of a double boiler.

Fabulous: With minced sun-dried tomatoes, cooked vegetables, seafood, ham, sausage, and/or minced fresh herbs added.

Further: Use leftovers cold in a salad or mixed into soups.

ZABAGLIONE MOUSSE WITH STRAWBERRIES AND ALMONDS

8 large egg yolks, at room temperature (see page 23)

2/3 cup sugar, plus extra for strawberries

3/4 cup marsala, Madeira, or sherry, warmed, plus extra for strawberries (optional)

Freshly grated nutmeg to taste

Grated zest of 2 to 4 lemons

2 cups heavy cream

2 pints strawberries, hulled and halved or whole

8 ounces slivered almonds, toasted (see page 29)

Shaved or grated bittersweet chocolate for garnish

A delicious and light way to end a big dinner.

1. Process the egg yolks and sugar in a food processor fitted with a metal blade until lemon-colored.
2. Add the warm marsala very slowly through the feed tube while the machine is running.
3. Season with the nutmeg and briefly process in the lemon zest. Transfer to the top of a double boiler set over simmering water and whisk until completely thickened. Taste and add more sugar and/or marsala if needed.
4. Transfer to a bowl and chill in the freezer for about 30 minutes.
5. Whip the cream until it holds soft peaks, then fold into the chilled mixture.
6. Refrigerate in a metal bowl, glass bowl, soufflé dish, or stemmed glasses until ready to serve.
7. To mascerate the strawberries, place in a large bowl and add sugar if needed and some marsala if desired. Let sit at room temperature for several hours or refrigerate for up to 1 day.

Fast: Can prepare zabaglione up to 2 days in advance and refrigerate, or freeze for up to 1 month. Thaw 2 days in the refrigerator. Can prepare strawberries up to 1 day in advance and refrigerate.

Flashy: Serve zabaglione in stemmed glasses or a large glass bowl, spoon the strawberries over it, then sprinkle with the almonds and some grated chocolate. Serve with Lemon-Butter Thins (see page 62).

Fabulous: On pound or angel food cake or in puff pastry. Use zabaglione to fill crêpes and top with strawberries, almonds, and chocolate. Substitute sliced fresh cherries or peaches, or any berry for the strawberries.

Further: Don't worry, there won't be any leftovers!

Poached Salmon Dinner

This is the first time I have ever thought of color-coordinating an entree with the tablecloth, but salmon instantly inspires me. This delicate fish not only has a delicious flavor, but its color is so perfect for spring. My flowers and tablecloth are both in salmon. To heighten the visual impact and create a feeling of drama, I use dinner plates, napkins, and a flower vase in black.

An arrangement of salmon-colored azaleas with asparagus ferns adds a wispy, delicate look to this table. For the final touch, scatter votive candles in glass holders down the table.

The menu is seductively flavorful, with a very light feel from the hors d'oeuvre to the dessert. Chèvre and Sun-Dried Tomato Cups start the evening off with style and a riot of thrilling flavors. Next comes a well-composed salad full of seasonal flavors. What could be more springlike than asparagus, shrimp, and celery root dressed with a tarragon-flavored vinaigrette?

The entree, poached salmon, cooks quickly. In fact, the sauce will take longer to reduce than the fish to cook. This last minute reduction is worth the effort, but if you are uncomfortable doing it, I've provided a delicious alternative that can be completely prepared in advance.

The salmon is served with two interesting side dishes. The risotto is flavored with saffron and fennel, both lovely flavor complements to salmon. The vegetable, Sugar Peas with Shiitake Mushrooms, is seasoned with a hint of fresh ginger and sesame seeds, providing a nice flavor and textural contrast to the other dishes. The color composition of the plate is as balanced as the flavors.

The grand finale is every bit as light and refreshingly seductive as the rest of the meal. The dessert consists of individual shell-shaped tarts filled with a lemon custard and topped with a combination of fresh berries and kiwi slices. As you can see, this menu is overflowing with glorious spring flavors and colors from start to finish!

MENU

Chèvre and Sun-Dried Tomato Cups

Asparagus, Shrimp, and Celery Root Salad

Sliced Baguette with Dill-Shallot Butter

Poached Salmon with Dill Cream Sauce

Fennel-Saffron Risotto

Sugar Peas with Shiitake Mushrooms

Strawberry and Kiwi Pastry Scallops

FASTER & FLASHIER MENU

Warm Chèvre (topped with minced green onions and sun-dried tomatoes)

Tossed Salad with Shrimp

Broiled Salmon Steaks with Dilled Mayonnaise

Rice with Saffron

Sugar Peas

Dessert (purchased)

WINES

Champagne or Sauvignon Blanc

Chardonnay

Late harvest Gewürztraminer or Champagne

Fast & Fabulous Timetable

Up to 6 Months in Advance and Frozen
   Won Ton Cups • Salmon Stock

Up to 3 Months in Advance and Frozen
   Pastry Scallops • Lemon-Almond Cream Filling

Up to 1 Week in Advance and Refrigerated
   Won Ton Cups

5 Days in Advance and Refrigerated
   Tarragon Vinaigrette

3 Days in Advance and Refrigerated
   Won Ton Cups • Salmon Stock (fresh made) • Pastry Scallops • Lemon-Almond Cream Filling • Thaw frozen prepared-ahead foods

1 Day in Advance and Refrigerated
   Assemble Chèvre and Sun-Dried Tomato Cups • Asparagus, Shrimp, and Celery Root Salad • Start salmon, risotto, and sugar peas • Set table

Bake Chèvre and Sun-Dried Tomato Cups • Arrange salads • Poach salmon and prepare sauce before serving • Finish risotto and sugar peas • Assemble dessert • Warm bread

CHÈVRE AND SUN-DRIED TOMATO CUPS

1 pound chèvre

1/4 to 1/2 cup pine nuts, toasted (see page 29)

1 cup minced sun-dried tomatoes or cut into small pieces

1/2 cup minced fresh basil leaves

Won Ton Cups (recipe follows)

Sprigs of fresh parsley, basil leaves, and/or nontoxic flowers for garnish

Yield: about 60 cups

This is so simple—you will not believe the results!

1. Preheat the oven to 350°F.
2. Combine the pine nuts, tomatoes, and basil in a food processor fitted with a metal blade, using several quick on-and-off motions so as not to destroy the texture, or mix together in a bowl with a wooden spoon.
3. Place enough cheese in each won ton cup to fill them three-quarters full. Top each cup with a generous amount of the sun-dried tomato mixture.
4. Place on an ungreased baking sheet and bake until the cheese is hot, about 10 minutes.

Fast: Can assemble up to 1 day in advance and refrigerate. Bring to room temperature before baking.

Flashy: Serve on a platter garnished with sprigs of parsley or fresh basil leaves and flowers.

Fabulous: The variations are endless! Try different cheeses and herbs. One of my favorite combinations is teleme cheese with chopped roasted red peppers and minced red onions.

WON TON CUPS

1 package won ton or sui
   mai wrappers
Olive oil for pan and cups

Yield: about 60

You will love these crisp tartlet shells and be delighted by how quickly they can be prepared.

1. Preheat the oven to 350°F.
2. Oil a mini muffin tin.
3. Fit one wrapper into each cup. Brush with oil.
4. Place in the oven and bake until crisp, about 10 to 15 minutes.

Fast: Can prepare up to 1 week in advance and store in plastic bag(s) or in airtight jar(s), or freeze for up to 6 months.

Fabulous: Filled with anything from peanut butter to lobster.

TARRAGON VINAIGRETTE

1/2 cup tarragon vinegar
2 cups extra virgin olive oil
2 to 4 cloves garlic
Salt and freshly ground white
   and black pepper to taste
Fresh lime juice to taste

Yield: about 2 1/2 cups

This is one of my favorite dressings to serve with a large, rich meal. It is very refreshing.

1. Combine all the ingredients in a food processor fitted with a metal blade, or in a blender.
2. Taste and adjust the seasonings.

Fast: Can prepare up to 5 days in advance and refrigerate.

Fabulous: On any salad or as a sauce for fish or seafood. As a dip for artichokes.

ASPARAGUS, SHRIMP, AND CELERY ROOT SALAD

Juice from 1 lemon

1 small to medium-size celery root, peeled and cut into 1/2-inch thick rounds

3/4 to 1 pound cooked baby shrimp

2 tablespoons minced fresh tarragon

Tarragon Vinaigrette (see page 47)

Salt and freshly ground black pepper to taste

24 asparagus spears, trimmed

Crumbled bleu cheese for garnish

1. Fill a small saucepan with water. Lightly salt it and squeeze the lemon juice into it. Bring to a boil.
2. Add the celery root to the boiling water and blanch for about 2 minutes. Remove and refresh under cold running water. This will prevent discoloration. Slice into thin matchstick strips. If the celery root is old and tough, cook it fully, until tender, about 5 minutes.
3. Toss together the celery root, shrimp, tarragon, and desired amount of vinaigrette. Taste, season with salt and pepper, cover with plastic wrap, and refrigerate.
4. Blanch the asparagus in a large nonaluminum pot of salted water until barely tender, about 4 to 5 minutes, then remove and refresh under cold running water. Drain well, transfer to a platter, and dress with the desired amount of vinaigrette. Cover with plastic wrap and refrigerate until chilled, for at least 30 minutes.

Fast: Can prepare up to 1 day in advance and refrigerate.

Flashy: Arrange decoratively on a large platter or individual plates with the asparagus surrounding or next to the shrimp mixture. Sprinkle crumbled bleu cheese on the asparagus.

Fabulous: With minced fresh dill instead of tarragon. With sliced canned hearts of palm, sliced raw fennel bulb, or celery instead of the celery root. With cooked mussels or scallops instead of the shrimp. With a slice of papaya or mango on each plate.

POACHED SALMON WITH DILL CREAM SAUCE

8 salmon fillets,
approximately 6 ounces
each, boned and skinned
2 tablespoons unsalted butter
2 shallots, minced
1/2 cup minced fresh dill
1 cup dry white wine or
vermouth
1 cup Salmon Stock (recipe
follows) or bottled clam
juice
1 cup heavy cream
2 teaspoons Dijon mustard
2 teaspoons cornstarch
dissolved in 2 tablespoons
dry white wine
2 tablespoons unsalted
butter, cold
2 large egg yolks mixed with
2 tablespoons heavy
cream
Salt and freshly ground white
pepper to taste
Fresh lemon juice to taste
Johnny-jump-ups for garnish

Delicate and luscious!

The salmon cooks in almost no time at all. Reducing the sauce requires a bit more patience. If you want to simplify the preparation, substitute the Dill-Caper Sauce on page 38. For added flavor excitement, I have provided an optional marinade.

1. Preheat the oven to 375°F. Butter a large baking dish or ovenproof skillet.
2. Place the salmon in the baking dish.
3. Melt the butter in a medium-size, heavy saucepan and sauté the shallots and dill over low heat until the shallots are tender
4. Add the wine and stock, bring to a boil, then pour over the salmon. Cover with aluminum foil and poach in the oven for 5 to 10 minutes, depending on the thickness of the salmon, taking care not to overcook it. To poach on top of the stove, use a large skillet and place over medium heat. Cook the salmon until it begins to turn opaque, but is still slightly pink in the center (I love just barely cooked salmon, so I undercook it).
5. Transfer the salmon to an ovenproof platter and tent with aluminum foil to keep warm.
6. Pour the cooking liquids into a large, heavy saucepan. Bring to a boil and reduce by half.
7. Add the cream and return to a boil. Reduce again until the flavors and consistency are pleasing.
8. While the sauce boils, whisk in the mustard and the cornstarch mixture. Continue to boil for a few minutes until the sauce thickens slightly.
9. Reduce the heat to medium and whisk in the yolk-and-cream mixture. Do not boil or the yolks will curdle. Continue to whisk and cook for a few minutes.
10. Swirl in the cold butter and season with salt, pepper, and lemon juice.

Fast: Can prepare through adding the wine and stock in step 4; boil and refrigerate, up to 1 day in advance. To cook, bring the liquid to a boil again and proceed.

Flashy: Served with the sauce drizzled over the salmon and a johnny-jump-up on top of each fillet.

Fabulous: Served cold, with dilled mayonnaise. Also fabulous with Lemon Cream Sauce (see page 68) instead of the reduction sauce.

SALMON STOCK

Salmon trimmings (tail, skin,
  backbone, and head if you
  are brave!)
1 onion, quartered
2 bay leaves
1 bunch celery, top third,
  including leaves

1. Place all the ingredients in a large saucepan and cover with water. Bring to a boil and simmer until the flavors develop to your liking, at least 20 minutes. Skim off the scum that rises to the top, using a strainer.
2. Strain the stock.

Fast: Can prepare up to 3 days in advance and refrigerate, or freeze for up to 6 months. Thaw in the refrigerator for 2 days or at room temperature for about 8 hours.

Flashy: In fish and seafood soups and sauces.

SALMON MARINADE

Olive oil
Fresh lemon juice
Salmon
Salt and freshly ground white
  pepper to taste
Minced shallots
Minced fresh dill

I marinate everything except brownies!

1. Drizzle olive oil and lemon juice over the salmon, season with salt and pepper, then scatter the shallots and dill on and around the salmon. Cover with plastic wrap and refrigerate for up to 1 day.

FENNEL-SAFFRON RISOTTO

4 to 6 tablespoons (1/2 to 3/4 stick) unsalted butter

1 small to medium-size fennel bulb, minced or thinly sliced

2 shallots, minced

2 cups uncooked arborio rice or short grain pearl rice

1/8 to 1/4 teaspoon saffron threads

3/4 cup dry vermouth

4 cups chicken broth, homemade or canned

Fennel leaves for garnish

Salt and freshly ground white pepper to taste

An interesting version of an Italian classic.

1. Melt the butter in large, heavy saucepan and sauté the fennel and shallots over medium-low heat until tender.
2. Stir in the rice and saffron. Cook, stirring, until the rice turns opaque.
3. Add the vermouth and stir frequently until it is absorbed.
4. Stir in one half of the broth and cook, stirring, until it is absorbed. Repeat with the remaining broth and stir until the rice is creamy, but al dente. The entire process should take about 20 minutes. Add more liquid if necessary.
5. Taste and season with salt and pepper.

Fast: Can prepare, adding only one half of the liquid, up to 1 day in advance and refrigerate. Bring to room temperature and proceed as directed.

Flashy: Top with fennel leaves.

Fabulous: With any dry white wine or champagne instead of the dry vermouth. Season with any herb that will complement your entree. With celery (sliced thinly) instead of fennel.

SUGAR PEAS WITH SHIITAKE MUSHROOMS

1 1/2 to 2 pounds sugar
   peas
4 tablespoons (1/2 stick)
   unsalted butter
4 green onions, minced
1 to 2 ounces dried shiitake
   mushrooms, rehydrated,
   stemmed, and thinly sliced
One 1/2-inch piece fresh
   ginger or to taste, minced
1/4 cup sesame seeds,
   toasted (see page 29)
Salt and freshly ground white
   pepper to taste

This side dish combines French cooking techniques with Asian ingredients.

1. Bring a large pot of water to a boil and blanch the sugar peas until they turn dark green (do not overcook). Remove and immediately place in a colander under cold running water. Drain well.
2. Melt 2 tablespoons of the butter in large skillet and sauté the green onions, mushrooms, and ginger over medium-low heat until tender.
3. Add the sugar peas and sesame seeds, raise the heat to high, and cook just until hot. Stir in the remaining butter and season with salt and pepper.

Fast: Can prepare through step 2 up to 1 day in advance and refrigerate. Bring to room temperature before cooking.

Fabulous: Seasoned with any minced fresh or dried herb instead of the ginger. With domestic or porcini mushrooms instead of shiitake. With green beans or pea pods if sugar peas are not available, blanched till dark green.

STRAWBERRY AND KIWI PASTRY SCALLOPS

PASTRY SHELLS
2 1/4 cups all-purpose flour
1/4 cup packed light brown
   sugar
Freshly grated nutmeg to
   taste
1/2 pound (2 sticks)
   unsalted butter, cut into
   small pieces
Grated zest of 2 lemons
1 teaspoon vanilla extract
1 large egg
1/4 cup ice water
12 scallop shells for baking
   the pastry

1. Combine the flour, sugar, and nutmeg in a food processor fitted with a metal blade, or in a bowl.
2. Add the butter and process until the mixture resembles coarse meal. If doing this by hand, cut the butter in using a pastry blender or the tines of a fork.
3. Process in the zest, vanilla, and egg, or mix it in using the pastry blender or tines of a fork.
4. While the machine is running, process in the water through the feed tube, one tablespoon at a time. Or add to the bowl, one tablespoon at a time, while tossing with a fork. Add only enough water to hold the dough together.
5. Use your hands to form the dough into a ball, then roll it into a cylinder, 1 inch in diameter. Wrap in plastic wrap and chill for 30 minutes in the freezer.

LEMON-ALMOND CREAM FILLING

8 ounces cream cheese, at room temperature

1 to 2 ounces almond paste

1/4 cup packed light brown sugar or to taste

Freshly grated nutmeg to taste

2 to 4 tablespoons orange-flavored liqueur

1 teaspoon vanilla extract

1/2 cup slivered almonds, toasted (see page 29)

Grated zest of 2 lemons

1 cup heavy cream, beaten until it holds soft peaks

GLAZE

1/3 cup orange or lemon marmalade

2 tablespoons orange-flavored liqueur

ASSEMBLY

2 pints fresh strawberries, sliced or whole

4 kiwi, peeled and sliced

2 tablespoons brandy

6. While the pastry is chilling, process the cream cheese with the almond paste, sugar, nutmeg, liqueur, and vanilla in a food processor fitted with a metal blade, or in a bowl using an electric mixer.

7. Process in the almonds and zest briefly, using several quick on-and-off motions so as not to destroy the texture.

8. Transfer to bowl and fold in the whipped cream. Chill until ready to use.

9. Preheat the oven to 400°F.

10. Cut the dough horizontally into twelve pieces. On a lightly floured surface roll each piece out to a thickness of 1/8 inch.

11. Press each pastry onto the back of a scallop shell and pierce with a fork.

12. Place on an ungreased baking sheet and bake for 12 minutes or until golden. Place the shells on a rack for about 10 minutes to cool. Remove the pastry from the shells.

13. Place the ingredients for the glaze in a small saucepan and heat until the marmalade dissolves. This can also be done in a microwave.

14. Strain through a fine strainer or leave as is.

15. To assemble, fill the pastry shells with the whipped cream mixture, top with the fruit, then brush with the glaze and serve.

Fast: Can prepare pastry up to 1 day in advance, or freeze for up to 3 months. Thaw in the refrigerator for 2 days or at room temperature for about 8 hours. Can prepare the filling up to 3 days in advance and refrigerate or freeze for up to 3 months. Assemble up to 4 hours in advance and refrigerate.

Flashy: Serve on top of fresh grape leaves, with a sprig of fresh mint and/or with violas.

Fabulous: With any fruit in season. With pastry shells dipped in melted bittersweet chocolate.

Brandied Chicken Breast with Shrimp Dinner

For this dinner party, I recommend dressing your table in a very light peach-colored cloth with a wide, fern-green ribbon running down the center. This provides instant drama. Arrange white azaleas, mixed with sprigs of asparagus fern and parsley in three crystal vases and place them on the ribbon. Scatter matching peach napkins, along with white candles in glass candlesticks down the center of the table to provide the finishing touches.

The evening begins with two wonderful hors d'oeuvres. Choose one or both. They have a carefree but impressive feel. Brie-Stuffed Mushrooms is one of those amazing recipes that will make a culinary star out of even the most amateur of cooks. The Smoked Ham Mousse is a rich but quick alternative to preparing a baked pâté. Rather than salad, I serve a luscious Cream of Roasted Red Pepper and Red Onion Soup—exquisite in flavor as well as color. The mousse and soup are probably items that you will want to prepare in large quantities and keep in your freezer.

Lowly chicken breasts are transformed into an elegant entree by marinating them with shrimp. Their moist texture as well as their shrimp flavor will delight you. The carrots and pilaf complement the chicken without overshadowing it. A very light-in-texture, but big-in-flavor Cheesecake Mousse, along with fresh fruit, completes the meal on a note as elegant as it began.

MENU

Brie-Stuffed Mushrooms

Smoked Ham Mousse

Cream of Roasted Red Pepper and Red Onion Soup

Sliced Baguette with Green Onion Lemon Butter (see page 158)

Brandied Chicken Breasts with Shrimp in Wine Sauce

Carrots with Fennel

Lemon Pilaf

Cheesecake Mousse

Praline-Butter Thins

FASTER & FLASHIER MENU

Brie and Crackers

Pâté (purchased)

Cream of Roasted Red Pepper Soup (prepared with purchased roasted peppers)

Brandied Chicken Breasts with Wine Sauce (buy chicken breasts already boned and skinned)

Carrots with Dill (use frozen baby carrots)

Dessert (purchased)

WINES

Sauvignon Blanc or Champagne

Chardonnay

Orange Muscat or Champagne

Fast & Fabulous Timetable

Up to 6 Months in Advance and Frozen
Cream of Roasted Red Pepper and Red Onion Soup through step 3 • Wine Sauce • Pecan-Praline Powder

Up to 3 Months in Advance and Frozen
Smoked Ham Mousse • Cheesecake Mousse • Praline-Butter Thins

2 Weeks in Advance and Refrigerated
Pecan-Praline Powder

4 Days in Advance and Refrigerated
Praline-Butter Thins

3 Days in Advance and Refrigerated
Smoked Ham Mousse • Cream of Roasted Red Pepper and Red Onion Soup through step 3 • Wine Sauce

2 Days in Advance and Refrigerated
Cheesecake Mousse • Thaw frozen prepared-ahead foods

1 Day in Advance and Refrigerated
Brie-Stuffed Mushrooms • Start Brandied Chicken Breasts with Shrimp • Carrots with Fennel • Lemon Pilaf • Set table

Party Day!
Heat mushrooms • Finish cooking soup, chicken, carrots, and pilaf • Warm bread

SMOKED HAM MOUSSE

2 to 3 chicken livers,
 trimmed of fat
1 cup milk or wine
6 tablespoons (3/4 stick)
 unsalted butter
2 to 4 tablespoons minced
 shallots
2 cloves garlic, minced
1/4 cup Madeira
1 1/2 envelopes unflavored
 gelatin
12 ounces smoked ham,
 trimmed and cut in 1-inch
 pieces
2 teaspoons Dijon mustard
 or to taste
1 3/4 cups heavy cream
1/4 teaspoon dried thyme
1 teaspoon dried dillweed
Grated zest of 2 lemons
1 ounce dried shiitake
 mushrooms, rehydrated,
 stemmed, and thinly sliced
Salt and freshly ground white
 pepper to taste
Thinly sliced cucumber,
 cornichons, watercress,
 assorted mustards,
 crackers, melbas, and/or
 thinly sliced baguette for
 garnish and to serve

Yield: about 12 servings

I made my debut on national TV with this.

1. Soak the livers in the milk for at least 1 hour at room temperature, or refrigerate overnight.
2. Melt 2 tablespoons of the butter in a large skillet. Sauté the shallots and garlic over low heat until soft.
3. Add the livers and sauté until just pink on the inside.
4. Combine the Madeira and gelatin in a bowl and place in a larger bowl of hot water, or place it in the microwave for 30 seconds on low power, to dissolve.
5. Process the liver, ham, the remaining butter, the dissolved gelatin, and the mustard in a food processor fitted with a metal blade until smooth.
6. Add the cream and process until just blended, being careful not to overprocess, or the cream will curdle.
7. Add the herbs, zest, mushrooms, salt, and pepper. Process briefly with several quick on-and-off motions so as not to destroy the texture of the zest or mushrooms.
8. Pour into a 6- to 8-cup oiled mold, or several smaller molds, and chill until set, about 6 hours.

Fast: Can prepare up to 3 days in advance and refrigerate, or freeze for up to 3 months. Thaw in the refrigerator for 2 days.

Flashy: Garnish with cucumber, cornichons, and watercress. Serve with an assortment of interesting mustards, crackers, melbas, and/or baguette slices.

Fabulous: With about 1 tablespoon or more of minced fresh dill, thyme, rosemary, and/or sage, instead of the dried herbs. With about 1/2 cup toasted (see page 29) and chopped nuts. With porcini mushrooms instead of the shiitake. With chicken broth used to replace some or all of the cream.

BRIE-STUFFED MUSHROOMS

6 tablespoons (3/4 stick)
   unsalted butter

3 cloves garlic, minced

1/4 cup minced fresh parsley

1/4 cup minced green onion

Salt and freshly ground white
   pepper to taste

16 medium-size to large
   mushrooms, stemmed

16 pieces Brie (about 1/2
   pound), cut to fit into the
   mushroom caps

1/2 cup chopped walnuts,
   sautéed in 2 tablespoons
   butter

This will get raves.

1. Preheat the oven to 350°F.
2. Melt the butter in a large saucepan over low heat. Add the garlic, parsley, onions, salt, and pepper, and sauté over medium heat until the onions are tender.
3. Add the mushrooms and briefly sauté (they should not be fully cooked), coating them well with the butter mixture.
4. Remove the mushrooms to an ovenproof serving platter and place a piece of brie into each cap.
5. Place the platter in the oven until the cheese melts, about 10 minutes. Sprinkle with the walnuts and serve.

Fast: Can assemble up to 1 day in advance and refrigerate.

Fabulous: With different cheeses, such as teleme, whole milk mozzarella, Camembert, or chèvre.

CREAM OF ROASTED RED PEPPER AND RED ONION SOUP

2 tablespoons unsalted butter

2 red onions, minced

4 cloves garlic, minced

1/4 cup minced fresh parsley

6 cups chicken broth,
homemade or canned

5 red bell peppers, roasted
(see page 28), skinned,
seeded, and pureed

1 bay leaf

1 cup Madeira

1 cup plus 2 tablespoons
heavy cream

2 large egg yolks

Salt and freshly ground white
pepper to taste

Minced fresh parsley, chives,
or green onions for garnish

1. Melt the butter in 3-quart saucepan and gently sauté the onions over low heat until soft.
2. Stir in the garlic and parsley and continue to cook over low heat until the garlic is tender, about 5 minutes.
3. Add the chicken broth, pureed red pepper, and bay leaf. Bring the soup to a boil over high heat, then reduce to medium-low and stir in the Madeira. Simmer for 10 to 30 minutes, or until the flavors and consistency are pleasing.
4. Stir in the cup of cream and simmer for another 5 minutes.
5. Mix together the remaining cream and the yolks. Stir several table-spoons of the hot soup into the yolk mixture, then stir the yolk mixture back into the soup. Continue cooking until the soup thickens slightly. Season with salt and pepper. Do not boil or the soup will curdle.

Fast: Can prepare through step 3 up to 3 days in advance and refrigerate, or freeze for up to 6 months. Finish cooking right before serving. Thaw in the refrigerator for 2 to 3 days.

Flashy: Garnish with a sprinkle of minced parsley, chives, or green onions.

Fabulous: Seasoned with fresh or dried thyme, dill, basil, or oregano.

BRANDIED CHICKEN BREASTS WITH SHRIMP IN WINE SAUCE

BRANDY MARINADE

1/4 cup brandy or to taste

1/2 cup olive or peanut oil

1/2 cup buttermilk

Several sprigs fresh thyme or
dried thyme to taste

1/4 cup minced shallots

1/4 cup minced fresh parsley

1. Combine all the ingredients for the marinade in a food processor fitted with a metal blade or whisk together in a large bowl. Taste and adjust the seasonings.
2. Place the chicken and shrimp in a large glass or ceramic pan and coat with the marinade. Cover with plastic wrap and refrigerate for 4 to 24 hours.
3. To make the wine sauce, bring the vermouth, brandy, shallots, and thyme to a boil in a saucepan over high heat and let boil until reduced by half, about 5 minutes.

Salt and freshly ground white
pepper to taste

4 chicken breasts,
approximately 6 ounces
each, boned, skinned,
halved, and pounded to
1/4 inch thickness

8 to 16 large shrimp, shelled
and deveined (or whatever
amount your budget
allows)

WINE SAUCE
1 cup dry vermouth
1/4 cup brandy
1/4 cup minced shallots
Several sprigs fresh thyme,
minced
3 cups chicken broth,
homemade or canned
1 cup heavy cream
Salt and freshly ground white
pepper to taste

1/4 pound (1 stick) unsalted
butter
1/2 cup peanut oil
All-purpose flour for dredging
Salt and freshly ground white
pepper to taste
2 tablespoons unsalted
butter, cold and cut into
pieces
Minced fresh parsley or
thyme sprigs for garnish

4. Lower the heat to medium-high, then add the broth and cream and reduce by half again, about 10 minutes. Season with the salt and pepper. Taste and adjust the seasonings. Set aside.

5. To finish the dish, melt 2 tablespoons of the butter with 2 table-spoons of the peanut or olive oil in a large skillet.

6. Remove the chicken and shrimp from the marinade and pat dry. Lightly dredge the chicken in the flour, and sauté on each side over medium heat until the chicken turns opaque and firm, but is still pink inside, several minutes per side. Season with salt and pepper while cooking. Do not crowd the chicken pieces. Sauté in batches, adding more butter and oil as needed. Transfer the finished chicken to a baking pan.

7. Add more butter and oil to the skillet, and briefly sauté the shrimp only until they turn opaque, about 3 to 5 minutes.

8. Place a shrimp on top of each chicken breast in the baking pan.

9. Strain the wine sauce through a fine wire mesh strainer over the chicken and shrimp and cover with aluminum foil.

10. Finish the cooking in a preheated 350°F oven for 15 to 30 minutes, until just cooked.

11. Remove the chicken breasts to a warm serving platter. Place the baking pan with the sauce on a burner over medium heat (or transfer the sauce to a saucepan). Stir the cold butter into the sauce before serving.

Fast: Can prepare up to 1 day in advance, through step 9 and refrigerate. Bring to room temperature before finishing. Can prepare wine sauce up to 3 days in advance and refrigerate or freeze for up to 6 months and thaw at room temperature for 4 hours or 1 day in the refrigerator.

Flashy: Garnish with minced fresh parsley and/or sprigs of fresh thyme.

Fabulous: With fresh or dried tarragon and/or dill.

CARROTS WITH FENNEL

1 pound carrots, trimmed,
    peeled, and cut into
    matchstick strips
1 fennel bulb, trimmed and
    cut into matchstick strips
3/4 cup chicken broth,
    homemade or canned
2 cloves garlic, minced
2 shallots, minced
1/4 cup sherry
1 teaspoon dried dillweed or
    to taste
1/2 bay leaf
Salt and freshly ground white
    pepper to taste
2 to 4 tablespoons (1/4 to
    1/2 stick) unsalted butter
2 tablespoons minced fresh
    parsley

1. Place all but the last three ingredients in a large skillet. Bring to a boil over high heat, cover, reduce heat to medium, and simmer for 5 minutes.
2. Season with salt and pepper and continue to cook for a few minutes, until the liquid cooks away. Stir in the butter and parsley, then taste and adjust the seasonings.

Fast: Can prepare through step 1 up to 1 day in advance and refrigerate. Bring to room temperature before finishing.

Fabulous: With any herb.

LEMON PILAF

6 tablespoons (3/4 stick)
    unsalted butter
1/2 cup minced red onions
1 1/2 cups uncooked long
    grain white rice
1/2 cup uncooked bulgur
2 1/2 cups chicken broth,
    homemade or canned
1/2 cup dry vermouth
Grated zest of 2 to 3 lemons
Salt and freshly ground white
    pepper to taste

1. Melt the butter in a large saucepan and sauté the onions over low to medium-low heat until tender, but not brown.
2. Stir in the rice and bulgur. Cook, stirring, until the rice becomes opaque.
3. Add the chicken broth, vermouth, and zest, and bring to a boil over high heat. Reduce the heat to low, cover, and cook for 20 minutes. Season with salt and pepper.

Fast: Can prepare through step 2 up to 1 day in advance and refrigerate. Can fully prepare up to 1 day in advance, refrigerate, and reheat in a double boiler or microwave.

Fabulous: With different kinds of rice and grains, such as couscous, polenta, brown rice, barley, basmati rice. With one large stalk lemon grass instead of lemon zest. With toasted pine nuts stirred in.

CHEESECAKE MOUSSE

4 large egg yolks (see page
  23)
6 tablespoons sugar
3 tablespoons fresh lemon
  juice
1 tablespoon brandy
Grated zest of 2 to 3 lemons
1/2 cup plain yogurt
1 1/4 cups sour cream
2 1/2 cups heavy cream
1 teaspoon vanilla extract
Sliced almonds, strawberries,
  and kiwi for garnish

Yield: 8 to 12 servings

A rich and opulent dessert with a light texture.

1. Combine the egg yolks and 1/4 cup of the sugar in the top of a double boiler over simmering water. Whisk until thick and lemon-colored.
2. Add the lemon juice, brandy, and zest, and whisk for several minutes.
3. Transfer the mixture to a metal bowl and place in the freezer to chill, about 15 to 30 minutes.
4. Stir the yogurt and sour cream into the chilled mixture.
5. In the meantime, whip the heavy cream with the remaining sugar and the vanilla in a food processor fitted with a metal blade, or with an electric mixer, until it holds soft peaks.
6. Fold the whipped cream into the yolk mixture and chill for at least 1 hour before serving.

Fast: Can prepare up to 2 days in advance and refrigerate, or freeze for up to 3 months. Thaw in the refrigerator for 2 days.

Flashy: Serve with a sprinkling of almonds and fresh fruit, in stemmed glasses, with Praline-Butter Thins (recipe follows).

Fabulous: With any liqueur instead of the brandy. With orange zest instead of lemon, and/or with 4 ounces semisweet or bittersweet chocolate, melted, and added at step 2 with 1 teaspoon espresso powder.

PRALINE-BUTTER THINS

1/2 pound (2 sticks)
   unsalted butter, frozen
   and cut into small pieces
1/4 teaspoon salt
1/4 cup sugar
1/2 cup plus 2 tablespoons
   Pecan-Praline Powder
   (recipe follows)
1 teaspoon vanilla extract
2 large egg yolks
2 1/4 cups all-purpose flour

Yield: about 5 dozen

Yet another twist on the Swedish classic. Watch out, they tend to disappear rapidly.

1. Preheat the oven to 400°F and butter a cookie sheet.
2. Combine all the ingredients, except the flour, in a food processor fitted with a metal blade or place in a bowl and combine using an electric mixer until the butter is creamed.
3. Add the flour and process until a ball begins to form or add the flour to the bowl and blend in using the electric mixer until a dough forms.
4. Place the dough in a cookie press fitted with a ribbon disk. Press into 2-inch lengths.
5. Bake until the edges begin to brown, but the cookies are still pale, about 8 minutes. Cool for about 5 minutes, then remove from the cookie sheet to a rack and cool to room temperature. Repeat with the remaining dough, baking one cookie sheet at a time.

Fast: Can prepare up to 4 days in advance and store in an airtight jar(s), or freeze for up to 3 months. Defrost at room temperature for about 1 hour.

Fabulous: Modified as **Lemon-Butter Thins**. Use 3/4 cup sugar and substitute the grated zest of one lemon and freshly grated nutmeg to taste for the praline powder.

PECAN-PRALINE POWDER

2 cups sugar

1/2 cup brandy

2 cups pecans, toasted (see page 29)

This is wonderful to keep on hand for creating instant magic.

1. Place the sugar and brandy in a heavy saucepan over medium heat and dissolve the sugar. Don't stir; rather, hold the pan by the handle and swirl it throughout the process.
2. Add the pecans and cook over medium-high heat, covered with a tight-fitting lid, for 1 to 2 minutes. Remove the lid when the boiling bubbles are thick. Continue to boil until the mixture turns a light caramel color, about 3 to 5 minutes, swirling frequently. Remove the pan from the heat and continue swirling until it becomes a rich caramel color.
3. Pour the mixture onto a buttered piece of aluminum foil and let harden, about 20 minutes.
4. Break up the hardened praline and process it in a food processor fitted with a metal blade or a blender until ground to a powder.

Fast: Can prepare up to 2 weeks in advance and store in an airtight container, or freeze for up to 6 months. Thaw in the refrigerator for 2 days or at room temperature for about 8 hours.

Flashy: Sprinkled on almost anything from ice cream to frosting.

Fabulous: With any nut, instead of pecans, or bourbon instead of brandy.

CASUAL SPRING MENUS

. . . .

Spring Pasta Dinner Party

Casual dinner parties need not, and should not, be any less stylized than more elaborate ones. This party is built around a simple, yet sophisticated menu. It focuses on a few luxurious dishes, providing the opportunity for everyone to fully enjoy themselves.

The party begins with Marinated Shrimp, a refreshingly herbal hors d'oeuvre that stimulates the appetite. Instead of a predictable tossed salad, I serve a delicious vegetable terrine. Besides being a wonderful dish, it is extremely convenient. It can be completely arranged on an oven-proof platter and held at room temperature before your guests arrive. At serving time, place it in the oven for a minute and *voila!* Next comes the entree, a fantasy pasta designed to feature spring's starring vegetable, asparagus. Complementing this vegetable's assertive quality is the sweet, delicate flavor of sautéed scallops. The addition of pine nuts provides textural interest plus a rich nutty flavor. All of these ingredients are enhanced by a silken lemon sauce. Let's hear it for giving in to fantasies such as this!

Our party concludes with yet another culinary fantasy . . . Aphrodite's Parfait. It highlights the season's starring fruit—strawberries. Who could resist this combination of French vanilla ice cream, fresh, sweet strawberries, and whipped cream, along with a warm bittersweet chocolate sauce flavored with brandy?

As for the ambiance, I suggest creating a fresh crisp spring look—the emphasis on fun rather than fancy. Instead of a tablecloth use textured deep purple placemats with hot pink napkins. Pink azaleas are beautiful when mixed with cuttings of onion blossoms and arranged in a large white porcelain flower pot. To complete the look, surround the flowers with white porcelain candlesticks filled with white candles. This will create a "City Casual" spring look.

MENU

Marinated Shrimp with Garlic Crouton Rounds

Mediterranean Vegetable Terrine with Goat Cheese and Pecans

Sourdough French Bread with Sweet Butter

Asparagus and Scallop Pasta

Aphrodite's Parfait

Lemon-Butter Thins (see page 62)

FASTER & FLASHIER MENU

Marinated Shrimp (buy shrimp already cooked and peeled; marinate them as directed)

Tossed Salad

Asparagus and Scallop Pasta (use premade alfredo sauce)

Aphrodite's Parfait (buy chocolate sauce)

Butter Cookies (purchased)

WINES

Gewürztraminer

Sauvignon Blanc or Champagne

Black Muscat

Fast & Fabulous Timetable

Up to 3 Months in Advance and Frozen
  Garlic Crouton Rounds • Lemon-Butter Thins

5 Days in Advance and Refrigerated
  Vinaigrette

3 Days in Advance and Refrigerated
  Mediterranean Vegetable Terrine • Lemon Cream Sauce

2 Days in Advance and Refrigerated
  Marinated Shrimp • Thaw frozen prepared-ahead foods

1 Day in Advance and Refrigerated
  Prepare strawberries and whipped cream for dessert • Brandied Chocolate Sauce • Set table

Party Day!
  Heat terrine • Warm bread • Cook scallops, asparagus, and pasta • Warm sauce and assemble entree • Assemble Aphrodite's Parfait

MARINATED SHRIMP

16 to 24 medium-size to
  large shrimp, shelled and
  deveined
1/4 cup minced fresh parsley
1/4 cup minced green onions
1/4 cup sliced celery
Fresh lemon juice to taste
1/2 cup Tarragon-Caper
  Vinaigrette (recipe follows)
Garlic Crouton Rounds (see
  page 192)

Yield: 4 to 8 servings

1. To cook the shrimp, bring a large pot of salted water to a boil. Drop the shrimp in and watch carefully to avoid overcooking. The minute they turn pink and start to curl up, they should be removed from the water. This will only take about 3 minutes.
2. Combine all the ingredients in a large bowl and marinate in the refrigerator for at least 4 hours.
3. Taste and adjust the seasonings. Serve at room temperature.

Fast: Can prepare up to 2 days in advance and refrigerate.

Flashy: Serve with toothpicks and Garlic Crouton Rounds

Fabulous: The water that the shrimp are cooked in can be seasoned with: parsley, onions, garlic, black peppercorns, celery leaves, fresh lemon juice, a bay leaf, and/or fresh or dried tarragon leaves. Wine or a combination of wine and chicken, vegetable, or seafood broth can be used instead of the water.

   You can also substitute the same amount of medium to large scallops or mussels for the shrimp. If using small scallops or mussels, use double or triple the amount. To cook the scallops or mussels, proceed as directed above, but reduce the amount of liquid used to about 2 to 4 cups. The scallops are cooked as soon as they begin to firm up and turn opaque, about 3 to 5 minutes; the mussels when their shells open.

TARRAGON-CAPER VINAIGRETTE

1/2 cup tarragon vinegar
1/4 cup fresh lemon juice
1/4 cup capers, rinsed and
  drained
1 1/4 cups grapeseed oil or
  your favorite oil
Salt and freshly ground white
  pepper to taste
Minced fresh or dried
  tarragon to taste

Yield: about 2 1/4 cups

1. Combine all the ingredients in a food processor fitted with a metal blade, or in a blender. Taste and adjust the seasonings.
2. Store in the refrigerator in an airtight container. Stir or shake before using.

Fast: Can prepare up to 5 days in advance and refrigerate.

Fabulous: Used to marinate mushrooms, fish, chicken, or pork.

MEDITERRANEAN VEGETABLE TERRINE

1 eggplant, thinly sliced

2 to 4 zucchini, thinly sliced

Salt to taste

2 tablespoons extra virgin olive oil, plus extra for tossing

1 onion, thinly sliced

4 to 8 cloves garlic, minced

Freshly ground white pepper to taste

Dried or minced fresh herbs of your choice

2 red bell peppers, roasted (see page 28), peeled, and seeded

2 yellow bell peppers, roasted, peeled, and seeded

1/4 to 1/2 cup minced fresh parsley

4 ounces chèvre (plain or with herbs)

1/2 cup pecans, or more, sautéed in 2 to 4 tablespoons olive oil for 5 to 10 minutes over medium heat, until very fragrant

Raspberry Vinaigrette (see page 228)

Yield: One 4-cup terrine (any leftovers are delicious added to salads, pasta, or rice dishes)

A vegetable pâté, well seasoned with herbs and olive oil. This evokes the essence of sunny Mediterranean flavors.

1. Place the eggplant and zucchini slices in a colander in the sink, sprinkle with salt, and let drain for at least 1 hour. Rinse well and blot dry with paper towels.
2. In a large skillet, heat the oil over very low heat, toss in the onions and garlic, and cook until soft, about 20 minutes.
3. Toss the zucchini and eggplant with just enough olive oil to coat them. Season with the salt, pepper, and herbs. Place on an aluminum foil–lined baking sheet. Bake in a preheated 350°F oven until just tender, about 20 minutes.
4. Oil a 4- to 6-cup terrine or loaf pan and layer in the zucchini and eggplant, then the red and yellow peppers, then the onion and garlic mixture along with the minced parsley.
5. Reduce the oven temperature to 300°F. Place the terrine, covered with a sheet of aluminum foil, in a large pan filled with hot water that reaches halfway up the sides of the terrine. Bake for 1 hour.
6. Remove the terrine from the water and cool to room temperature.
7. Cover with plastic wrap and place a weight on top. Refrigerate for 24 hours.
8. Blot up any excess oil and juices. Unmold onto an ovenproof platter. Top with pieces of chèvre and pecans.

Fast: Can prepare through step 7 up to 3 days in advance and refrigerate.

Flashy: Pour the vinaigrette over the top and around the base of the terrine. Place extra pecans around the base as well. Before serving, place in a preheated 350°F oven until the cheese is hot. Serve with lots of crusty French bread to sop up the vinaigrette.

Fabulous: In summer take advantage of the availability of fresh herbs. Layer in fresh basil leaves or even pesto. For another variation, alternate layers of 4 cups pureed white or garbanzo beans (seasoned with an egg, salt, and chèvre) with layers of vegetables.

ASPARAGUS AND SCALLOP PASTA WITH LEMON CREAM SAUCE

LEMON CREAM SAUCE

1/4 pound (1 stick) unsalted butter

3 shallots, minced

4 to 6 cloves garlic, minced

1/4 cup minced fresh parsley

Grated zest of 2 lemons, minced

1 cup dry vermouth

2 cups heavy cream

2 pounds uncooked angel hair, fettucine, or linguini

1 pound asparagus, trimmed and cut into 1 1/2- to 2-inch lengths

1 pound sea scallops, sliced into 1/4-inch-thick rounds, soaked in milk for at least 1 hour in refrigerator, and drained

Salt and freshly ground white pepper to taste

Freshly grated nutmeg to taste

Fresh lemon juice to taste

1/2 to 1 cup pistachios, chopped

Freshly grated mizithra or Parmesan cheese to taste

Yield: 8 to 12 servings

If you like alfredo sauce, you will adore this.

1. For the sauce, melt half of the butter in a large saucepan and sauté the shallots, garlic, parsley, and zest over low heat until the shallots are tender, but not brown.
2. Add the vermouth, bring to a boil over high heat, and reduce by half.
3. Stir in the cream and reduce by about a third or until slightly thickened. Season with salt and pepper.
4. Meanwhile, bring a large pot of salted water to a boil.
5. Blanch the asparagus until barely tender, about 3 to 4 minutes. Remove the pieces with a strainer and add them to the sauce.
6. Cook the pasta until al dente
7. At the same time, melt the remaining butter in a large, heavy skillet and sauté the scallops with the pistachios briefly over medium-high heat, until the scallops are just opaque. Season with salt, pepper, nutmeg, and lemon juice while cooking.
8. Drain the pasta and transfer to a large warm bowl. Toss with the scallops, sauce, and desired amount of grated cheese.

Fast: Can prepare sauce up to 3 days in advance and refrigerate. Reheat over medium heat.

Flashy: Served over rice, bulgur, or couscous instead of pasta.

Fabulous: Seasoned with almost any fresh herb such as basil, dill, tarragon, or thyme. With shrimp, lobster, or steamed mussels instead of, or with, the scallops. With 1/4 cup capers, rinsed and drained, add to the sauce. With any nut instead of the pistachios.

APHRODITE'S PARFAIT

*2 pints fresh strawberries,
hulled and sliced*

*Grand Marnier, or any
orange-flavored liqueur, to
taste*

*1 quart French vanilla ice
cream*

*Brandied Chocolate Sauce
(see page 141)*

*1 cup walnuts, toasted (see
page 29)*

*2 cups heavy cream,
whipped to soft peaks*

As soon as you taste this you'll understand why I dedicated it to the goddess of love.

1. Combine the strawberries with the Grand Marnier in a large glass bowl. Let macerate for about 1 hour at room temperature, or up to 1 day refrigerated, and spoon into goblets.
2. Next add desired amount of ice cream.
3. Top with the chocolate sauce, walnuts, and whipped cream.

Fast: Can prepare strawberries and whipped cream up to 1 day in advance and refrigerate. Assemble right before serving.

Flashy: Serve with Lemon-Butter Thins (see page 62).

Fabulous: With fresh or frozen raspberries instead of strawberries, or any other berry in season.

Mediterranean Spring Stew Dinner

Here is a dinner party made-to-order for brisk spring weather. It is a menu best described as country casual, getting its inspiration from the marvelous Mediterranean cuisines. The flavors are bold and robust, while requiring very little effort to prepare or present. As a matter of fact, this menu is equally enjoyable served at room temperature, which makes it a great choice for a picnic!

Simply omit the chicken and shrimp from this entree if you want to serve a vegetarian meal. Besides all the other good and tasty qualities this menu has, it is *very* low in fat and calories.

This dinner menu eliminates a separate salad and vegetable course. Instead the hors d'oeuvre acts as both an hors d'oeuvre and a salad. The entree also does double-duty and combines a vegetable with the shrimp and chicken. Such simplification allows you to focus fully on each dish.

Once again, I suggest taking your cues for the table design from the feeling that the menu projects. The goal is to capture the rich, exuberant mood of the Mediterranean countryside. A brilliant yellow tablecloth with a bit of texture helps to establish a rustic but fresh country feel.

Daisies along with stems of daylilies that are about to bloom can be arranged in a simple white porcelain pitcher. For added excitement surround this by fresh, whole artichokes and red bell peppers. Use white pillar candles placed on terra-cotta saucers on each side of the centerpiece. Bulky, simple Spanish wineglasses along with earthy Spanish pottery, and bright orange napkins helped to create a special Mediterranean feeling.

MENU

Pickled Mushrooms

Caesar Sauce with Jicama, Belgian Endive, and Asparagus

Mediterranean Spring Stew

Grilled Polenta

French Bread with Butter or Olive oil

Grapes and Walnuts with Bleu Cheese and Madeira Spread

Orange Almond Biscotti

FASTER & FLASHIER MENU

Marinated Mushrooms (purchased from a deli)

Mediterranean Spring Stew on Rice

Grapes and Walnuts with Bleu Cheese

Biscotti (purchased)

WINES

Sauvignon Blanc

Chardonnay

Late harvest Riesling or Champagne

Fast & Fabulous Timetable

Up to 6 Months in Advance and Frozen
  Mediterranean Spring Stew through step 6 • Orange Almond Biscotti

Up to 3 Months in Advance and Frozen
  Grilled Polenta through step 4 • Bleu Cheese and Madeira Spread

Up to 2 Weeks in Advance and Refrigerated
Pickled Mushrooms

5 Days in Advance and Refrigerated
Bleu Cheese and Madeira Spread • Orange Almond Biscotti

3 Days in Advance and Refrigerated
Mediterranean Spring Stew through step 6 • Caesar Sauce

2 Days in Advance and Refrigerated
Start polenta • Thaw frozen prepared-ahead foods

1 Day in Advance
Set table

Party Day!
Finish Mediterranean Spring Stew • Grill or reheat polenta • Arrange dessert on a platter • Warm bread

PICKLED MUSHROOMS

1 cup white wine vinegar
1/2 cup chicken broth, homemade or canned
1/2 to 1 cup olive oil
2 to 4 cloves garlic, whole or minced
1 carrot, thinly sliced
4 to 8 green onions, cut into 1-inch pieces
1/4 cup minced fresh parsley
Dried marjoram, rosemary, and oregano to taste
5 black peppercorns
1/2 bay leaf
1 1/2 teaspoons salt or to taste
1 pound small to medium-size mushrooms, stemmed

Yield: about 3 cups

Also great for picnics and barbecues!

1. Combine all the ingredients, except the mushrooms, in a large saucepan and bring to a boil over high heat. Reduce the heat to medium-low and simmer for 5 minutes.
2. Add the mushrooms and simmer for 5 to 10 minutes. Taste and adjust the seasonings.
3. Cool. Transfer to a glass jar and refrigerate, covered, for several days to allow the mushrooms to absorb the flavors.

Fast: Can prepare up to 2 weeks in advance and refrigerate.

Flashy: Serve with toothpicks and a sliced baguette.

Fabulous: With about a pound of celery, fennel, artichoke hearts, carrots, green beans, zucchini, or peppers cut into bite-size pieces instead of the mushrooms.

CAESAR SAUCE

1 cup olive oil
2 tablespoons crumbled feta
  cheese
1 teaspoon Dijon mustard or
  to taste
2 cloves garlic, minced, or to
  taste
4 to 8 anchovy fillets
1 teaspoon Worcestershire
  sauce
1/2 cup freshly grated
  Parmesan cheese or to
  taste
Fresh lemon or lime juice to
  taste
Salt and freshly ground black
  pepper to taste

Yield: about 1 3/4 cups

If the anchovies worry you, relax—they just act as a subtle seasoning, not a pronounced flavor. Instead of egg, this Caesar is enriched with feta cheese.

1. Combine all the ingredients in a food processor fitted with a metal blade, or in a blender.
2. Taste and adjust the seasonings. Serve chilled or at room temperature.

Fast: Can prepare up to 3 days in advance and refrigerate.

Flashy: Dunk romaine, endive, jicama, or cooked artichoke leaves, cooked or raw asparagus, broccoli or cauliflower florets, melba toast, or French bread. Even fingers are sensational dunked in this!

Fabulous: As a cold sauce for grilled chicken, beef, pork, fish, or lamb.

MEDITERRANEAN SPRING STEW

10 tablespoons olive oil
2 onions, thinly sliced
2 fennel bulbs, thinly sliced
  (reserve the stalks and
  feathery leaves)
2 yellow wax peppers,
  stemmed, seeded, and
  minced
6 cloves garlic, minced
Two 10-ounce packages
  frozen baby artichokes,
  thawed, or 6 medium-size
  fresh artichokes (see note
  page 73)

Yield: 8 to 12 servings

This is an exciting rustic dish full of seasonal vegetables that is perfect for cool evenings when casual fare is called for. Don't let all the ingredients scare you—it is very easy to prepare.

1. Heat 1/4 cup of the olive oil in a large skillet or wok.
2. Add the onions, fennel, peppers, garlic, artichokes, and chard stalks. Sauté over medium-low heat, stirring frequently, until very tender, about 30 to 40 minutes.
3. In the meantime, toss the eggplant with about 1/4 cup of the olive oil. Place on a baking sheet and bake in a preheated 400°F oven for about 20 minutes, until tender and fully cooked. Remove from the oven and add it along with the tomatoes to the sautéed vegetables.

Red chard stalks from 1
bunch chard, thinly sliced

1 eggplant, cut into 1/2- to
1-inch cubes

Two 16-ounce cans pear
tomatoes, drained and
chopped

1 pound medium-size to
large shrimp, peeled and
deveined (reserve the
shells)

1 cup bottled clam juice
(optional)

1/2 teaspoon saffron threads

1/4 cup sherry, plus a little
extra

Calamata olives to taste

2 pounds chicken thighs or
breasts, boned, skinned,
and cut into bite-size
pieces

Salt and freshly ground white
pepper to taste

Crumbled feta cheese for
garnish

Grilled Polenta (recipe
follows)

4. At the same time, prepare a shrimp stock. Toast the reserved shrimp shells in a saucepan over medium to high heat until they become very fragrant and turn pink. Add water to cover, at least 2 cups, and bring to a boil. Add several of the reserved fennel stalks. Continue to simmer until the flavors develop and the liquid reduces by at least half. (Can use the bottled clam juice instead.) Strain the stock through a fine wire mesh strainer into the vegetable mixture. Discard the shells and fennel stalks.

5. Put the saffron in small skillet and heat over medium to high heat for a minute or so, until it becomes very fragrant. Add the sherry and cook until the sherry is infused with the saffron. Add this to the tomato-vegetable mixture.

6. Stir in the olives, along with a bit more sherry. Continue to simmer over medium-low heat for about 20 minutes until the flavors are pleasing.

7. Heat the remaining olive oil in another large, heavy skillet or wok, and sauté the chicken and shrimp until both are opaque. Do not overcrowd; cook in several small batches if necessary. Season with salt and pepper while cooking.

8. Combine the chicken and shrimp with the tomato mixture. Cook over low heat for several minutes to allow the flavors to mix. Taste and adjust the seasonings.

Fast: Can prepare through step 6 up to 3 days in advance, or freeze for up to 6 months. Thaw in the refrigerator for 2 days. Sauté the chicken and shrimp before serving or undercook up to 1 day in advance and refrigerate. Warm gently in the tomato mixture.

Flashy: Place grilled polenta on a large platter or on individual dishes. Top with the chicken and shrimp mixture and a sprinkling of crumbled feta cheese.

Fabulous: All by itself, without anything but vegetables. With just shrimp or with monkfish or scallops. With mussels and/or clams, added in step 8 and cooked just until their shells open. Can also serve on white beans, pasta, couscous, or rice instead of polenta.

Further: Add broth to leftovers to create a soup. Toss leftovers into pasta, or serve on white beans, rice, or couscous.

NOTE: If using fresh artichokes, cut the top third from the artichokes, removing all sharp, prickly tips. Immediately rub the cut portion with half of a lemon to prevent discoloration. Repeat this on any cut that you make on the artichoke. Next cut away any portion of the stem that looks like it should be discarded. Cut the artichoke in half and cut away and discard the thistle in the middle along with the leaves. Cut into long, thin pieces all the way through to the stem. Place the pieces in a bowl of acidulated water containing the juice of 1 lemon. When finished, drain the artichokes and prepare as directed.

GRILLED POLENTA

8 cups chicken broth, homemade or canned

1 cup dry white wine

2 cloves garlic, minced, or to taste

1/4 cup minced green onions or to taste

1/4 cup minced fresh parsley or to taste

Sprigs fresh rosemary or dried rosemary to taste

3 cups uncooked polenta or instant polenta

1/4 cup olive oil

Italian soul food!

1. Add all the ingredients, except the polenta and olive oil, to a large pot, and bring to a boil over high heat.
2. Slowly stir the polenta into the boiling liquid. Reduce the heat to medium-high and cook, stirring frequently, until the polenta comes away cleanly from the sides of the pot when stirred, about 30 to 50 minutes, or 5 minutes for instant polenta.
3. Transfer the polenta to an oiled rimmed cookie sheet. Cool to room temperature, then chill in the refrigerator.
4. When firm, cut the polenta into squares.
5. Oil the barbecue grill and brush the squares of polenta with the oil. Grill until hot, or broil in the oven.

Fast: Can prepare through step 4 up to 2 days in advance and refrigerate, or freeze up to 3 months. Thaw in the refrigerator for 2 days.

Flashy: Cut into small pieces and served as an hors d'oeuvre.

Fabulous: With fresh minced basil rather than rosemary. Cut into small pieces and served as an hors d'oeuvre.

GRAPES AND WALNUTS WITH BLEU CHEESE
AND MADEIRA SPREAD

*Bleu Cheese and Madeira
(recipe follows)*
*Grape leaves, sprigs fresh
mint, and/or marigolds for
garnish*
Water crackers
*Walnut halves, toasted (see
page 29)*
*Assorted clusters of grapes
(green, purple, black),
chilled*

A lovely combination of flavors and textures, this is a refreshing and satisfying end to any meal. As you can see, no amounts are given—it's up to you.

1. Present this on a large wooden or ceramic platter. Place the cheese spread in the middle on several grape leaves, surrounded with crackers. Place the walnut halves attractively, then the grapes. Remember, grapes should be chilled. Make sure to put several small spreading knives on the platter for the cheese.

Fast: Can assemble the cheese and garnishes up to 1 day in advance and refrigerate.

Fabulous: With a wedge of almost any cheese (from Brie to gorgonzola) instead of or in addition to the Bleu Cheese and Madeira.

BLEU CHEESE AND MADEIRA

*1/2 pound bleu cheese or
gorgonzola, at room
temperature*
*1/4 pound (1 stick) unsalted
butter, at room
temperature*
2 tablespoons Madeira
*Salt and freshly ground white
pepper to taste*
*1 teaspoon green peppercorns
or to taste*
*Grapes or sliced fruit and
crackers or French bread
for garnish*

Yield: about 1 1/2 cups

A delicious hors d'oeuvre or dessert!

1. Cream all the ingredients together, except the peppercorns, in a food processor fitted with a metal blade or with a wooden spoon in a large bowl.
2. Add the peppercorns and process with several quick on-and-off motions, taking care not to destroy their texture. If mixing by hand, cream into the mixture.
3. Pack the cheese mixture into an oiled, plastic wrap–lined mold. Refrigerate until firm, about 4 hours.

Fast: Can prepare up to 5 days in advance and refrigerate, or freeze for up to 3 months. Thaw in the refrigerator for 2 days or at room temperature for 8 hours.

Flashy: To serve, invert mold onto platter. Garnish with grapes and/or any sliced fruit of the season. Serve with crackers, French bread, and/or apple slices.

Fabulous: Add nuts and/or herbs.

ORANGE ALMOND BISCOTTI

3/4 to 1 cup sugar
4 1/2 cups all-purpose flour
Freshly grated nutmeg to
 taste
1/2 teaspoon salt
1/2 pound (2 sticks)
 unsalted butter, cut into
 small pieces
2 large eggs
1 teaspoon vanilla extract
1/4 cup orange-flavored
 liqueur
1/2 cup water
1 1/2 cup almonds, toasted
 (see page 29) and
 chopped
Grated zest of 2 oranges

Yield: about 7 dozen

One of my favorites!

1. Preheat the oven to 375°F.
2. Combine the sugar, 4 cups of the flour, the nutmeg, and salt in a food processor fitted with a metal blade.
3. Process in the butter until the mixture resembles a coarse meal, then process in the eggs, vanilla, liqueur, and enough water to form a dough.
4. Add the almonds and zest. Process with several quick on-and-off motions so as not to destroy their texture.
5. Dust the work area with the remaining flour and lightly flour your hands. Divide the dough in half and form two loaves.
6. Place the loaves on an ungreased cookie sheet and bake until a tester inserted into the middle comes out clean, about 35 to 45 minutes.
7. Remove from the oven and cool slightly. Cut the loaves into 1/2-inch slices. You can cut each slice in half lengthwise for long narrow slices.
8. Return the slices to the cookie sheet, reduce the temperature to 300°F and bake, until crisp 15 to 20 minutes more. Turn the oven off and leave the cookies in the oven with the door ajar for another 15 minutes.

Fast: Can prepare up to 5 days in advance and store in airtight jar(s) or in plastic bag(s), or freeze for up to 6 months. Thaw in the refrigerator for 2 days or at room temperature for a few hours.

Fabulous: With half of each cookie dipped in melted milk or semisweet chocolate after baking.

. . . .

CHAPTER FOUR

Summer Dinner Parties

SUMMER DINNER PARTIES AT A GLANCE

. . . .

The Setting

ELEGANT
- Outdoors or indoors, but with a cool, fresh, gardenlike feel
- Impact results from the juxtaposition of formal treatments with natural elements, such as silver candlesticks near a swimming pool

CASUAL
- Often outdoors
- Country charm, or with a strong emphasis on nature
- Primitive, rustic and/or exotic with a playful, youthful exuberance

Party Props

ELEGANT
- Colors are more refined and subdued pastels: gray, pink, mauve, light green, peach, lilac
- Silver, china, crystal serving pieces . . . all your best!
- Simple, bold floral arrangements with an Oriental feel or lush country bouquets
- Champagne flutes, glass bowls, or traditional vases
- Candelabra or masses of votive candles in clear glass holders

CASUAL
- Bright, pure colors: red, green, yellow, orange, purple, blue
- Cast-iron skillets, pottery, clear or colored glass, and/or vivid contemporary plastic for serving pieces

- Boldly patterned, checkered picnic cloths or brightly colored floral, print, or solid tablecloths
- Solid or patterned sheets or cotton bedspreads used as tablecloths
- Oversized napkins or fresh and brightly colored kitchen towels
- Unstructured country bouquets mixing flowers with fresh herb cuttings
- Jelly-jar glasses, French canning jars, baskets, tin pails, wine carafes, pottery crocks, terra-cotta pots, and/or ceramic pitchers as vases
- Simple heavy glassware
- Votive candles on bricks or chunks of wood, in terra-cotta pots, or in terra-cotta saucers filled with sand, or mini tin pails, or imported tin candle holders

Foods for Decorating

- Fresh fruits: grapes, melons, lemons, limes, peaches, nectarines, plums, apricots—anything!
- Fresh vegetables: tomatoes, onions, garlic, eggplant, zucchini, peppers, cucumbers—anything!
- Fresh herb cuttings

Cuisine

ELEGANT
- Contrasts elegance and refinement in presentation with fresh, bold summer flavors
- Emphasis on fresh herbs and produce
- Intense, vibrant colors and flavors
- Requires less time in the kitchen than in winter

CASUAL
- Glorifies the backyard barbecue
- Simplified and unrestrained in style
- Jubilant in spirit
- Flavors are as big and intense as the season
- Requires limited time in a hot kitchen
- Emphasis on fresh and herbal flavors

ELEGANT SUMMER MENUS

. . . .

Grilled Lamb Dinner

I gave this party over the Labor Day Weekend. It was a fabulous evening. The menu exemplifies an elegant summer barbecue. Summer cooking and entertaining demand a special vitality, along with a carefree spirit that I was able to capture with this menu. I wanted to savor every remaining minute of the season.

My table design reflected this spirit. The tablecloth, a pale pink, was the only subtle touch. Napkins and candles were hot pink. The centerpiece was one of my favorites. I used an unstained flower basket—you know, the classic style used to harvest fruits and vegetables. An arrangement of purple and pink stock, mixed with baby's breath, was arranged in a clear glass pitcher. Surrounding this was an arrangement of yellow summer squash, purple Japanese eggplant, and baby artichokes, along with red, yellow, and green bell peppers. It turned out to be an exciting and colorful tribute to the season. After the party, the vegetables were sautéed and tossed into pasta.

The party started off on a luxurious note with Stuffed Romaine and Prosciutto and Vegetables. The raw vegetables were especially welcomed, as the menu did not include a salad. The simplicity and flamboyance of these hors d'oeuvres will amaze and delight you.

Zucchini Soup with Double Pesto followed. Soups are often overlooked during the summer, but they can be delightful. This is a light and fresh-tasting soup which can be served either hot or cold, depending upon the temperature of summer evenings in your locale. Serving two different pesto sauces makes this course especially memorable, and allows your guests to add their own flavoring.

The entree plate is a composition of brilliant colors, interesting shapes, and bold flavors. Serve Grilled Skewers of Lamb, infused with garlic and herbal flavors from an olive oil–based marinade, with a brilliant Roasted Red Pepper Sauce as well as a cool and tangy Tarragon Mayonnaise Sauce. I halved big, gorgeous, juicy summer tomatoes and stuffed them with a mixture of sourdough bread crumbs, fresh dill, grated Romano cheese, and, for that special flavor punch, marinated artichoke hearts. This is a great way to enjoy tomatoes and can be completely assembled in advance. Lemon and Pine Nut Bulgur provides a complement for both dishes. The fresh, cleansing quality of the lemon zest, along with the smoky flavor of the pine nuts is delicious. An added bonus is its complete ease of preparation.

The menu concludes with a fresh Raspberry Sorbet in Peach Puree and Brandied Chocolate Sauce and Walnut Florentine cookies. As you can see, even the dessert focuses on seasonal produce, treating it with reverence. From hors d'oeuvres to dessert, this party is a marvelously indulgent tribute to the final days of summer.

MENU

Stuffed Romaine

Prosciutto and Vegetables

Zucchini Soup with Double Pesto

Sliced Baguette with Sweet Butter

Skewers of Lamb with Two Sauces

Baked Stuffed Tomatoes

Lemon and Pine Nut Bulgur

Raspberry Sorbet in Peach Puree and Brandied Chocolate Sauce

Walnut Florentines

FAST & FLASHIER MENU

Warm Chèvre with French Bread

Skewers of Lamb with Roasted Red Pepper Sauce (prepare with purchased roasted red peppers)

Bulgur with Lemon Zest

Raspberry Sorbet with Chocolate Sauce and Butter Cookies (purchased)

WINES

Champagne or Chardonnay

Sauvignon Blanc

Petite Sirah

Champagne

Fast & Fabulous Timetable

Up to 6 Months in Advance and Frozen
Zucchini Soup • Pesto • Chile and Sun-Dried Tomato Pesto • Lamb marinade • Simple Syrup (just refrigerated) • Peach Puree

Up to 3 Months in Advance and Frozen
Tomato Stuffing • Walnut Florentines

Up to 1 Month in Advance and Frozen
Raspberry Sorbet

Up to 2 Weeks in Advance and Refrigerated
Lamb marinade

Up to 7 Days in Advance and Refrigerated
Tarragon Mayonnaise Sauce

4 Days in Advance and Refrigerated
Pesto • Roasted Red Pepper Sauce

3 Days in Advance and Refrigerated
Zucchini Soup • Marinate lamb

2 Days in Advance and Refrigerated
Chile and Sun-Dried Tomato Pesto • Assemble stuffed tomatoes • Thaw frozen prepared-ahead foods

1 Day in Advance and Refrigerated
Prosciutto and Vegetables • Lemon and Pine Nut Bulgur • Peach Puree • Walnut Florentines • Set table

Party Day!
Stuffed Romaine • Heat soup and bread • Broil tomatoes • Finish bulgur • Grill lamb

STUFFED ROMAINE

Romaine lettuce, inner
  leaves, washed and dried
Brie, at room temperature
Saint André cheese, at room
  temperature
Caviar
Minced green onions
Smoked oysters
Walnuts, toasted (see page
  29) and chopped or left in
  halves
Minced fresh parsley

Great as a summer hors d'oeuvre or for an unusual salad course. There are no amounts—just have fun and create!

1. Spread one half of the lettuce leaves with the Brie, the other half with the Saint André.
2. Top the Saint André with a dollop of caviar and a sprinkle of minced green onions.
3. Top the Brie with a smoked oyster and sprinkle with walnuts and parsley.

Fast: Can assemble up to 4 hours in advance and refrigerate.

Fabulous: Brie with roasted red pepper or pesto; Saint André or Brie topped with a slice of prosciutto, chèvre, and sun-dried tomatoes. Substitute Belgian endive for the romaine.

PROSCIUTTO AND VEGETABLES

Thinly sliced prosciutto
Asparagus spears, blanched
  until barely tender, about
  3 minutes
Zucchini spears
Baby corn, canned or fresh,
  blanched until barely
  tender, about 3 minutes
Cucumber spears
Jicama spears
Tiny red potatoes, blanched
  until barely tender, about
  10 to 15 minutes

An unusual variation of the classic prosciutto with melon.

1. Wrap a slice of prosciutto around the vegatable(s) of your choice, and *voilà!*

Fast: Can prepare up to 1 day in advance and refrigerate.

Fabulous: Substitute thinly sliced Westphalian ham, smoked salmon, and/or pastrami for prosciutto.

ZUCCHINI SOUP WITH DOUBLE PESTO

1/4 cup olive oil
1 red onion, chopped
8 small zucchini, chopped
  (about 4 cups)
1 bunch parsley, chopped
7 3/4 cups chicken broth,
  homemade or canned
1/4 cup sherry
1 bay leaf
Salt and freshly ground white
  pepper to taste
Freshly grated nutmeg to
  taste
1/4 to 1/2 cup sour cream,
  plus extra for garnish
Pesto (recipe follows) for
  garnish
Chile and Sun-Dried
  Tomato Pesto (recipe
  follows) for garnish

A refreshing summer soup that offers your guests flavor options.

1. Heat the oil in a large soup pot and sauté the onion and zucchini over medium-low heat until softened, but not browned, about 10 minutes.
2. Transfer them to a food processor fitted with a metal blade or to a blender and puree with the parsley.
3. Add the chicken broth, sherry, and bay leaf to the soup pot and bring to a boil over high heat.
4. Stir the pureed mixture into the boiling liquid and simmer over medium to medium-high heat until the flavors are pleasing. Add the salt, pepper, and nutmeg, then remove and discard the bay leaf.
5. Reduce the heat to low and stir in the sour cream. Do not allow this to boil or the sour cream will curdle.

Fast: Can prepare up to 3 days in advance and refrigerate, or freeze for up to 6 months. Thaw in the refrigerator for 2 days or at room temperature for about 8 hours.

Flashy: Serve hot or cold with a dollop of sour cream and both pesto sauces, or pass separately and have your guests help themselves.

Fabulous: With broccoli (blanched until barely tender), yellow squash, mushrooms, or eggplant instead of the zucchini.

PESTO

2 cups packed fresh basil
    leaves
1/2 cup minced fresh parsley
2 to 4 cloves garlic
1/2 cup grated Romano
    cheese or to taste
1/2 cup olive oil or to taste
1/2 cup walnuts, toasted
    (see page 29)
Salt and freshly ground white
    pepper to taste

Yield: about 3 cups

This is one of my favorite summer flavors. Make extra, store it in the freezer, and enjoy it all year long.

1. Puree the first five ingredients in a food processor fitted with a metal blade, or in a blender.
2. Process in the walnuts with quick on-and-off motions, so as not to destroy their texture.
3. Taste and add salt and pepper.

Fast: Can prepare up to 4 days in advance and refrigerate, or freeze for up to 6 months. Thaw in the refrigerator for 2 days or at room temperature for about 4 hours.

Flashy: As an hors d'oeuvre mixed into sour cream for a dunk or smothered over a wedge of Brie, feta, or chèvre and warmed in a preheated 350°F oven for about 10 minutes. Accompany this with Garlic Crouton Rounds (see page 192) or thinly sliced pieces of baguette.

Fabulous: On pasta, in sauces, soups, or stews. For an hors d'oeuvre, spread on thinly sliced baguettes topped with Brie or chèvre. With pine nuts, pecans, pistachios, or pumpkin seeds instead of the walnuts.

Further: Store leftovers in the freezer and use as a general seasoning.

CHILE AND SUN-DRIED TOMATO PESTO

2 dried red California chiles
3 dried pasilla chiles
1 cup sun-dried tomatoes
2 cups water
3 green onions
1/2 to 1 bunch fresh
    cilantro, including stems
Salt and freshly ground white
    pepper to taste
Fresh lemon or lime juice to
    taste
1/2 cup extra virgin olive oil
1/4 cup almonds, toasted
    (see page 29)

Yield: about 2 cups

Great summer flavors!

1. Place the chiles and tomatoes in a small saucepan with the water. Bring to a boil over high heat, then reduce the heat to medium, cover, and let simmer, until softened 15 to 20 minutes. To do this in a microwave, place the chiles and tomatoes in a glass, ceramic, or plastic bowl with just 1 cup of water and cover with a lid or plastic wrap. Cook on regular power for 3 to 5 minutes. In both cases, strain and reserve the cooking liquid.
2. Pull the stems off the chiles, remove the seeds, and cut each one into several pieces.
3. Place all of the ingredients into a food processor fitted with a metal blade, or in a blender. Process until a smooth consistency is reached. Add some or all of the reserved cooking liquid to thin the flavor of the mixture.

Fast: Can prepare up to 2 days in advance and refrigerate or freeze for up to 6 months. Thaw in the refrigerator for 2 days or at room temperature for about 4 hours.

Flashy: Serve instead of a sauce with grilled or roasted beef, pork, chicken, or fish, or with soups. Served as is, or with Brie, feta or chèvre as an hors d'oeuvre.

Fabulous: With fresh or dried basil, thyme, or tarragon instead of the cilantro. Combined with 1/2 cup of sour cream or mayonnaise.

SKEWERS OF LAMB WITH TWO SAUCES

MARINADE

5 to 8 cloves garlic

Salt to taste

1 cup olive oil

1/4 cup minced fresh parsley

1 red onion, minced

1/4 cup soy sauce

1/4 cup Dijon mustard

1/4 cup fresh lemon juice or
to taste

Minced fresh rosemary, dill,
thyme, and mint to taste

Freshly ground black pepper
to taste

3 pounds boned leg of lamb,
cut into 1 1/4-inch cubes

Roasted Red Pepper Sauce
(recipe follows)

Tarragon Mayonnaise Sauce
(recipe follows)

Sprigs fresh thyme, parsley,
mint, and/or rosemary for
garnish

Simple but exotic, with brilliant flavors!

1. Place the garlic in a small saucepan with salted water, bring to boil, and drain. Repeat the process. This will mellow the garlic.
2. Combine all the marinade ingredients in a food processor fitted with a metal blade, or a blender, and puree.
3. Place the lamb in a large glass or ceramic pan with the marinade. Cover with plastic wrap and refrigerate for 4 to 72 hours.
4. Remove the lamb from the marinade, pat dry with paper towels, skewer, and grill over hot coals until browned on the outside, but still pink on the inside, about 8 minutes.

Fast: Can marinate up to 3 days in advance and refrigerate. Can prepare marinade up to 2 weeks in advance and refrigerate, or freeze for up to 6 months. Thaw in the refrigerator for 2 days or at room temperature for about 4 hours.

Flashy: Serve on a puddle of Roasted Red Pepper Sauce and Tarragon Mayonnaise Sauce. Garnish with sprigs of fresh parsley, mint, thyme, and/or rosemary.

Fabulous: With chicken or pork instead of lamb. With rehydrated shiitake mushrooms added to the skewers.

Further: Use leftover lamb cold in a salad with couscous, rice, or bulgur.

ROASTED RED PEPPER SAUCE

4 red bell peppers, roasted
(see page 28), peeled, and
seeded
2 cloves garlic
1 to 2 cups extra virgin olive
oil
Salt and freshly ground white
pepper to taste
Fresh lemon or lime juice to
taste

This is a favorite of mine. When I prepared it on national television, I splashed it all over the host, Gary Collins.

1. Puree all the ingredients in a food processor fitted with a metal blade, or in a blender.
2. Taste and adjust the seasonings.

Fast: Can prepare up to 4 days in advance and refrigerate, or freeze for up to 6 months. Thaw in the refrigerator for 2 days or at room temperature for about 4 hours.

Flashy: On anything from potatoes to fish.

Fabulous: With heavy cream or chicken broth instead of the oil, and served hot.

TARRAGON MAYONNAISE SAUCE

1 cup mayonnaise
2 tablespoons tarragon
vinegar
4 ounces cream cheese
(optional)
1 tablespoon fresh tarragon,
minced (optional)

Fantastic flavors!

1. Combine all the ingredients in a bowl by hand, or in a food processor fitted with a metal blade, or in a saucepan.

Fast: Can prepare up to 7 days in advance and refrigerate.

Flashy: As a sauce for cooked or raw vegetables, fish, lamb, pork, or poultry.

Fabulous: With all or half lowfat yogurt instead of mayonnaise to reduce the calorie count.

BAKED STUFFED TOMATOES

4 large tomatoes, halved,
  with some of the pulp
  scooped out and reserved
One 6-ounce jar marinated
  artichoke hearts (reserve
  the marinade)
1 1/2 cups dried sourdough
  bread crumbs
1/4 cup minced fresh dill
1/4 cup minced fresh parsley
1 to 2 cloves garlic, minced
1/4 cup freshly grated
  Parmesan cheese
2 to 4 tablespoons sesame
  seeds, toasted (see page
  29)
Salt and freshly ground white
  pepper to taste

This is a lovely way to enjoy sweet summer tomatoes.

1. Combine the tomato pulp with all the ingredients, except the to-
    mato halves and reserved marinade, in a food processor fitted with
    a metal blade, or in a blender. Taste and adjust the seasonings.
2. Place the tomato halves in a baking dish, top with the bread-crumb
    mixture, and drizzle the reserved artichoke marinade over them.
3. Place in a preheated 425°F oven until hot and bread-crumb mixture
    is golden, about 10 minutes.

Fast: Can prepare through step 2 up to 2 days in advance and refrigerate.
Can prepare bread-crumb mixture up to 3 months in advance and
freeze. Thaw in the refrigerator for 2 days or at room temperature for
about 4 hours.

Fabulous: With feta, Gruyère, Romano, or chèvre instead of the Parmesan. Use any fresh or dried herb instead of the dill.

Further: Use extra stuffing to stuff mushrooms, zucchini, eggplant,
chicken, or pork chops.

LEMON AND PINE NUT BULGUR

4 tablespoons (1/2 stick)
  unsalted butter
2 shallots, minced
2 1/2 cups uncooked bulgur
1/2 cup dry vermouth
5 cups chicken broth,
  homemade or canned
Grated zest of 2 lemons
1/4 to 1/2 cup pine nuts,
  toasted (see page 29)
Salt and freshly ground white
  pepper to taste
Minced fresh parsley for
  garnish

This is a great change-of-pace from rice.

1. Melt the butter in a large saucepan and sauté the shallots over low heat until tender.
2. Add the bulgur and sauté over low heat, stirring, until it is well coated with butter. Do not brown.
3. Stir in the vermouth, broth, and zest. Bring to a boil, reduce the heat to low, and cover. Cook until the liquid is absorbed, about 10 to 15 minutes.
4. Taste and add more liquid if the bulgar isn't tender enough.
5. Stir in the pine nuts. Season with salt and pepper.

Fast: Can prepare up to 1 day in advance and refrigerate. Reheat, covered, in a microwave or in a preheated 350°F oven before serving.

Flashy: Garnish with a sprinkling of minced parsley.

Fabulous: Prepared with equal amounts of couscous, orzo, and bulgur. With sautéed mushrooms and seasoned with any fresh or dried herb.

Further: Add leftovers to soups, stuffings, or salads.

RASPBERRY SORBET IN PEACH PUREE AND BRANDIED CHOCOLATE SAUCE

1 1/2 pints raspberries, fresh
　or frozen
2 tablespoons rum
1 tablespoon fresh lemon
　juice
1 1/4 cups Simple Syrup
　(recipe follows)
Peach Puree (recipe follows)
Brandied Chocolate Sauce
　(see page 141)
Fresh mint leaves, berries,
　grapes, and/or sliced fruit
　for garnish

Cool, refreshing, and beautiful!

1. If using fresh raspberries, rinse gently and drain well. Freeze solid before proceeding.
2. Place the frozen raspberries in a food processor fitted with a metal blade, or a blender, and puree.
3. Process in the rum, lemon juice, and syrup. Taste and adjust the flavors.
4. Transfer to a plastic container and freeze. When frozen, return to the food processor or blender and process again. Serve or return to the container and store in the freezer.

Fast: Can prepare up to 1 month in advance and freeze. You can serve directly from the freezer, but for a lighter texture, reprocess before serving.

Flashy: Spoon Peach Puree onto a plate or in a goblet, top with a scoop of the sorbet and drizzle Brandied Chocolate Sauce over the top. Garnish with fresh mint leaves and berries, grapes, and/or thinly sliced fruit arranged attractively.

Fabulous: This recipe is a basic formula for sorbet, and will work with almost any fruit: berries, melons, peaches, mangoes, apricots, nectarines, pears—anything. By freezing the fruit first you speed up the entire process.

SIMPLE SYRUP

3 cups sugar
2 cups water
1 cup rum
Juice of 1/2 lemon
1 vanilla bean, cut up

Yield: about 4 1/2 cups

Prepare this in large quantities and keep it on hand so you can prepare sorbet at the drop of a hat!

1. Place all the ingredients, except the vanilla bean, in a heavy saucepan over low heat and stir until the sugar dissolves.
2. Bring to a boil over high heat, then remove from the heat, add the vanilla bean, and let cool. Refrigerate until ready to use.

Fast: Can prepare up to 6 months in advance and refrigerate in an airtight jar.

Fabulous: Substitute sprigs of rosemary or thyme for the vanilla, to use as a palate-cleansing sorbet.

PEACH PUREE

3 1/2 to 4 cups sliced
   peaches
1/2 cup orange-flavored
   liqueur
Sugar, if needed, to taste

Yield: about 2 1/2 cups

Here is another item to prepare in large batches during the season.

1. Puree all the ingredients in a food processor fitted with a metal blade, or in a blender. Taste and adjust the flavors.

Fast: Can prepare up to 1 day in advance and refrigerate, or freeze for up to 6 months. Thaw in the refrigerator for 2 days or at room temperature for about 8 hours.

Flashy: On ice cream, pound or sponge cake, pancakes, or crêpes.

Fabulous: Prepared with any kind of fruit instead of the peaches. With 1/2 cup heavy cream and fresh mint leaves mixed in.

WALNUT FLORENTINES

1/2 cup all-purpose flour
1/4 cup plus 2 tablespoons
  sugar
1 cup heavy cream
2/3 cup walnuts, toasted
  (see page 29) and
  chopped
Grated zest of 1 orange
Grated zest of 1 lemon
8 ounces semisweet
  chocolate, melted (see
  page 25)

Yield: about 4 dozen

A sophisticated, but simple cookie.

1. Preheat the oven to 350°F. Butter and flour a cookie sheet.
2. Combine the flour and sugar in a food processor fitted with a metal blade.
3. Process in the cream.
4. Add the walnuts and zests, using quick on-and-off motions, so as not to destroy their texture.
5. Drop the batter by teaspoonful onto the prepared cookie sheet, about 1 inch apart.
6. Bake until golden, about 10 to 15 minutes.
7. Transfer to a wire rack and cool.
8. Spread half of the top of each cookie with the melted chocolate and let set or freeze until firm.

Fast: Can prepare up to 1 day in advance and refrigerate, or flash freeze for up to 3 months. Thaw at room temperature for several hours.

A Summer Celebration

I created this menu to celebrate a very special occasion, and wanted it to be full of summery, herbal flavors and brilliant colors—all served with a jubilant feeling. To achieve this, I focused on foods that symbolize opulence and flamboyance.

Our evening began on the patio with champagne and hors d'oeuvres. We moved into the dining room for dinner, but took a break between the salad and entree. While the entree, duck breast, was being grilled, everyone went outside for another glass of champagne. I really enjoy being able to stage dinner parties this way. The leisurely pace is a welcome break from our workaday routines, and greatly adds to the enjoyment of the food.

Everyone raved about the table and I know you'll get the same response! It was done in a light peach cloth, black napkins, and glass candlesticks with black candles placed down the center of the table. Three champagne flutes filled with a mixture of purple statice, fresh oregano cuttings, and pink zinnias were interspersed. In the very center of the table was an arrangement of grape leaves, green grapes, and glossy purple Japanese eggplants. All of these elements came together to create an elegant, yet free-spirited look.

MENU

Feta and Sun-Dried Tomato Torta

Gravlax with Gingered Dill-Mustard Sauce

Summer Spinach Salad with Duck Cracklings and Macadamia Nuts in an Orange-Tarragon Vinaigrette

Sliced Baguettes and Sweet Butter

Grilled Rosemary Marinated Duck Breasts with Three Sauces

Orzo Bulgur Risotto

Green Beans with Capers and Watercress

Mango and Berry Tart

WINES

Brut Champagne and/or Fumé Blanc

Pinot Noir or Sauvignon Blanc

Cabernet Sauvignon

Late harvest Gewürztraminer or Champagne

FASTER & FLASHIER MENU

Sliced Smoked Salmon (served with lemon and cucumber slices, minced fresh dill, and capers on small squares of pumpernickel or baguette slices)

Salad of Spinach, Baby Corn, and Macadamia Nuts

Grilled Chicken Breast with Mango Chutney (purchased or homemade)

Buttered Orzo

Sautéed Green Beans with Capers

Chocolate Ice Cream with Brandied Whipped Cream, Berries, and Mangoes

Butter Cookies (purchased)

Fast & Fabulous Timetable

Up to 6 Months in Advance and Frozen
Gingered Dill-Mustard Sauce • Duck marinade • Mango Chutney • Ancho Chile Paste

Up to 3 Months in Advance and Frozen
Feta and Sun-Dried Tomato Torta • Duck Cracklings • Pastry Cream and Glaze

Up to 2 Weeks in Advance and Refrigerated
Gingered Dill-Mustard Sauce

5 Days in Advance and Refrigerated
Feta and Sun-Dried Tomato Torta • Orange-Tarragon Vinaigrette • Duck Marinade

4 Days in Advance and Refrigerated
Prepare gravlax through step 4 • Mango Chutney • Ancho Chile Paste • Ancho Chile Chutney • Prepare tart shell, pastry cream, and glaze

3 Days in Advance and Refrigerated
Marinate duck breasts and make cracklings • Start Rosemary-Red Wine Sauce

2 Days in Advance and Refrigerated
Thaw frozen prepared-ahead foods

1 Day in Advance and Refrigerated
Prepare tomato-and-cucumber mixture for salad • Blanch green beans • Start risotto • Set table • Tart shell

Party Day!
Heat cracklings, toss and assemble salads • Warm bread • Grill duck and finish sauce after salad course • Finish risotto • Sauté green beans • Assemble tart

FETA AND SUN-DRIED TOMATO TORTA

1/2 pound (2 sticks) cold
   unsalted butter, cut into
   pieces
12 ounces feta cheese, cut
   into pieces
8 ounces cream cheese, cut
   into pieces
2 cloves garlic
1 shallot
2 to 4 tablespoons dry
   vermouth
Freshly ground white pepper
   and/or hot pepper sauce
   or minced fresh red
   jalapeño pepper (seeded
   and deveined) to taste
1/2 cup pine nuts, toasted
   (see page 29)
1 cup minced sun-dried
   tomatoes
1 cup Pesto (see page 84) or
   purchased

Yield: about 4 cups

A delicious indulgence!

1. Combine the butter, cheeses, garlic, shallot, and vermouth thoroughly in a food processor fitted with a metal blade, or using an electric mixer, then season with white pepper and/or hot pepper sauce or red jalapeño pepper.
2. Oil a 4- or 5-cup straight-sided mold, bowl, container, or pâté terrine. Line with plastic wrap.
3. Layer in the ingredients in any order you wish. I start with 1/2-inch layers of pine nuts, then sun-dried tomatoes, pesto, and the cheese mixture. Repeat until the mold is full.
4. Fold plastic over the top, press gently to compact the layers, and chill until firm, at least 1 hour.
5. Unmold and enjoy!

Fast: Can prepare up to 5 days in advance and refrigerate or freeze for up to 3 months. Thaw in the refrigerator for 2 days.

Flashy: Serve with Bagel Chips (see page 203), crackers, and/or breads.

Fabulous: With all layered ingredients mixed into the cheese and then molded. With roasted red peppers and pesto instead of sun-dried tomatoes

Further: Use leftovers tossed into hot pasta, on rice, in baked potatoes.

GRAVLAX WITH GINGERED DILL-MUSTARD SAUCE

One 2-pound salmon fillet,
   with skin on
2 tablespoons kosher salt
1/4 cup sugar
1/2 cup minced fresh dill or
   to taste
1/4 cup pickled ginger,
   drained and minced, or to
   taste
Freshly ground black pepper
   to taste
2 tablespoons gin
Grated zest and juice of 1
   lemon
Gingered Dill-Mustard Sauce
   (recipe follows)
Sprigs fresh dill, lemon slices,
   watercress leaves for
   garnish

Yield: up to 24 servings

This is cured raw salmon. It is absolutely delicious and very elegant!

1. Slash the salmon skin about four times with a knife, being careful not to cut all the way through.
2. Place the salmon in a glass or ceramic pan that the salmon just fits in, skin-side up.
3. Pour the salt, sugar, dill, ginger, and pepper over the salmon. Pat it in gently over both sides. Add the gin, zest, and lemon juice.
4. Cover with plastic wrap and place jars or cans on top to weight it down. Refrigerate for 1 day with the weights. Remove the weights and place the salmon and its curing mixture in a sealed plastic bag. Return to the refrigerator for up to 3 days, frequently turning the salmon.
5. Wipe off the curing mixture with paper towels, then thinly slice against grain.

Fast: Can prepare through step 4 up to 4 days in advance and refrigerate.

Flashy: Serve on ceramic, glass, or wooden platter and garnish with minced fresh dill, watercress leaves, and/or lemon slices. Serve with Gingered Dill-Mustard Sauce on the side, thinly sliced baguettes, and/or pumpernickel squares.

Fabulous: With fresh tarragon instead of, or in addition to, the dill.

Further: Mince leftovers and toss into a salad or hot or cold pasta.

GINGERED DILL-MUSTARD SAUCE

*1/2 cup pickled ginger,
    drained*
1/2 cup Dijon mustard
2 teaspoons dry mustard
*3 to 4 tablespoons packed
    light or dark brown sugar*
*4 to 6 tablespoons rice
    vinegar*
*1/2 cup minced fresh dill or
    to taste*
2/3 cup grapeseed oil

Yield: about 2 cups

You will find a million uses for this wonderful sauce.

1. Combine all the ingredients in a food processor fitted with a metal blade, or in a blender. Taste and adjust the seasonings.

Fast: Can prepare up to 2 weeks in advance and refrigerate or freeze for up to 6 months. Thaw in the refrigerator for 2 days or at room temperature for about 8 hours.

Fabulous: With duck, lamb, poultry, or sausages. Use in sauces or marinades. Makes a great gift!

SUMMER SPINACH SALAD WITH DUCK CRACKLINGS AND MACADAMIA NUTS IN AN ORANGE-TARRAGON VINAIGRETTE

1 red onion, thinly sliced

Salt to taste

3 large, ripe tomatoes, peeled and thinly sliced

1 cup packed fresh basil leaves, cut into thin strips

Freshly ground black pepper to taste

Extra virgin olive oil

1 European or seedless cucumber, thinly sliced

Orange-Tarragon Vinaigrette (recipe follows)

2 to 3 bunches baby spinach leaves, washed and dried

One 6- or 8-ounce can baby corn

1/2 cup macadamia nuts, chopped

Duck Cracklings, heated (recipe follows)

4 to 8 ounces feta cheese, crumbled

Definitely not an everyday salad! This is a wonderful luncheon dish.

1. Put the onions in a glass or ceramic bowl with lightly salt water and soak for about 1 hour, changing the salt water several times, until the onions are sweet. Drain and rinse.

2. Place the tomato slices on a platter with the basil and onions. Season with salt and pepper and drizzle olive oil over the top. Let sit for at least 1 hour, or for up to 24 hours, refrigerated.

3. Toss the cucumber with a small amount of vinaigrette in a bowl. Let sit for at least 1 hour, or up to 24 hours, refrigerated.

4. Toss the spinach, corn, macadamia nuts, hot cracklings, and feta with the desired amount of vinaigrette at serving time.

Fast: Can prepare through step 3 up to 1 day in advance and refrigerate. Can arrange the tomato and onion mixtures up to 4 hours in advance and refrigerate. Toss, dress, and add hot cracklings to the spinach immediately before serving.

Flashy: Place small amount of spinach salad on each plate. Flank with tomato salad on one side and cucumber salad on the other.

Fabulous: As a main course!

ORANGE-TARRAGON VINAIGRETTE

1 cup orange juice

1 sprig fresh tarragon or 1/4
    to 1/2 teaspoon dried

4 cloves garlic

2 to 4 tablespoons
    orange-flavored liqueur

1/2 cup olive oil

1/2 cup peanut oil

1/4 cup sherry wine vinegar

2 tablespoons sesame oil

1 teaspoon white
    Worcestershire sauce
    (optional)

1 teaspoon Dijon mustard or
    to taste

Salt and freshly ground white
    pepper to taste

Yield: about 2 1/4 cups

1. Place the orange juice, tarragon, and garlic in saucepan, and bring to a boil over medium-high to high heat. Cook until reduced to about 1/4 cup.
2. Combine the reduced mixture with the remaining ingredients in a food processor fitted with a metal blade, in a blender, or in a bowl with a whisk. Taste and adjust the seasonings.

Fast: Can prepare up to 5 days in advance and refrigerate.

Fabulous: With cilantro, dill, rosemary, or thyme instead of the tarragon. As a marinade or cold sauce for seafood, poultry, pork, lamb, or fish.

DUCK CRACKLINGS

Duck skin (reserved from the
    duck breasts)

Salt to taste

If your cholesterol level will allow this splurge, it will be well worth it!

1. Place the skin in a large stock pot, cover with a lid, and cook over low heat until a great deal of the fat is rendered.
2. Remove the skin and place on paper towels to drain off the excess fat.
3. Transfer the skin to an aluminum foil–lined baking pan, then salt it and place in a preheated 300°F oven. Bake until the skin is crisped, about 30 minutes. Watch carefully to make sure it doesn't burn.
4. Remove the crisped skin and drain on paper towels.
5. Cut the skin, or crumble, and serve hot.

Fast: Can prepare up to 3 days in advance and refrigerate or freeze for up to 3 months. Thaw in the refrigerator for 1 day. Rewarm in a 350°F oven or the microwave before serving.

Fabulous: In pasta or rice dishes.

GRILLED ROSEMARY MARINATED DUCK BREASTS WITH THREE SAUCES

ROSEMARY MARINADE

Minced fresh rosemary to
   taste
2 cups olive oil
6 cloves garlic, minced, or to
   taste
Fresh lemon juice to taste
Fresh mint leaves, minced, to
   taste
Salt and freshly ground black
   pepper to taste

8 to 16 boneless duck
   breasts, about 4 to 8
   ounces each, (depending
   upon their size), skinned
   (reserve skin for cracklings)
Rosemary-Red Wine Sauce
   (recipe follows)
Mango Chutney (recipe
   follows)
Ancho Chile Chutney (see
   page 102)
Sprigs fresh rosemary, fresh
   mint leaves, and/or strips
   of lemon zest for garnish

This dish offers a huge variety of tastes and colors. Do not feel compelled to use all three sauces. Any one can stand alone but I find that offering variety is an exciting way to eat and a great point of conversation. Remember, this recipe also works well for chicken breasts.

1. Combine all the marinade ingredients in a food processor fitted with a metal blade, or a blender. Taste and adjust the seasonings.
2. Place the duck breasts in a ceramic or glass pan and cover with the marinade. Cover with plastic wrap and refrigerate for at least 24 hours. Bring to room temperature before cooking.
3. To grill, have coals red hot and watch carefully to avoid overcooking. Baste the duck with the marinade while grilling. This should only take a few minutes on each side. To sauté, heat several tablespoons of olive oil or peanut oil in a large skillet. Add the duck breasts and cook for just a few minutes on each side. When done, they should be slightly pink on the inside. Use two skillets or do this in batches so as not to overcrowd the breasts.

Fast: Can prepare the marinade up to 5 days in advance and refrigerate, or freeze for up to 6 months. Thaw in the refrigerator for 2 days or at room temperature for about 8 hours.

Flashy: Drizzle Rosemary-Red Wine Sauce over the duck breasts and top with a dollop of Mango Chutney and Ancho Chile Chutney. Garnish with sprigs of rosemary, fresh mint leaves, and thin strips of lemon zest.

Fabulous: With thyme instead of rosemary.

Further: Cold in salad or thinly sliced in pasta or rice.

ROSEMARY-RED WINE SAUCE

1 cup dry red wine,
   preferably a cabernet or
   zinfandel
3 to 4 tablespoons minced
   shallots
3 tablespoons minced fresh
   parsley
1 tablespoon minced fresh
   rosemary or to taste
1/2 pound (2 sticks)
   unsalted butter, cold and
   cut into small pieces

Yield: about 1 1/2 cups

Rich and intense.

1.   Combine the wine, shallots, parsley, and rosemary in a small sauce-
     pan and reduce by one third over high heat.
2.   Reduce the heat to low, and slowly whisk in the butter, piece by
     piece.
3.   Strain through a fine mesh strainer and enjoy.

Fast: Can prepare through step 1 up to 3 days in advance and refrigerate.
   Can fully prepare up to 2 hours in advance. Place over a double boiler
   or in a thermos to keep warm.

Flashy: On beef, lamb, pork, poultry, or salmon.

Fabulous: With minced fresh ginger or your choice of herbs.

MANGO CHUTNEY

1 large mango, peeled and
   cut into small cubes or
   chopped
1/2 cup minced red onion
1/4 to 1/2 cup packed fresh
   mint leaves, minced
2 tablespoons sugar or to
   taste
1/2 to 1 teaspoon salt or to
   taste
1/4 cup sherry wine vinegar
Freshly ground white pepper
   to taste

Yield: about 1 1/2 cups

This is very exotic and tropical in feeling.

1.   Combine all the ingredients in a large bowl. Taste and adjust the
     flavors.

Fast: Can prepare up to 4 days in advance and refrigerate, or freeze for
   up to 6 months. Thaw in the refrigerator for 2 days or at room temperature for about 8 hours.

Flashy: Serve with any roasted or grilled poultry, pork, fish, seafood, or
   beef dish.

Fabulous: With minced cilantro, minced, rehydrated and seeded ancho
   chiles, rosemary, oregano, and/or basil. With 1/2 to 1 cup sour cream
   added. As a dressing for pasta, rice, spinach, or potato salads.

ANCHO CHILE CHUTNEY

1/4 cup Ancho Chile Paste
  (recipe follows) or to taste
2 large bunches fresh
  cilantro, chopped
1/4 cup sesame oil
1/2 cup rice vinegar
Sugar and salt to taste

Yield: about 2 cups

A tasty cross-cultural marriage between Mexico and China

1. Combine all the ingredients in a food processor fitted with a metal blade, in a blender, or whisk together in a bowl. Taste and adjust the seasonings.

Fast: Can prepare up to 4 days in advance and refrigerate.

Flashy: On any roasted or grilled seafood, fish, pork, or poultry dish.

Fabulous: As a marinade for pork, poultry, fish, or seafood. As a dressing for Napa cabbage, spinach, pasta, or rice salads.

ANCHO CHILE PASTE

3 ounces medium-hot dried
  Ancho chiles
1 cup hot water

Yield: about 1 cup

A basic seasoning to keep on hand in your refrigerator or freezer. In case you are a chile novice, make sure you either wear gloves when handling them or wash your hands immediately after working with them. You only need to forget this rule once to have it permanently imprinted on your brain. To soothe burning hands, try soaking them in milk or in a mixture of baking soda and water. Never touch your eyes while handling them—if you do, the burning sensation will be unforgettable.

1. Rinse the chile pods under water. Pull off the stems and shake out the seeds.
2. Place the pods in a glass or ceramic bowl and cover with the hot water. Let sit until the chiles soften, about 30 minutes, or microwave to speed up the process, about 5 minutes.
3. Cut the chiles and place in a food processor fitted with a metal blade, or a blender, along with enough of the strained soaking liquid to form a paste. Transfer to a glass jar or plastic container.

Fast: Can prepare up to 4 days in advance and refrigerate or freeze for up to 6 months. Thaw in the refrigerator for 2 days or at room temperature for about 8 hours.

Fabulous: As a seasoning ingredient for soups, sauces, or marinades. Prepared with red California chiles instead of anchos.

ORZO BULGUR RISOTTO

4 tablespoons (1/2 stick)
  unsalted butter
2 cloves garlic, minced
1/2 cup chopped red onion
1 cup uncooked orzo
1 cup uncooked bulgur
1/4 cup dry white wine
1 tablespoon minced fresh
  thyme or lemon thyme
4 cups chicken broth,
  homemade or canned
1/4 cup heavy cream
2 to 4 tablespoons minced
  fresh parsley
Salt and freshly ground white
  pepper to taste

An interesting twist on a classic Italian rice dish.

1. Melt the butter in a large saucepan and gently sauté the garlic and onion over low heat until tender.
2. Stir in the orzo and bulgur and sauté until coated with butter; do not brown.
3. Stir in the wine and thyme and increase the heat to medium. Cook, stirring frequently, until absorbed.
4. Add half of the chicken broth and cook, stirring frequently, until absorbed.
5. Add the remaining broth and the cream. Cook, stirring frequently, until absorbed. If the orzo is not tender, add more liquid and continue cooking a bit longer. The entire process should about 20 minutes.
6. Stir in the parsley and season with salt and pepper. The risotto should have a moist, creamy consistency, with the rice al dente.

Fast: Can prepare through step 4 up to 1 day in advance and refrigerate. Bring to room temperature and finish cooking before serving.

Flashy: With almost any entree, from lamb to seafood.

Fabulous: With shallots instead of onions. Substitute any herb for the thyme. Add cooked minced pancetta or bacon to the sautéed onions.

GREEN BEANS WITH CAPERS AND WATERCRESS

2 pounds green beans,
   stringed
4 tablespoons (1/2 stick)
   unsalted butter
2 shallots, minced
1/4 cup capers, rinsed and
   drained
Salt and freshly ground white
   pepper to taste
Fresh lemon juice to taste
Minced fresh or dried thyme
   to taste
Freshly grated nutmeg to
   taste
1 or 2 bunches watercress,
   stemmed

A lovely way to treat green beans!

1. Blanch the green beans in a large pot of boiling salted water until barely tender, about 3 to 5 minutes. Remove the beans and place in a strainer or colander under cold running water until no longer warm. Drain well.
2. In a large skillet, melt the butter and sauté the shallots until tender over low heat.
3. Add the capers, green beans, salt, pepper, lemon juice, thyme, and nutmeg. Toss over medium-high heat with the watercress leaves until the beans are hot. Taste and adjust the seasonings, then serve.

Fast: Can blanch beans up to 1 day in advance and refrigerate. Bring to room temperature before sautéing.

Fabulous: With chopped walnuts, sesame seeds, hazelnuts, pecans, almonds, or other seeds or nuts, mixed in.

MANGO AND BERRY TART

WALNUT PASTRY

4 1/2 teaspoons sugar

1/4 teaspoon salt

1 1/2 cups all-purpose flour

1/4 pound (1 stick) unsalted butter, frozen and cut into small pieces

2 tablespoons ice water

1/2 cup walnuts, toasted (see page 29) and chopped

GLAZE

1/2 cup apricot preserves or orange marmalade

2 tablespoons liqueur, rum, brandy, bourbon, or Scotch

PASTRY CREAM

1 cup heavy cream, less 2 tablespoons

1 teaspoon unflavored gelatin

1 large egg (see page 23)

2 large egg yolks (see page 23)

1/3 cup sugar

2 tablespoons cornstarch

Finely grated zest of 1 lemon

2 tablespoons Scotch

1 teaspoon vanilla extract

Freshly grated nutmeg to taste

1 or 2 mangoes, peeled and sliced

1 pint berries (blueberries, strawberries, raspberries, or other berries)

Sprigs fresh mint for garnish

Yield: one 11-inch tart

Great colors, flavors, and shapes!

1. Place the sugar, salt, flour, and butter in a food processor fitted with a metal blade and process until the mixture resembles a coarse meal.
2. While the machine is running, slowly add the water through the feed tube. Process until the dough begins to form a ball. To prepare without using a food processor, combine the sugar, salt and flour in a bowl. Add the butter (chilled, not frozen) and cut it in, using two knives or a pastry blender, until the mixture resembles coarse meal. Stir in the ice water until the mixture holds together and can be gathered into a ball.
3. Take the dough from the processor, form into a ball, and roll it out on a lightly floured surface so it is 2 inches larger than the diameter of an 11-inch tart pan.
4. Fold the dough in half and place it in the pan. Unfold and lightly press it into the pan. Prick the bottom with a fork and scatter the walnuts over the pastry, gently pressing them in.
5. Refrigerate for 30 minutes. Preheat the oven to 400°F.
6. Line the crust with aluminum foil and fill with uncooked beans or pastry weights.
7. Bake for 12 minutes.
8. Meanwhile make the glaze by heating the preserves with the liqueur in a microwave or small saucepan over low heat until the preserves melt. Strain through a fine mesh strainer or use as is.
9. Remove the foil and lightly brush the pastry with the glaze. Bake for 12 minutes more or until golden. Let the crust cool awhile.
10. For the pastry cream, bring the cream and gelatin to a boil over medium-high heat in saucepan.
11. Combine the egg, egg yolks, sugar, cornstarch, zest, and Scotch in a food processor fitted with a metal blade or in a mixing bowl using an electric mixer.
12. Process several tablespoons of the hot cream through the feed tube while the machine is running or beat in with an electric mixer.
13. Transfer the contents of the food processor or mixing bowl into the saucepan containing the cream, whisking all the while.

14. Cook, while whisking, over medium heat until the mixture is thickened, about 3 to 8 minutes.
15. Stir in the vanilla and nutmeg.
16. Cool for at least 30 minutes before filling the tart shell. Use the freezer to speed up the process.
17. Fill tart shell with pastry cream and arrange fruit on top. Brush glaze over the fruit. Enjoy!

Fast: Can prepare pastry cream and glaze up to 4 days in advance and refrigerate or freeze for up to 3 months. Prepare the tart shell up to 1 day in advance and hold covered with plastic wrap at room temperature or freeze for up to 3 months.

Flashy: Garnish with sprig of fresh mint.

Fabulous: Use pastry cream as a filling for crêpes or cakes. Flavor the pastry cream with any liqueur, bourbon, or rum, minced dried apricots, or chocolate, or with any fruit.

CASUAL SUMMER MENUS

• • • • • • • • • • • • • • • • • •

Barbecued Ribs and Wings Dinner

Ribs and chicken wings are a perfect choice for a summer barbecue, as they instantly signal fun and the abandonment of all pretense. Here they are treated to a fabulous red wine barbecue sauce, of Chinese inspiration. Two exotic, made-in-advance salads round out the menu. Peach Bombe with Boysenberry Sauce is a cooling and dramatic grand finale that will fit in nicely at any party, whether it be casual or elegant.

This menu embodies the essence of casual cool and can easily be used to serve large groups. To reinforce the mood, dress your table in a classic blue-and-white checkered cloth with matching napkins. Use small tin pails to hold bouquets of white daisies mixed with mint and oregano cuttings. Instead of using traditional candlesticks, use bulky, white pillar candles directly in terra-cotta saucers and set them in hurricane lanterns. All these elements will come together to create a country look with a fresh, fun feel.

MENU

Avocado Dipping Sauce and Salsa with Tortilla Chips

Marinated Barbecued Ribs and Wings with Ginger-Merlot Sauce

Shiitake Mushroom and Cucumber Salad

Papaya Potato Salad with Mango Chutney Vinaigrette

Garlic-Rosemary Bread

Peach Bombe with Boysenberry Sauce

Red Wine Fennel Biscotti

FASTER & FLASHIER MENU

Salsa (purchased) with Tortilla Chips

Marinated Barbecued Ribs and Wings with Chinese Barbecue Sauce (purchased)

Potato Salad (purchased, with papaya and garnishes added)

Sliced Cucumbers and Tomatoes (dressed with olive oil and fresh lemon juice)

Ice cream, fresh fruit, and cookies (purchased)

WINES

Brut Champagne or Assorted Beers

Merlot, Champagne, or Assorted Beers

Late harvest Chenin Blanc or Champagne

Fast & Fabulous Timetable

Up to 1 Year in Advance and Frozen
  Salsa

Up to 6 Months in Advance and Frozen
  Ginger-Merlot Sauce • Boysenberry Sauce • Red Wine Fennel Biscotti

Up to 1 Month in Advance and Frozen
  Peach Bombe

5 Days in Advance and Refrigerated
  Ginger-Merlot Sauce • Mango Chutney Vinaigrette • Salsa • Garlic oil
  for bread • Red Wine Fennel Biscotti

4 Days in Advance and Refrigerated
Boysenberry Sauce

3 Days in Advance and Refrigerated
Marinate ribs and wings • Shiitake Mushroom and Cucumber Salad

2 Days in Advance and Refrigerated
Avocado Dipping Sauce • Papaya Potato Salad • Garlic-Rosemary
Bread • Thaw frozen prepared-ahead foods

1 Day in Advance
Set table

Party Day!
Barbecue ribs and wings • Heat sauce and bread

AVOCADO DIPPING SAUCE

2 ripe avocados, peeled and
   stoned
2 large tomatillos, husked, or
   to taste
2 to 6 green onions, minced
1/2 to 1 cup Salsa (recipe
   follows) or your favorite
   brand
1 bunch fresh cilantro,
   chopped
1/2 cup sour cream or
   low-fat yogurt
2 cloves garlic
1 tablespoon ground cumin
Salt and freshly ground white
   pepper to taste
Fresh lime juice to taste
Sprigs fresh cilantro and a
   marigold for garnish

Yield: 3 to 4 cups

If you think guacamole is good, wait until you taste this!

1. Combine all the ingredients, except the garnish, in a food processor
    fitted with a metal blade, or in a blender. Taste and adjust the
    seasonings.

Fast: Can prepare up to 2 days in advance and refrigerate.

Flashy: With tortilla chips, cold cooked shrimp, and/or spears of jicama.
   Garnish with sprigs of cilantro and a marigold.

Fabulous: As a dressing for pasta, couscous, potato, rice, or bulgur salad.

SALSA

3 large, ripe tomatoes,
    chopped
1/2 cup chopped onions
1/2 cup chopped fresh
    cilantro
2 to 4 green canned chiles,
    seeded and deveined
2 to 4 tomatillos, husked
    and chopped
2 cloves garlic or to taste
Fresh red jalapeño, as big a
    piece as you can handle,
    seeded and deveined
2 tablespoons olive oil
Salt and freshly ground white
    pepper to taste
Dried oregano to taste
Sugar to taste

Yield: 2 to 3 cups

Another marvelous summer mixture to fill your freezer with. Remember, when working with hot peppers, wear plastic gloves or wash your hands immediately afterwards. *Never* touch your eyes while handling hot peppers.

1. Combine all the ingredients in a food processor fitted with a metal blade, or in a blender. Taste and adjust the seasonings.

Fast: Can prepare up to 5 days in advance and refrigerate, or freeze for up to 1 year. Thaw in the refrigerator for 2 days or at room temperature for about 8 hours.

Flashy: Served with chips as an hors d'oeuvre.

Fabulous: To season anything or to use in place of rich sauces.

MARINATED BARBECUED RIBS AND WINGS WITH GINGER-MERLOT SAUCE

MARINADE

4 cups merlot or any dry
    full-bodied red wine
2 cups soy sauce
1/2 cup Chinese plum sauce
    or to taste
2 cups minced green onions
1/2 cup packed fresh mint
    leaves, minced
2 teaspoons dried thyme
6 to 12 cloves garlic, minced
2 to 4 tablespoons fermented
    black beans (optional)

3 to 5 pounds chicken wings
8 pounds spareribs
Ginger-Merlot Sauce (recipe
    follows)
Grape leaves, sprigs fresh
    mint, and/or nasturtiums
    for garnish

Yield: 6 to 8 servings

This is considered by many to be a religious experience!

1. Combine all the marinade ingredients in a bowl.
2. Place the chicken wings in a glass or ceramic baking pan, add half of the marinade, and cover with plastic wrap.
3. Place the ribs in another glass or ceramic pan, add the remaining marinade, and cover with plastic wrap. Allow both items to sit at room temperature for two hours or marinate in the refrigerator for up to 3 days.
4. To barbecue, have the coals hot and set them on each side of a kettle-type barbecue. For a smokier flavor, add several handfuls of smoke chips before putting the ribs and wings on. Cover and let cook for about 45 minutes, or until fully cooked. The cooking time will vary greatly, depending on the meatiness of the ribs and the intensity of the fire. Serve with the ginger-merlot sauce on the side.

Fast: Can marinate up to 3 days in advance.

Flashy: Serve on a huge wooden platter or cutting board. Garnish with grape leaves, sprigs of mint, and/or nasturtiums.

Fabulous: Undeniably!

Further: Don't worry, there won't be any.

GINGER-MERLOT SAUCE

2 tablespoons unsalted butter
2 to 4 cloves garlic, minced
1/4 cup minced fresh ginger
   or to taste
4 green onions, minced
1 cup merlot or any
   full-bodied dry red wine
1 1/2 cups chicken broth,
   homemade or canned
1/4 cup soy sauce
1/4 cup packed light or dark
   brown sugar or to taste
Salt and freshly ground white
   pepper to taste
1 tablespoon cornstarch
   dissolved in 2 tablespoons
   red wine or soy sauce

Yield: about 2 cups

It's impossible to describe this rich, intense flavor.

1. Melt the butter in a large saucepan and briefly sauté the garlic, ginger, and green onions over low heat until tender, about 5 minutes.
2. Add all the remaining ingredients, except the dissolved cornstarch, and bring to a boil. Cook over medium heat until the flavors develop to your liking, about 10 minutes.
3. Return the sauce to a boil and stir in the cornstarch mixture. Cook for another 30 seconds. Taste and adjust the seasonings.

Fast: Can prepare up to 5 days in advance and refrigerate, or freeze for up to 6 months. Thaw in the refrigerator for 2 days or at room temperature for about 8 hours.

Fabulous: Strain sauce before serving for a more elegant look.

SHIITAKE MUSHROOM AND CUCUMBER SALAD

8 dried shiitake mushrooms,
   rehydrated, stemmed, and
   thinly sliced, or to taste
3 to 4 cucumbers, peeled
   and thinly sliced
1/4 to 1/2 cup sesame
   seeds, toasted (see page 29)
2 cloves garlic, minced
4 green onions, minced
1/4 cup chopped fresh dill,
   or 1 teaspoon dried
1 tablespoon sugar
2/3 cup rice vinegar
3 tablespoons sesame oil
Salt and freshly ground white
   pepper to taste

An East meets West mixture of flavors and seasonings.

1. Combine all the ingredients in a large salad bowl and toss. Taste and adjust the flavors. Chill before serving.

Fast: Can prepare up to 3 days in advance and refrigerate. The flavors improve after it has set for several hours.

Fabulous: You may need more vinegar and seasonings, depending upon the cucumbers. With 2 cups shredded cabbage instead of cucumbers. With cooked baby shrimp added!

PAPAYA POTATO SALAD WITH MANGO CHUTNEY VINAIGRETTE

2 to 4 pounds new potatoes,
  unpeeled
6 thin slices smoked ham,
  cut into thin strips
1 red onion, thinly sliced
2 papayas, peeled, seeded,
  and thinly sliced
3 cucumbers, peeled, seeded,
  scored, and thinly sliced
Mango Chutney Vinaigrette
  (recipe follows)
Broccoli florets, nasturtium
  flowers and leaves, and/or
  grape leaves for garnish
3 ripe avocados, peeled,
  stoned, sliced lengthwise,
  and sprinkled with fresh
  lemon juice to prevent
  discoloration, for garnish

An extraordinary potato salad with a real exotic touch.

1. Place the potatoes in large pot with enough water to cover them and bring to a boil. Reduce the heat to medium and simmer until fork tender, about 25 minutes.
2. Drain and cut into 1/4-inch thick slices.
3. Place the potato slices, along with smoked ham, onion, papaya, and cucumber slices in a large bowl. Toss with the desired amount of vinaigrette, then cover with plastic wrap and refrigerate for at least 2 hours before serving.

Fast: Can prepare up to 2 days in advance and refrigerate.

Flashy: Place potato salad on a large platter. Surround with grape leaves, nasturtiums, and broccoli florets. Top with avocado slices.

Fabulous: With minced parsley, cubed jicama, sliced bamboo shoots, and/or toasted slivered almonds.

MANGO CHUTNEY VINAIGRETTE

2 canned mild green chiles,
  deveined and seeded
1 cup olive oil
1/3 cup apple cider vinegar
1/3 cup Mango Chutney
  (see page 101) or
  purchased
1 clove garlic
1 teaspoon Dijon mustard
1 teaspoon salt
Freshly ground white pepper
  to taste

Yield: about 2 2/3 cups

A tropical dressing.

1. Combine all the ingredients in a food processor fitted with a metal blade, or in a blender, and process until almost smooth. Taste and adjust the seasonings.

Fast: Can prepare up to 5 days in advance and refrigerate.

Flashy: On any salad.

Fabulous: As a cold sauce for fish, seafood, pork, or chicken. With fresh or dried herbs added.

GARLIC-ROSEMARY BREAD

1 loaf sourdough French
   bread
2 cloves garlic or to taste
1 cup olive oil
Salt and minced fresh or
   dried rosemary to taste

A delicious and zero-cholesterol way to prepare garlic bread. The seasoned oil is something you may want to keep on hand in your refrigerator as a cooking oil for use in and on almost anything.

1. Preheat the oven to 350°F.
2. Slice the bread. Combine the remaining ingredients in a food processor fitted with a metal blade, or in a blender. Taste and adjust the seasonings.
3. Line a cookie sheet with aluminum foil. Brush the slices of bread with the seasoned oil and place on the sheet.
4. Bake until warm, about 20 minutes.

Fast: Can prepare the oil up to 5 days in advance and refrigerate in a jar. Can prepare bread through step 3 up to 2 days in advance and refrigerate, covered with aluminum foil or plastic wrap.

Flashy: Serve in a napkin-lined basket.

Fabulous: With any herb. With butter or a combination of butter and oil. Top with grated Parmesean, Romano, and/or Mizithra cheese.

PEACH BOMBE WITH BOYSENBERRY SAUCE

1 quart French vanilla ice
  cream, softened
6 large peaches, peeled,
  pitted, and pureed (about
  1 1/2 cups of puree)
4 ounces bittersweet
  chocolate, shaved or
  chopped
2 cups almonds, toasted (see
  page 29) and chopped
2/3 cup orange-flavored
  liqueur
1/3 cup brandy
1 cup heavy cream, whipped
  to firm peaks
Freshly grated nutmeg to
  taste
Boysenberry Sauce (recipe
  follows)
Whipped cream and sprigs
  fresh mint for garnish

Yield: 8 to 12 servings

Cool and beautiful, this is a molded, flavored ice cream dessert.

1. Oil 2-quart mold with vegetable or other flavorless oil.
2. Combine all the ingredients, except the Boysenberry Sauce and
    garnishes, in a large bowl, blending well.
3. Pour into the prepared mold. Cover with plastic wrap and freeze
    until firm, at least 3 hours. Let sit at room temperature for about
    15 minutes before serving.

Fast: Can prepare up to 1 month in advance and freeze.

Flashy: To serve, run a sharp knife dipped in hot water around the mold.
    Dip the bottom of the mold in hot water quickly and invert onto a
    platter. Top with Boysenberry Sauce and whipped cream. Garnish with
    sprigs or leaves of mint.

Fabulous: With nectarines, cantaloupe, bananas, papaya, kiwi, and/or
    mangoes instead of the peaches.

BOYSENBERRY SAUCE

3 cups (1 1/2 pints) fresh or
    unsweetened frozen
    boysenberries, pureed and
    strained
1/2 cup orange-flavored
    liqueur
1/4 cup brandy
1/2 cup sugar or to taste
1/2 cup heavy cream,
    whipped to soft peaks

Yield: about 4 1/2 cups

Make large batches of this wonderful sauce, and freeze it, so you can enjoy the taste of summer anytime.

1. Combine all the ingredients, except the cream, in a food processor fitted with a metal blade, or in a bowl.
2. Gently fold in the whipped cream and let stand at room temperature for about 1 hour before serving.

Fast: Can prepare up to 4 days in advance and refrigerate, or freeze for up to 6 months. Thaw in the refrigerator for 2 days or at room temperature for about 8 hours.

Fabulous: Prepared with any berry, especially raspberries, and seasoned with fresh mint leaves.

RED WINE FENNEL BISCOTTI

4 cups all-purpose flour
3/4 cup sugar
1/2 teaspoon salt
4 1/2 teaspoons fennel seeds
1 cup full-bodied red wine,
    such as merlot or cabernet
    sauvignon
1 cup olive oil
Grated zest of 2 oranges
Freshly grated nutmeg to
    taste

Yield: about 70 biscotti

A version of the classic Italian cookie, designed to be dunked in coffee or red wine. It is baked twice to achieve a crisp texture. Great for breakfast or dessert!

1. Preheat the oven to 350°F and oil a cookie sheet.
2. Combine the flour with the sugar, salt, and fennel seeds in a food processor fitted with a metal blade or a bowl.
3. While the machine is running, add the wine, olive oil, zest, and nutmeg through the feed tube or add to the bowl and combine with an electric mixer.
4. Process until a soft dough forms.
5. Dust the work surface with flour and lightly flour your hands. Divide the dough in half and form two loaves.
6. Place the loaves on the cookie sheet and bake until a tester inserted into the middle of a loaf comes out clean, about 35 to 45 minutes
7. Remove the loaves from the oven, let cool slightly, and cut into

slices about 1/2 inch thick at an angle. Each slice can be cut in half lengthwise to make long, narrow cookies.

8. Return the cookie sheet to the oven, reduce the temperature to 300°F, and bake for 15 to 20 minutes more, until golden and crisp. Turn the oven off and leave the cookies in the oven with the door open for another 15 minutes.

Fast: Can prepare up to 5 days in advance and store in airtight jar(s) or in plastic bag(s), or freeze for up to 6 months. Thaw in the refrigerator for 2 days or at room temperature for about 8 hours.

Flashy: To serve with and dunk in red wine or coffee.

Fabulous: With chopped almonds or walnuts mixed in. Rolled in chopped nuts or sesame seeds before baking. Or dip half of each biscotti in melted milk or semisweet chocolate after baking, and coat with chopped nuts or sesame seeds. With minced fresh rosemary and crushed green peppercorns to create an hors d'oeuvre.

Grilled Swordfish Dinner

Yes, I do classify this as a "casual menu," but it is a difficult call. As it now stands, it is "casually elegant," or in today's lingo, "up-scale casual." For a more casual party, simply eliminate a dish or two.

The flavors are vivid and the dishes simple, with almost half of the menu grilled. For some unknown reason, bringing the barbecue into the act puts everyone in a relaxed, upbeat mood. It is natural to stage this evening outside on the patio. I especially like serving hors d'oeuvres that my guests can grill themselves; it is a surefire icebreaker. The Cheese-Stuffed Mushrooms in Grape Leaves are totally different from standard hors d'oeuvres, and absolutely delicious. The salad, a composition of papaya, jicama, cucumbers, red onions, and feta, with a zingy cilantro-flavored dressing, is just as interesting. From there the action returns to the grill, with the marinated swordfish and polenta. The eggplant dish can be served at room temperature. Keep in mind that this entire menu is wonderful served at room temperature—a real luxury for any cook.

The menu concludes with a dessert that focuses on the season's glorious fresh fruit. Shortbread is bathed with a Scotch-flavored custard sauce and topped with fresh fruit decoratively arranged. A beautiful and refreshing finish!

This party calls for a table that is just as upbeat and fun as the menu. Here is one possibility: Use an off-white cotton cloth with bright orange, red, blue, and yellow stripes. Instead of napkins, buy blue cotton kitchen towels. Roll them up with the silverware and use white yarn to tie them. For flowers, how about bright zinnias with stalks of blue lily-of-the-Nile arranged in French jelly-jar glasses? Use these glasses to hold votive candles. Glossy Japanese eggplants, green grapes, and lemons scattered around the center of the table also assist in creating a summer-in-the-country feeling!

MENU

Cheese-Stuffed Mushrooms in Grape Leaves

Cold Guacamole Soufflé with Tortilla Chips

Papaya, Jicama, Cucumber, and Red Onion Salad with Feta

French Rolls

Grilled Marinated Swordfish with Anchovy-Basil Mayonnaise

Baked Eggplant and Artichoke Hearts

Grilled Polenta with Sun-Dried Tomatoes and Garlic

Fresh Fruit and Shortbread with Scotch-Custard Sauce

FASTER & FLASHIER MENU

Tossed Salad with Red Onions and Feta

Grilled Swordfish with Anchovy-Basil Mayonnaise

Rice with Lemon and Dill

French Vanilla Ice Cream with Raspberries and Kahlua

Shortbread (purchased)

WINES

Champagne

Chardonnay or Sauvignon Blanc

Orange Muscat

Fast & Fabulous Timetable

Up to 6 Months in Advance and Frozen
Cold Guacamole Soufflé • Scotch-Custard Sauce

Up to 3 Months in Advance and Frozen
Lemon-Sesame Shortbread

Up to 1 Month in Advance and Frozen
Start Grilled Polenta with Sun-Dried Tomatoes and Garlic

Up to 1 Week in Advance and Refrigerated
Swordfish marinade

5 Days in Advance and Refrigerated
Cilantro Vinaigrette • Lemon-Sesame Shortbread

4 Days in Advance and Refrigerated
Scotch-Custard Sauce

3 Days in Advance and Refrigerated
Anchovy-Basil Mayonnaise

2 Days in Advance and Refrigerated
Assemble Cheese-Stuffed Mushrooms in Grape Leaves • Cold Guacamole Soufflé • Papaya, Jicama, Cucumber, and Red Onion Salad with Feta • Baked Eggplant and Artichoke Hearts • Start Grilled Polenta with Sun-Dried Tomatoes and Garlic • Thaw frozen prepared-ahead foods

1 Day in Advance and Refrigerated
Marinate swordfish • Slice peaches for dessert • Set table

Party Day!
Grill Cheese-Stuffed Mushrooms in Grape Leaves, swordfish, and polenta • Warm bread • Bring eggplant to room temperature • Assemble dessert

CHEESE-STUFFED MUSHROOMS IN GRAPE LEAVES

Mushrooms, stemmed

Olive oil

Teleme or muenster cheese,
  cubed to fit mushroom
  caps

Minced green onions

Minced fresh basil

Grape leaves in brine
  (purchased)

Here's a playful choice for summer!

1. Preheat the oven to 375°F or fire up the barbecue.
2. Brush each mushroom cap with olive oil and fill with a piece of cheese, some green onions, and basil.
3. Wrap the mushrooms in grape leaves and place on an oiled ovenproof pan. Bake or grill on the barbecue for 20 minutes, just until the mushrooms are hot and the cheese starts to melt. Use smoke chips if you enjoy smoky flavors.

Fast: Can assemble up to 2 days in advance and refrigerate.

Fabulous: Serve hot or at room temperature. Experiment with different cheeses and herbs for the stuffing. Feta and rosemary make a good combination.

COLD GUACAMOLE SOUFFLÉ

2 envelopes unflavored
   gelatin
1/4 cup fresh lemon juice or
   to taste
1 cup mashed ripe avocado
   (about 2 to 3 avocados)
1 cup sour cream
1 cup Salsa (see page 110)
   or purchased
1/2 cup chopped fresh
   cilantro
1/4 to 1/2 cup minced
   green onions
2 to 4 dried pasilla chiles,
   rehydrated, stemmed,
   seeded, and minced
2 cloves garlic, minced
1 cup grated sharp cheddar
   cheese
Salt and freshly ground white
   pepper to taste
Ground cumin to taste
Minced fresh cilantro, black
   olives, marigolds, and/or
   sour cream for garnish

Yield: about 4 cups

A refreshing, cool summer hors d'oeuvre!

1. Oil a 4- to 6-cup soufflé dish, flan tin, or container of your choice.
2. Dissolve the gelatin by sprinkling it over the lemon juice in a small bowl set in a larger bowl of hot water (or dissolve in a microwave on low power).
3. Combine the avocado, sour cream, salsa, and dissolved gelatin in a food processor fitted with a metal blade, or in a large bowl.
4. Process in the remaining ingredients with several quick on-and-off motions, using care not to destroy their texture, or combine with the ingredients in the bowl. Taste and adjust the seasonings.
5. Pour the mixture into the prepared mold and chill until firm, about 2 hours in the refrigerator or 1 hour in the freezer.

Fast: Can prepare up to 2 days in advance and refrigerate, or freeze up to 6 months. Thaw in the refrigerator for 2 days.

Flashy: Garnish with a dollop of sour cream on top and a sprinkling of minced cilantro or a marigold and/or black olives.

Fabulous: With minced fresh or dried chiles of your choice. To reduce fat content, substitute lowfat yogurt for the sour cream.

PAPAYA, JICAMA, CUCUMBER, AND RED ONION SALAD WITH FETA

1 large papaya, peeled, seeded, and thinly sliced

1 1/2 pounds jicama, peeled and cut into 1/2-inch cubes

1 large European cucumber, thinly sliced

1 large red onion, thinly sliced

8 ounces feta cheese, crumbled

Cilantro Vinaigrette (recipe follows)

Sprigs fresh cilantro and/or lettuce leaves for garnish

1. Combine all the ingredients, except the dressing and garnish, in a large salad bowl.
2. Toss with the desired amount of dressing and let sit for at least 1 hour, at room temperature, or up to 2 days in the refrigerator.

Fast: Can prepare up to 2 days in advance and refrigerate.

Flashy: Arrange on salad plates or on a platter and garnish with sprigs of cilantro and/or serve on lettuce leaves.

Fabulous: With cooked shrimp, crab, or lobster added.

Further: Use leftovers in a tossed green salad or in cold pasta, rice, potato, or couscous salad.

CILANTRO VINAIGRETTE

1 cup olive oil

1/3 cup white wine vinegar

1/2 teaspoon chili powder or to taste

2 cloves garlic, minced

1/2 to 1 bunch fresh cilantro, stemmed and minced

1/2 to 1 teaspoon salt

1/2 teaspoon ground cumin or to taste

Freshly ground white pepper to taste

Yield: *about 2 cups*

A dressing with a Southwestern flair

1. Place all the ingredients in a food processor fitted with a metal blade, or whisk together in a large bowl.
2. Taste and adjust the seasonings.

Fast: Can prepare up to 5 days in advance and refrigerate.

Fabulous: As a marinade or cold sauce for poultry, fish, and/or seafood.

GRILLED MARINATED SWORDFISH WITH ANCHOVY-BASIL MAYONNAISE

MARINADE

1/4 cup soy sauce

1/2 cup orange juice

Juice of 1 or 2 lemons

1/4 cup olive oil

1/4 cup sesame oil

4 to 8 cloves garlic, minced

1 tablespoon minced fresh
   thyme or 1 teaspoon dried

2 to 4 tablespoons minced
   fresh mint

6 green onions, minced

1/4 cup minced fresh basil

1 teaspoon Szechuan
   peppercorns, crushed

Eight 3/4-inch thick
   swordfish steaks

Smoke chips, soaked in hot
   water (optional)

Anchovy-Basil Mayonnaise
   (recipe follows)

Sprigs fresh thyme or basil,
   black olives, and/or
   minced green onions for
   garnish

This entree evokes strong Mediteranean flavors with Asian undertones.

1. Combine all the marinade ingredients in a food processor fitted with a metal blade or whisk together in a large bowl.

2. Place the swordfish in a glass or ceramic pan, then pour the marinade over and cover with plastic wrap. Let sit at room temperature for 30 minutes or up to 24 hours in the refrigerator.

3. When ready to cook, heat the barbecue. If using smoke chips, scatter them over the top when the coals are hot. Oil the grill and cook the fillets for about 3 to 5 minutes on each side or until just firm.

Fast: Can marinate up to 1 day in advance and refrigerate. Can prepare marinade up to 1 week in advance and refrigerate.

Flashy: Serve hot or at room temperature. Garnish with sprigs of fresh thyme or basil, minced green onions, and/or olives. Serve with Anchovy-Basil Mayonnaise, separately or with a dollop on top.

Fabulous: Cold as a salad, with cold cooked zucchini and shredded spinach. With 2 to 4 tablespoons fermented black beans, mashed, and 1/4 cup minced fresh mint leaves and cilantro added to the marinade instead of basil. With Roasted Red Pepper Sauce (see page 87) in addition to, or instead of, the Anchovy-Basil Mayonnaise.

ANCHOVY-BASIL MAYONNAISE

3 to 6 cloves garlic, smashed
1 large egg (see page 23)
1 teaspoon anchovy paste or
   to taste
2 to 4 tablespoons minced
   fresh parsley
1 tablespoon fresh lemon
   juice or to taste
1/4 cup minced fresh basil
   or to taste
1/2 cup olive oil
1/2 cup peanut oil
Freshly ground white pepper
   to taste

Yield: about 1 cup

Basil is my favorite summer flavor.

1. Place the garlic in a small saucepan with lightly salted water and bring to a boil. Change the water and repeat. Drain. (This mellows the taste of the garlic.)
2. Puree the garlic with the next five ingredients in a food processor fitted with a metal blade or in a blender.
3. Slowly process the oils in through the feed tube or the cover while the machine is running. Taste and adjust the seasonings.

Fast: Can prepare up to 3 days in advance and refrigerate.

Flashy: With cooked or raw vegetables, or as a sauce for poultry, seafood, or fish.

Fabulous: To avoid any problems with salmonella, this recipe is just as delicious prepared with 1 cup purchased mayonnaise substituted for the egg and olive and peanut oil. You won't sacrifice any flavor.

BAKED EGGPLANT AND ARTICHOKE HEARTS

3 to 3 1/2 pounds eggplant, trimmed and cut into 1-inch cubes

Salt to taste

Two 6-ounce jars marinated artichoke hearts (reserve the marinade)

4 cloves garlic, minced, or to taste

1 red onion, thinly sliced

1 tablespoon capers, rinsed and drained

1/4 cup minced fresh parsley

1/4 cup minced fresh basil or to taste

1/4 to 1/2 cup pumpkin seeds, toasted (see page 29)

Freshly ground white pepper to taste

Fresh lemon juice to taste

A wonderful vegetable dish that is equally at home at a picnic or an elegant dinner.

1. Sprinkle the eggplant lightly with salt and place in a colander set in a bowl or the sink to drain off its bitter juices for about 1 hour. Rinse and spin or pat dry.

2. In a large bowl, combine the artichoke hearts and their marinade, with the eggplant, garlic, and onions. Place in a baking pan and bake in a preheated 400°F oven until tender, about 30 minutes.

3. Add the remaining ingredients, then taste and adjust the seasonings.

Fast: Can prepare up to 2 days in advance and refrigerate. (For best results, undercook by about 15 minutes if you are planning on reheating and serving this hot.) Reheat in a microwave or in a preheated 350°F oven for about 15 minutes.

Flashy: Serve at room temperature for this menu or serve hot for more elegant dinners.

Fabulous: With zucchini, instead of eggplant, and with roasted red peppers mixed in. With freshly grated Parmesan cheese.

Further: Use leftovers in soups, or in lettuce, rice, or pasta salads. Toss into hot pasta.

GRILLED POLENTA WITH SUN-DRIED TOMATOES AND GARLIC

10 to 20 cloves garlic
Salt to taste
1/2 cup minced fresh parsley
2 tablespoons olive oil
1 red onion, minced
1/4 to 1/2 cup sun-dried
  tomatoes, minced
9 cups chicken broth,
  homemade or canned
1 1/2 cups dry vermouth
1 bay leaf
Freshly ground white pepper
  to taste
1 1/2 cups uncooked polenta

This is my version of a wonderful Italian classic. It not only tastes great but is healthy.

1. Preheat the oven to 350°F.
2. Place the garlic in small saucepan of lightly salted water and bring to a boil. Drain and repeat the procedure once. Remove the garlic and puree with the parsley in a food processor fitted with a metal blade or in a blender.
3. Heat the olive oil in large saucepan over medium heat, and sauté the onion until tender.
4. Add all the ingredients, except the polenta, and bring to a boil. Slowly stir in the polenta and continue to stir from time to time until the polenta is tender and the liquid is absorbed, about 30 minutes. It should pull away from the sides of the pan when stirred.
5. Transfer the polenta to an oiled glass or ceramic loaf pan and let stand at room temperature until cool. Refrigerate until firm enough to slice. Cut into 1/2-inch thick slices.
6. Brush with olive oil and place on a hot grill or under a preheated broiler 3 to 5 minutes per side before serving.

Fast: Can prepare through step 5 up to 2 days in advance and refrigerate, or freeze for up to 1 month. Thaw in the refrigerator for 2 days or at room temperature for about 8 hours.

Fabulous: Add minced marinated artichoke hearts and/or fresh or dried herbs in step 5.

Further: Use leftovers cut up and added to salads or soups.

FRESH FRUIT AND SHORTBREAD WITH A SCOTCH-CUSTARD SAUCE

Scotch-Custard Sauce (recipe
  follows)
Lemon-Sesame Shortbread
  (see page 129) or
  purchased
4 to 6 peaches, sliced
1 pint blueberries
Fresh mint sprigs and/or
  grated chocolate for
  garnish

A nice alternative to fruit pies or tarts.

1. Pour the sauce on each dessert plate.
2. Place a piece of shortbread on top of the sauce and arrange the fruit
    over it.

Fast: Can prepare the fruit, shortbread, and sauce in advance, but
  assemble right before serving.

Flashy: Garnish with a sprig of mint and/or grated chocolate sprinkled
  over the top.

Fabulous: With purchased shortbread, French vanilla ice cream, and
  chocolate sauce instead of the Scotch-Custard Sauce.

SCOTCH-CUSTARD SAUCE

1/4 cup Scotch
6 large egg yolks (see page 23)
1/2 cup packed light brown sugar
1/4 teaspoon salt
1/4 cup pear liqueur or Kirsch
1 3/4 cups milk
One 1-inch piece vanilla bean, cut in half lengthwise or 2 teaspoons vanilla extract
Grated zest of 2 lemons
Freshly grated nutmeg to taste

Yield: about 2 cups

1. Combine the first five ingredients in a food processor fitted with a metal blade or beat with an electric mixer in a large bowl for about 5 minutes until lemon-colored.
2. Heat the milk with the vanilla bean, zest, and nutmeg in a double boiler over simmering water. Let cook until the milk is nicely flavored by the vanilla, about 5 minutes. Remove the vanilla bean, rinse and dry it off, and store in a jar of sugar. It will flavor it nicely.
3. Whisk the yolk mixture into the milk. Continue to cook until the custard begins to thicken. Do not boil or the yolks will curdle.
4. Fill a large bowl with ice and place a small bowl on top. Strain the custard into the small bowl through a fine mesh strainer and whisk frequently until cool.

Fast: Can prepare up to 4 days in advance and refrigerate, or freeze for up to 6 months. Thaw in the refrigerator for 2 days or at room temperature for about 4 hours.

Flashy: On crêpes, soufflés, pound or shortcake, or on any fruit.

Fabulous: With any liqueur instead of the pear, and with rum, brandy, or bourbon instead of the Scotch.

LEMON-SESAME SHORTBREAD

1/2 pound (2 sticks)
    unsalted butter, cut up
2 teaspoons vanilla extract
1/2 to 1 cup sugar, plus 2
    tablespoons, depending on
    desired sweetness
2 cups all-purpose flour
1/2 cup sesame seeds,
    toasted (see page 29)
Finely grated zest of 2 to 4
    lemons, depending on
    desired tartness
Freshly grated nutmeg to
    taste

Yield: about twelve 2-inch wedges

Shortbread is the ultimate buttery cookie, and literally takes only a few minutes to prepare. It's almost too good to be true!

1. Preheat the oven to 325°F.
2. Add the butter, vanilla, and the sugar, minus the 2 tablespoons, to a food processor fitted with a metal blade and process until well creamed, or beat together with an electric mixer until well creamed.
3. Process in the flour, sesame seeds, and zest until a ball forms, or beat in using an electric mixer until smooth. Then form dough into a ball.
4. Pat the dough into the bottom of two ungreased 8- or 9-inch square or round tart pans with removable bottoms. Sprinkle with the remaining sugar.
5. Use the tines of a fork to decorate the outer edge of the dough, and a knife to score the dough into wedges or squares.
6. Bake until pale golden, about 25 minutes, then cut into wedges or squares along scored lines and cool in the pan. Remove the rim of the pan and use a spatula to remove the cookies.

Fast: Can prepare up to 5 days in advance and store in airtight jar(s), or freeze in plastic bag(s) for up to 3 months. Thaw at room temperature for several hours.

Fabulous: With poppy seeds or chopped nuts instead of the sesame seeds.

· ·

CHAPTER FIVE

Fall Dinner Parties

FALL DINNER PARTIES AT A GLANCE

· ·

Setting

ELEGANT
- Refined, elegant, festive
- The official start of the indoor holiday entertaining season

CASUAL
- In kitchens, family rooms, and dens, the heart of the house
- Relaxed, warm, and cozy

Props

ELEGANT
- Traditional colors are earthy: rust, amber, gold, pumpkin, burgundy, olive, brown, tan
- Can use light colors or work with the colors of your choice if used with seasonal items
- Brass, copper, silver accessories add warmth and elegance

CASUAL
- Heavy textured, handwoven tablecloths, placemats, and napkins
- Cotton bedspreads, patterned or in solid colors, from import stores used as tablecloths
- New dish towels in fall colors for napkins

Foods for Decorating and Arrangements

- Persimmons, pomegranates, stalks of brussels sprouts, winter squashes, nuts, gourds, grapes, pears, flowering kale, and cabbage

Cuisine

- Cooler weather calls for heartier and richer dishes along with slower cooking methods

ELEGANT FALL MENUS

• • • • • • • • • • • • • • • • • • • •

Stuffed Chicken Breast Dinner

This is a menu deserving of a stately, refined tablescape. A black or charcoal gray cloth with dove gray napkins would work well. A rust cloth with peach napkins is another option. Arrange white mums in several small glass vases or champagne flutes. Bring out your best: china, crystal, and silver that have been overlooked for most of your summer entertaining.

The party begins with delectable Saint André and Shiitake Tartlets. As an added bonus, they are easy to prepare. I recommend preparing extra and freezing them for other parties. If you use this filling in a pie shell, it becomes a lovely entree for luncheons, brunches, and light suppers, served with crusty French bread, a tossed salad, and maybe a soup.

Your guests will be delighted by the Raw Beet and Watercress Salad with Baby Corn. It is refreshingly astringent, very attractive, and unusual. Stuffed Chicken Breast with Anchovy Cream Sauce is guaranteed to convert anchovy haters into anchovy lovers. The flavor is not harsh or dominant, the anchovies are used as a seasoning to provide flavor intrigue. As a matter of fact, most of your guests will not be able to identify them. The couscous makes a wonderful alternative to rice and takes only minutes to prepare. If you are not already familiar with couscous, you'll be amazed by its versatility! The plate composition is completed by the Brandied Carrots, which are also a flavor treat.

This menu concludes with a rich, yet refreshing medley of fresh pear sorbet, decadent chocolate sauce, and fabulous biscotti.

MENU

Saint André and Shiitake Tartlets

Raw Beet and Watercress Salad with Baby Corn

Sliced Baguette and Sweet Butter

Stuffed Chicken Breast with Anchovy Cream Sauce

Couscous with Saffron

Brandied Carrots

Pear Sorbet Helene

Lemon Sherry Biscotti

FASTER & FLASHIER MENU

Saint André and Crackers

Tossed Salad with Baby Corn and Beets (canned)

Chicken Breast with Anchovy Cream Sauce (not stuffed)

Couscous

French Vanilla Ice Cream with Pears and Chocolate Sauce (purchased)

Butter Cookies or Biscotti (purchased)

WINES

Chardonnay or Champagne

Sauvignon Blanc

Champagne

Fast & Fabulous Timetable

Up to 1 year in Advance and Frozen
   Brandied Chocolate Sauce

Up to 6 Months in Advance and Frozen
   Anchovy Cream Sauce • Lemon Sherry Biscotti • Croustades or Won
   Ton Cups

Up to 3 Months in Advance and Frozen
   Stuffed Chicken Breast

Up to 1 Month in Advance and Frozen
Saint André and Shiitake Filling or finished tartlets • Pear Sorbet

Up to 2 Weeks in Advance and Refrigerated
Brandied Chocolate Sauce

Up to 1 Week in Advance and Refrigerated
Won Ton Cups

5 Days in Advance and Refrigerated
Herbed Walnut Vinaigrette • Lemon Sherry Biscotti

3 Days in Advance and Refrigerated
Saint André and Shiitake filling • Anchovy Cream Sauce

2 Days in Advance and Refrigerated
Couscous through step 3 • Thaw frozen prepared-ahead foods

1 Day in Advance and Refrigerated
Stuffed Chicken Breast • Partially cook brandied carrots • Prepare beets and marinate • Set Table

Party Day!
Warm bread • Assemble salads • Heat chicken • Prepare Couscous with Saffron • Finish carrots • Bake tartlets

SAINT ANDRÉ AND SHIITAKE TARTLETS

2 tablespoons unsalted butter

1 ounce dried shiitake
    mushrooms, rehydrated,
    stemmed, and minced
    (strain and reserve the
    soaking liquid)

1 to 2 shallots, minced

2 tablespoons all-purpose
    flour

1/4 cup dry vermouth

1 teaspoon Dijon mustard

Grated zest of 1 lemon

3/4 cup heavy cream

4 ounces Saint André, rind
    removed and cut into
    chunks

1/4 cup pine nuts, toasted
    (see page 29), or to taste

1 large egg yolk combined
    with 2 tablespoons heavy
    cream

Salt and freshly ground white
    pepper to taste

Freshly grated nutmeg to
    taste

1 recipe Croustades or Won
    Ton Cups (see pages 146,
    47)

Sprigs fresh mint and
    nasturtiums for garnish

1. Preheat the oven to 350°F.
2. Melt the butter in a large saucepan and sauté the mushrooms and shallots over medium heat until tender.
3. Stir in the flour and cook for several minutes over low heat.
4. Whisk the reserved soaking liquid into the saucepan and bring to a boil over high heat. Whisk frequently and cook until reduced to less than 1/4 cup.
5. Whisk in the vermouth, mustard, and zest. Bring to a boil.
6. Whisk in the cream and cook until thickened.
7. Add the cheese and pine nuts. Cook over low heat until melted.
8. Stir several tablespoons of sauce into the yolk mixture. Stir the yolk mixture back into the sauce and continue to cook over low until thickened. Do not boil or the yolks will curdle. Taste and season with the salt, pepper, and nutmeg.
9. Fill the croustades or won ton cups. Place on a cookie sheet and bake for 10 to 15 minutes, until hot and firm.

Fast: Can prepare the filling up to 3 days in advance and refrigerate or freeze for up to 1 month. No thawing necessary. Can assemble tartlets up to 1 hour in advance and hold at room temperature until they are baked. Can assemble and flash freeze for up to 1 month. Bake frozen; if you let them thaw, they will get mushy.

Flashy: Serve on a platter with sprigs of mint and nasturtiums interspersed in the center.

Fabulous: With shrimp, crab, artichoke hearts, or hearts of palm, instead of shiitake mushrooms.

RAW BEET AND WATERCRESS SALAD WITH BABY CORN

1 pound beets, peeled and
cut into matchstick slices
or shredded (reserve the
greens)
One 15-ounce can baby corn
2 to 4 bunches watercress
leaves
Herbed Walnut Vinaigrette
(recipe follows)

Yield: 6 to 8 servings

1. Arrange beets, corn, and watercress leaves decoratively on salad plates.
2. Drizzle desired amount of vinaigrette over salad and serve.

Fast: For added flavor and convenience can prepare and marinate beets in the vinaigrette up to 1 day in advance and refrigerate. Can prepare vinaigrette up to 5 days in advance and refrigerate. Assemble salad up to 6 hours in advance and refrigerate. Dress before serving.

Fabulous: Top with a slice of chèvre and/or pecans or walnuts sautéed a minute or two in oil until they are fragrant. Mince and sauté the reserved beet greens in walnut oil until they wilt, and serve chilled or at room temperature on salad plates.

HERBED WALNUT VINAIGRETTE

1/4 cup walnut oil
3/4 cup olive oil
1/3 cup sherry wine vinegar
2 to 4 tablespoons minced
shallots
1/4 cup minced fresh parsley
1 tablespoon capers, rinsed
and drained
1 to 2 tablespoons fresh
thyme leaves
Salt and freshly ground white
pepper to taste

Yield: about 1 1/3 cups

1. Combine all the ingredients in a food processor fitted with a metal blade, or whisk together in a large bowl one ingredient at a time, slowly pouring in the oils and vinegar.
2. Taste and adjust the seasonings.

STUFFED CHICKEN BREAST WITH ANCHOVY CREAM SAUCE

STUFFING

2 large eggs

4 ounces chèvre or boursin
   cheese

1 pound ground pork or
   Italian sausage

2 to 4 cloves garlic, minced

2 shallots, minced

One 16-ounce package
   frozen chopped spinach,
   thawed and squeezed to
   remove all excess moisture

One 6-ounce jar marinated
   artichoke hearts, drained
   and chopped

One 8-ounce can water
   chestnuts, drained and
   chopped

Freshly grated nutmeg to taste

Salt and freshly ground white
   pepper to taste

Fresh or dried thyme, dried
   fines herbes, and/or sage
   to taste

4 large chicken breasts,
   boned, skinned, halved,
   and pounded to 1/4-inch
   thickness

1/2 cup all-purpose flour

Olive oil and unsalted butter
   as needed

Anchovy Cream Sauce
   (recipe follows)

2 tablespoons cornstarch

2 tablespoons dry vermouth

Minced green onions or fresh
   parsley for garnish

This is an elegant dish. Don't let the anchovies scare you away. They are subtle and contribute an interesting flavor.

1. Preheat the oven to 350°F.
2. To prepare the stuffing, combine the eggs, chèvre, and ground pork with the garlic and shallots in a food processor fitted with a metal blade or a large bowl.
3. Transfer the pork mixture to a bowl and mix in the remaining stuffing ingredients.
4. Fry 1 tablespoon of the mixture to check the seasonings.
5. To assemble, lay the chicken breasts out flat on a work surface. Top each one with the desired amount of filling and roll to enclose. Secure with toothpicks.
6. Place the flour in a shallow bowl. Roll each breast in the flour to coat fully. Shake off any excess.
7. Heat 2 tablespoons each of olive oil and butter in a skillet and quickly sauté the rolls over medium-high heat, turning frequently, until slightly golden. Add more oil and butter as needed. Do this in several batches, to avoid overcrowding. Transfer to a baking pan.
8. Strain the sauce through a fine mesh strainer over the rolls, cover with foil, and bake for 20 to 30 minutes, until hot and fully cooked.
9. Remove the chicken to a platter and tent with foil.
10. Transfer the sauce to a large saucepan and bring to a boil over high heat.
11. Dissolve the cornstarch in the dry vermouth and whisk into the boiling sauce. Only use as much of the cornstarch as needed to barely thicken it. Taste and adjust the seasonings.

Fast: Can prepare through step 8 up to 1 day in advance and refrigerate, or freeze for up to 3 months. Thaw in the refrigerator for 2 days. Bring to room temperature before baking.

Flashy: Serve the chicken on a puddle of sauce and garnish with minced green onions or parsley.

Further: Use extra stuffing to create a wonderful lasagna, or as a filling for ravioli, won tons, or cannelloni. To be Fast & Flashy, use egg roll wrappers for cannelloni, and won ton or *sui mai* wrappers for making ravioli.

ANCHOVY CREAM SAUCE

3/4 to 1 cup dry vermouth

1 to 2 tablespoons anchovy paste, or to taste

Grated zest of 2 lemons, minced

1/4 cup minced shallots

2 bay leaves

2 to 6 cloves garlic

2 teaspoons pink peppercorns crushed or to taste

2 cups chicken broth, homemade or canned

2 cups heavy cream

Salt and freshly ground white pepper to taste

Fresh lemon juice to taste

1. Bring the vermouth, anchovy paste, zest, shallots, bay leaves, garlic, and peppercorns to a boil in a large saucepan over high heat. Reduce by half while whisking frequently.

2. Add the chicken broth and cream and reduce by about a third until flavors develop. Taste and adjust the seasonings.

Fast: Can prepare up to 3 days in advance and refrigerate, or freeze for up to 6 months. Thaw in the refrigerator for 2 days or at room temperature for about 8 hours.

Fabulous: With fresh herbs, capers, green peppercorns, or mustard added to the sauce.

COUSCOUS WITH SAFFRON

2 tablespoons unsalted butter
2 to 4 shallots, minced
1/8 to 1/4 teaspoon saffron
   threads
2 cups uncooked couscous
2 cups chicken broth,
   homemade or canned
1/4 cup medium-dry sherry
Salt and freshly ground white
   pepper to taste
1/4 cup minced fresh parsley

Couscous is a perfect food: quick, delicious, versatile, and healthy. Sounds too good to be true!

1. Melt the butter in a large saucepan over low to medium-low heat and sauté the shallots until tender. Do not brown.
2. Add the saffron and sauté another minute.
3. Stir in the couscous and coat with the butter and shallots. Sauté for several minutes.
4. Add the broth, sherry, salt, and pepper, and bring to a boil.
5. Cover and remove from the heat. Let stand for 5 minutes, then stir in the parsley and serve.

Fast: Can prepare completely, or just through step 3, up to 2 days in advance, and refrigerate. Reheat over double boiler or in microwave for 5 to 10 minutes.

Fabulous: Season with any herb and add sautéed mushrooms, sun-dried tomatoes, and/or skinned, seeded, and minced fresh tomatoes.

Further: Use leftovers as a salad or added to soups.

BRANDIED CARROTS

6 tablespoons (3/4 stick)
  unsalted butter
2 pounds young carrots,
  washed, blanched 5 to 10
  minutes, peeled, and sliced
2 shallots, minced
Salt and freshly ground white
  pepper to taste
Freshly grated nutmeg to
  taste
1 teaspoon sugar or to taste
1/3 cup brandy
1/2 teaspoon dried thyme
2 tablespoons minced fresh
  parsley for garnish

This vegetable is often handled without inspiration. Here you'll see how delicious carrots can be.

1. Melt the butter in a large, heavy saucepan over medium heat, then add the carrots and shallots. Season with the salt, pepper, nutmeg, and sugar. Cook over medium-high heat until the glaze is a rich caramel color, stirring frequently, about 5 to 10 minutes.

2. Add the brandy and thyme. Cook over high heat for a few minutes until the brandy evaporates. Stir frequently. Taste and adjust the seasonings.

Fast: Can blanch carrots up to 1 day in advance and refrigerate. Bring to room temperature and finish cooking before serving.

Flashy: Garnish with minced parsley.

Fabulous: Seasoned with dillweed and sesame seeds, or any kind of nuts, or with minced Chinese black fungus (see page 22).

PEAR SORBET HELENE

2 cups dry white wine
1/2 cup sugar
1 3/4 pounds pears
Fresh lemon juice to taste
1/4 cup Poire Williams or
  other pear liqueur
Brandied Chocolate Sauce
  (recipe follows)
Fresh mint sprigs and kiwi
  slices for garnish

Yield: about 5 cups

This is my take-off on Pears Helene, a classic!

1. Combine the wine and sugar in small saucepan over low to medium-low heat and stir until the sugar dissolves; *do not boil.* Reduce the heat, and simmer, uncovered, for 5 minutes. Place this syrup, except for 1/4 cup, in the freezer until cold.
2. Peel and core the pears. Combine with the reserved syrup and lemon juice and cook, covered, in a large enamel or stainless steel saucepan over low to medium-low heat or in a microwave until tender.
3. Puree the pears in a food processor and chill.
4. Combine the liqueur, pears, and syrup. Freeze for about 2 hours.
5. Puree again and freeze for another 2 hours.

Fast: Can prepare up to 1 month in advance and freeze.

Flashy: Served in stemmed glasses with chocolate sauce drizzled over the top. Garnish with a sprig of mint and a slice of kiwi.

Fabulous: With apples instead of pears.

BRANDIED CHOCOLATE SAUCE

2 cups heavy cream
2/3 cup sugar or to taste
Grated zest of 2 oranges
1/3 cup brandy
16 ounces semisweet
chocolate, broken into
pieces, or chocolate chips
2 teaspoons vanilla extract
2 tablespoons orange-flavored
liqueur
Freshly grated nutmeg to
taste

Yield: about 3 cups

This makes a great Christmas gift!

1. Combine the cream, sugar, zest, and brandy in a medium-size saucepan and bring to a boil over medium-high to high heat. Cook until the sugar dissolves.
2. Meanwhile, chop the chocolate in a food processor fitted with metal blade.
3. Add the cream mixture through the feed tube while the machine is running.
4. Process in the vanilla, liqueur, and nutmeg.

Fast: Can prepare up to 2 weeks in advance and refrigerate, or freeze for up to 1 year. Thaw in the refrigerator for 2 days or at room temperature for several hours.

Flashy: On ice cream, pound cake, brownies, strawberries, anything your imagination suggests.

Fabulous: Substitute any kind of liqueur for the brandy and/or orange liqueur.

Further: Use leftovers to cure those unexpected chocolate attacks!

LEMON SHERRY BISCOTTI

3/4 cup confectioners' sugar
1/4 pound (1 stick) unsalted
   butter
1/2 teaspoon salt
4 1/2 cups all-purpose flour
1 tablespoon baking powder
Grated zest of 2 to 4 lemons
1 cup cream sherry
Freshly grated nutmeg to
   taste

Yield: about 70

If you are a biscotti fan, you will love this.

1. Preheat the oven to 350°F.
2. Combine the sugar, butter, and salt until fluffy in a food processor fitted with a metal blade, or in a bowl with an electric mixer.
3. Process in 4 cups of the flour and the baking powder.
4. Add the zest, sherry, and nutmeg while the machine or mixer is running and process until a soft dough forms.
5. Dust the work surface with the remaining flour and lightly flour your hands. Divide the dough in half and form into two cylinders about 2 inches wide. Place on an oiled cookie sheet and bake until the tester comes out clean, about 35 minutes
6. Let cool and cut each loaf into 1/2-inch thick slices at an angle. Cut each slice in half lengthwise and return to the cookie sheet.
7. Reduce the oven temperature to 300°F and bake until crisp, for 15 to 20 minutes more. Turn the oven off and let sit for 15 minutes more, with the door open.

Fast: Can prepare up to 5 days in advance and store in an airtight jar or plastic bag or freeze for up to 6 months. Thaw for 2 days in the refrigerator or at room temperature for a few hours.

Fabulous: With any chopped nut mixed in or dipped in chocolate.

Gingered Pork Dinner

An unusual but intriguing hors d'oeuvre, Chard and Chèvre Croustades start this evening off and immediately set an elegant tone. A Cream of Fennel Soup with Crab follows. Simply put, it is a killer. The fennel is refreshing, while the crab contributes a sweet richness. What a duo! The next course is a salad that, like most of my salads, functions as a palate cleanser. It is incredibly exotic. Just as is the rest of the menu, it is a composition of classic fall flavors, uniquely combined. No better way to illustrate this point than with the entree, Gingered Pork Cutlets with

Pears. Apple Walnut Egg Rolls for dessert further dramatize the menu.

I can almost see your eyes popping out, wondering how it could be humanly possible to enjoy all of these fabulous flavors and many courses at one meal. Fear not! The secret is simple. Each course must be only large enough to tease, never enough to satisfy. Serving more than the usual number of courses is a luxury reserved for elegant evenings, and when done properly will not cause anyone discomfort.

If you want your table to be just as interesting and unusual as the menu, think in terms of the season's produce. I used one of my favorite cloths, a very light pastel pink, not a typical fall color. My centerpiece was an arrangement of flowering kale, with its glorious green to magenta leaves, in a glass bowl. Mixed in were clusters of dark purple grapes along with wine-colored mums.

Stalks of brussels sprouts, placed directly on the table, radiated in a starlike pattern. For the final seasonal touch, persimmons were interspersed on the table along with brass candlesticks holding pale pink candles. All these decorative and flavor elements come together to create a fabulous party that is anything but predictable.

MENU

Chard and Chèvre Croustades

Cream of Fennel Soup with Crab

Sliced Baguettes and Sweet Butter

Salad of Watercress and Papaya

Gingered Pork with Pears

Potato and Onion Timbale

Sautéed Zucchini and Red Peppers

Apple Walnut Egg Rolls with Caramel Sauce

FASTER & FLASHIER MENU

Warm Chèvre with Sliced Baguette

Tossed Salad

Gingered Pork with Pears

Parsleyed Rice

Dessert (purchased)

WINES

Sauvignon Blanc

Gewürztraminer or Pinot Noir

Late harvest Riesling or Champagne

Fast & Fabulous Timetable

Up to 6 Months in Advance and Frozen
Croustades • Cream of Fennel Soup with Crab through step 4 • Apple Walnut Egg Roll filling • Caramel Sauce

Up to 3 Months in Advance and Frozen
Apple Walnut Egg Rolls through step 4 • Chard and Chèvre Won Ton Cups

5 Days in Advance and Refrigerated
Apple Walnut Egg Roll filling • Caramel Sauce

4 Days in Advance and Refrigerated
Salad dressing

3 Days in Advance and Refrigerated
Cream of Fennel Soup with Crab through step 4

2 Days in Advance and Refrigerated
Thaw frozen prepared-ahead foods

1 Day in Advance and Refrigerated
Chard and Chèvre filling • Apple Walnut Egg Rolls through step 4 • Prep salad • Gingered Pork with Pears through step 10 • Cut up vegetables for Sauteed Zucchini and Red Peppers • Potato and Onion Timbale through step 4 • Set table

Party Day!
Bake Chard and Chèvre Croustades • Bake timbale • Finish soup and zucchini • Heat pork • Prep salad and assemble • Bake Apple Walnut Egg Rolls • Toss salad • Warm bread

Elegant Spring Dinner Party. *Front to back: Poached Salmon with Dill Cream Sauce, Fennel-Saffron Risotto, and Sugar Peas with Shiitake Mushrooms; Strawberry and Kiwi Pastry Scallops; and Asparagus, Shrimp, and Celery Root Salad. For wines, try Dry Creek Vineyard Fumé Blanc or Reserve Chardonnay, or Segura Viudas sparkling wine.*

Casual Spring Dinner Party. *Asparagus and Scallop Pasta with Lemon Cream Sauce, Mediterranean Vegetable Terrine, Marinated Shrimp with Garlic Crouton Rounds, and Aphrodite's Parfait. Good companion wines would be Freixenet Brut Sparkling Wine and R & J Cook Winery or Dry Creek Vineyard Fumé Blanc.*

Casual Summer Dinner Party. *Marinated Barbecued Ribs and Wings with Ginger-Merlot Sauce, Shiitake Mushroom and Cucumber Salad, Papaya Potato Salad with Mango Chutney Vinaigrette, and Garlic-Rosemary Bread. Partner with Dry Creek Vineyard Meritage, Freixenet Brut Sparkling Wine, or Dry Creek Vineyard Chenin Blanc.*

Elegant Summer Hors d'Oeuvres. *Left: Stuffed Romaine; right: Prosciutto and Vegetables, and Fruit.*

Elegant Fall Dinner Party. *Cornish Game Hen, Barley and Wild Rice Pilaf, and Beet Shreds; Green Onion Lemon Butter; Cranberry Ginger Sauce; and Harvest Salad Platter with Gingered Mustard Vinaigrette. Partner with Dry Creek Vineyard Meritage and R & J Cook Winery Petite Sirah.*

Casual Fall Dinner Party. *Front to back: Chile con Queso with Chips, Southwestern Bulgur, Pasilla Chile and Pork Ragout, and Escarole Salad with Avocado, Tangerines, and Olives. Good companion wines are Freixenet Brut Sparkling Wine, Dry Creek Vineyard Meritage, and R & J Cook Winery Petite Sirah.*

Elegant Winter Hors d'Oeuvres and Desserts. *Clockwise from the back: Chèvre and Sun-Dried Tomato Croustades, Almond Mocha Ecstasy, Almond-Pear Cake on Brandied Chocolate Sauce, and Caviar Mousse with Bagel Chips. With the hors d'oeuvres, serve Gloria Ferrer Royal Cuvée Brut Sparkling Wine or Dry Creek Vineyard Fumé Blanc; with the desserts, R & J Cook Winery Moonlight Mist, Dry Creek Vineyard Cabernet Sauvignon, or Gloria Ferrer Royal Cuvée Brut Sparkling Wine.*

Casual Winter Dinner Party. *Left to right: Escarole, Endive, and Watercress Salad with Red Wine Vinaigrette, Seafood Cannelloni, Peas with Pancetta and Pine Nuts, and Potted Camembert with Garlic Crouton Rounds. Partner with Dry Creek Vineyard or R & J Cook Winery Chardonnay.*

CHARD AND CHÈVRE CROUSTADES

1 bunch chard
8 ounces chèvre
2 cloves garlic, minced
1 teaspoon dried Italian
  herbs
1/2 cup mayonnaise
3/4 cup milk
1/4 cup sherry
Salt and freshly ground white
  pepper to taste
Freshly grated nutmeg to
  taste
2 large egg yolks
1 large egg
Croustades (recipe follows)
Sprigs of fresh herbs and
  grapes for garnish

If you thought spinach quiche was delicious, just wait until you taste this!

1. In a large pot of boiling salted water, blanch the chard until it just turns dark green, about 2 minutes. Remove it from the pot with a slotted spoon and place in a colander under cold running water to stop the cooking process and lock in the color. Using your hands, squeeze out as much excess moisture as possible.

2. Preheat the oven to 350°F.

3. Combine all the ingredients, except the eggs, in a food processor fitted with metal blade or in a blender.

4. Process in the eggs until they are just combined; be careful not to overprocess.

5. Place the croustades on baking sheet and fill each one with the filling. Bake until just set, about 20 minutes.

Fast: Can prepare filling up to 1 day in advance and refrigerate, or freeze for up to 3 months. Can assemble up to 2 hours in advance and hold at room temperature or flash freeze for up to 3 months (bake frozen, allowing for an extra 10 minutes cooking time).

Flashy: Serve on a platter with a cluster of grapes in the center along with sprigs of fresh herbs.

Fabulous: With spinach or escarole instead of chard and feta instead of chèvre. In mushrooms or tartlet shells instead of croustades. As an entree for brunch or lunch, simply enlarge the cups using egg roll wrappers fitted into cup cake pans.

CROUSTADES

1 cup olive oil
2 to 4 cloves garlic
1/2 teaspoon salt or to taste
1 loaf very fresh sourdough
  bread, sliced

Yield: about 35 croustades

This is a quick, low-cholesterol alternative to rich pastry tartlets.

1. Preheat the oven to 350°F.
2. Puree the olive oil with the garlic and salt in a food processor fitted with a metal blade or in a blender.
3. Using a cookie cutter or wineglass, cut the bread into 2- to 2 1/2-inch rounds.
4. Roll out the bread rounds with a rolling pin.
5. Brush mini-muffin tins with the garlic oil. Press the bread rounds into the cups and brush them with garlic oil.
6. Bake until completely crisp, about 15 minutes. They are now ready to be filled.

Fast: Can store in airtight jar(s) or plastic bag(s) for up to 1 week, or freeze for up to 6 months. No thawing necessary.

Fabulous: With minced fresh or dried herbs added to the garlic oil.

CREAM OF FENNEL SOUP WITH CRAB

3 tablespoons unsalted butter

1 onion, chopped

1 1/2 pounds fennel bulb, chopped (reserve the feathery leaves for garnish)

2 cloves garlic, minced

3 tablespoons all-purpose flour

6 cups chicken broth, homemade or canned

1/2 cup Madeira

1/2 teaspoon dried tarragon

1 teaspoon dried thyme

1 bay leaf

Salt and freshly ground white pepper to taste

Freshly grated nutmeg to taste

1 cup heavy cream

1 pound crabmeat or more

2 large egg yolks (see page 23)

2 tablespoons unsalted butter, softened

Minced fresh parsley or chives and fennel leaves for garnish

Yield: *about 2 quarts*

A very refreshing and tasty soup.

1. Melt the 3 tablespoons butter in a large saucepan and sauté the onion, fennel, and garlic over low to medium-low heat until tender. Puree in a food processor fitted with a metal blade.
2. Return the mixture to the saucepan and stir in the flour. Cook for 1 minute over medium heat, while stirring.
3. Stir in the broth and Madeira. Bring to a boil, while stirring.
4. Add the seasonings, half of the cream, and the crab, and simmer until the flavors develop, at least 15 minutes.
5. Combine the egg yolks with the remaining cream in a small bowl. Add 2 tablespoons of the soup and mix well.
6. Lower the temperature to medium-low and stir the yolk mixture into the soup. Do not boil or the yolks will curdle. Continue to cook until the soup thickens, about 5 minutes. Taste and adjust the seasonings. Stir in the softened butter and serve.

Fast: Can prepare through step 4 up to 3 days in advance and refrigerate, or freeze for up to 6 months. Thaw in the refrigerator for 2 days or at room temperature for about 8 hours. Finish before serving.

Flashy: Garnish with a sprinkling of minced parsley or chives and the fennel leaves.

Fabulous: Prepared with any vegetable or with shrimp, scallops, clams, or mussels instead of crab.

SALAD OF WATERCRESS AND PAPAYA

*2 to 3 bunches watercress,
  leaves only*
*1 to 2 ripe papayas, peeled,
  seeded, and sliced*
*Tarragon-Sherry or Herbed
  Walnut Vinaigrette (see
  pages 204, 135)*

Besides being delicious and having beautiful colors, this salad also acts as a palate cleanser.

1. Place the watercress leaves and papaya slices in a bowl and toss with the desired amount of dressing. Taste and adjust the seasonings.

Fast: Can prep ingredients up to 8 hours in advance and refrigerate.

Flashy: Arrange attractively on salad plates with papaya slices fanned.

Fabulous: With roasted red bell peppers, toasted sesame seeds, and/or grilled slices of Japanese eggplant.

Further: Add leftovers to a rice or tossed green salad.

GINGERED PORK WITH PEARS

2 tablespoons unsalted butter
  or more

2 tablespoons olive oil or
  more

8 pork cutlets, from the loin,
  1/2- to 1-inch thick,
  rinsed in cold water and
  patted dry

Salt and freshly ground white
  pepper to taste

3 to 4 red bosc pears, cored,
  stemmed, and sliced

2 tablespoons minced fresh
  ginger or to taste

2 large shallots, minced

2 heads roasted (see page
  27) garlic

3/4 cup dry red wine

1/4 cup Madeira

2 tablespoons minced fresh
  lemon thyme or regular
  thyme (optional)

3 cups beef broth, homemade
  or canned

2 tablespoons unsalted
  butter, cold and cut into
  pieces

Freshly grated nutmeg to
  taste

Sprigs fresh parsley or
  watercress for garnish

An exotic dish with Asian influences.

1. Melt the butter with the oil in a large heavy skillet over medium-high heat.

2. Place several cutlets, without crowding, in the skillet. Gently sauté over medium-high heat until lightly browned on each side. Season with salt and pepper while cooking. Remove and place in an oven-proof pan. Repeat, until all the cutlets are browned, adding more butter and oil as needed. Cutlets should be very rare at this point.

3. Add the pear slices to the saucepan and gently sauté over medium-low heat for about 5 minutes.

4. Top each cutlet with pear slices.

5. Add the ginger and shallots to the remaining pears in the skillet and sauté until tender. Add more butter if needed.

6. Squeeze the garlic out of the skins into the skillet.

7. Add the wine, Madeira, and thyme, bring the mixture to a boil, and reduce by half.

8. Stir in the beef broth, return to a boil over medium-high to high heat, and reduce by one third. Season to taste.

9. Transfer the sauce to a blender or food processor and puree.

10. Pour the sauce through a fine strainer over the cutlets.

11. Cover the cutlets with aluminum foil and bake until hot and the pork is cooked to your liking, about 10 minutes.

12. Remove the pork to warm platter and tent with foil to keep warm.

13. Strain the sauce through a fine mesh strainer into a saucepan and bring to a boil over high heat. Stir in the cold butter until melted.

14. Serve the pork on the platter or individual plates, surrounded with the sauce.

Fast: Can prepare through step 10 up to 1 day in advance and refrigerate. Bring to room temperature before finishing.

Flashy: Garnish with sprigs of parsley or watercress.

Fabulous: With apples instead of pears, and rosemary instead of thyme.

POTATO AND ONION TIMBALE

2 red onions, thinly sliced
4 cloves garlic, minced
1/2 cup olive oil
5 russet potatoes, thinly
  sliced, blanched about 7
  to 10 minutes and patted
  dry
Salt and freshly ground white
  pepper to taste
1/4 cup fresh rosemary
  leaves or to taste
Minced fresh chives or
  parsley, and sprigs of fresh
  rosemary for garnish

A wonderful and very unique way to serve potatoes.

1. Preheat the oven to 400°F.
2. Sauté the onions and garlic in 2 to 4 tablespoons of the olive oil
    until golden.
3. Toss the potatoes in a large bowl with the remaining olive oil and
    coat them. Season with the salt, pepper, and rosemary. Toss again.
4. Oil eight small soufflé dishes or one large soufflé and add half of
    potatoes. Top with the onions and garlic and cover with the remain-
    ing potatoes.
5. Place the soufflé(s) on a baking sheet and bake until crisp, about 40
    minutes or 1 hour and 15 minutes for a large soufflé.
6. Unmold onto a platter or individual dinner plates.

Fast: Can prepare up to 1 day in advance through step 4 and refrigerate.
Bring to room temperature before baking.

Flashy: Garnish with a sprinkling of parsley or chives and a sprig of
rosemary.

Fabulous: With sweet potatoes or any other kind of potato and prepared
in a cast-iron skillet instead of a soufflé dish. With potatoes blanched
in 2 quarts of chicken broth seasoned with 6 cloves of garlic and 2
tablespoons of rosemary, instead of using plain water. With leftover
mashed or grated blanched potatoes instead of sliced, blanched
potatoes.

SAUTÉED ZUCCHINI AND RED PEPPERS

1/4 cup olive oil

1 or 2 red bell peppers,
  cored, halved, seeded, and
  cut into long, thin strips

2 to 4 cloves garlic, minced

2 pounds zucchini, cut into
  matchstick pieces

Salt and freshly ground white
  pepper to taste

Fresh lemon juice to taste

Looks as good as it tastes.

1. Heat the olive oil in a large skillet or wok over medium heat, then add the pepper strips and garlic and sauté until almost tender, about 3 to 5 minutes.

2. Add the zucchini and season with salt, pepper, and lemon. Sauté until just tender, about 5 to 7 minutes.

Fast: Can prepare vegetables up to 1 day in advance and refrigerate. Bring to room temperature and cook before serving.

Fabulous: Seasoned with almost any herb, nut, and/or capers.

Further: Serve leftovers chilled mixed into or on a bed of greens, pasta, rice, bulgur, or beans as a salad.

APPLE WALNUT EGG ROLLS WITH CARAMEL SAUCE

FILLING

2 1/2 to 3 pounds tart green
    apples, peeled, cored, and
    thinly sliced
1/4 cup bourbon
1/4 to 1/2 cup sugar, plus
    extra for sprinkling
1/2 cup apricot jam
Grated zest of 1 to 2 lemons
Freshly grated nutmeg to
    taste
Apple pie spice to taste
1 cup walnuts, toasted (see
    page 29) and chopped
1/2 cup unsalted butter,
    melted

1 package egg roll wrappers
Caramel Sauce (recipe
    follows)

Yield: about 24 rolls

So good and so simple!

1. Place all the filling ingredients, except the melted butter and walnuts, in a large, heavy skillet. Cook over medium-high heat, covered, until the apples reach the desired degree of tenderness, about 10 to 15 minutes.
2. Stir in the walnuts, then taste and adjust the seasonings.
3. Place several tablespoons of the filling, at an angle, in the center of a wrapper. Roll up like an envelope, lightly moistening the edges with water to seal. Place it seam-side down on a buttered baking sheet. Repeat until all the filling is used.
4. Brush the tops with the melted butter and sprinkle with sugar.
5. Place under a hot broiler until golden, about 3 to 5 minutes.

Fast: Can prepare filling up to 5 days in advance and refrigerate, or freeze for up to 6 months. Can prepare through step 4 up to 1 day in advance and refrigerate or flash freeze for up to 3 months. Do not thaw before baking in a preheated 350°F oven for 15 to 20 minutes. If not brown enough at that point, place under a broiler for a few minutes.

Flashy: Ladle sauce onto individual dessert plates. Top with one or two egg rolls. Add a dollop of Brandied Whipped Cream (see page 247), if you dare. Enjoy!

Fabulous: Use filling hot or cold to top French vanilla ice cream, on crêpes, or on pound cake. Works with almost any fruit in season . . . What about Peach and Pecan Egg Rolls?!

CARAMEL SAUCE

1 1/2 teaspoons unsalted
   butter
1 1/2 cups sugar
6 tablespoons rum
1/2 cup strong coffee
1/4 teaspoon salt
3/4 cup heavy cream
2 teaspoons vanilla extract

Yield: about 2 cups

I burned the midnight oil to come up with a killer caramel sauce—not too sweet with a deep complex flavor.

1. Place the butter, sugar, and rum in a heavy saucepan over medium heat until the sugar dissolves and turns a nutty golden color. Do not stir; instead, hold the pan by the handle and shake it. Cool until it reaches the soft ball stage (234° to 240°F), about 3 minutes more.
2. Stir in the coffee and salt. Return the saucepan to the burner and cook over medium heat until the caramel dissolves, stirring as necessary.
3. Remove from the heat, allow the sauce to cool slightly, then add the cream, otherwise it will curdle. Stir in the vanilla.

Fast: Can prepare up to 5 days in advance and refrigerate, or freeze for up to 6 months. Thaw in the refrigerator for 2 days or at room temperature for about 8 hours.

Flashy: Serve hot or cold.

Fabulous: With bourbon or brandy instead of rum.

Cornish Game Hen Dinner

The menu for this party is eclectic. You will find traditional fall foods, seasoned with interesting culinary twists. This is another big menu with an important feel. Keeping this in mind, our party gets off to an impressive start with Caviar Pastries. They can best be described as simply sublime. As a matter of fact, they are not only the quintessential hors d'oeuvre, but something that will allow even the noncook to shine. On to the salad, which is designed to be presented on a large platter. Have your guests serve themselves. It has a very grand look with a marvelous range of flavors, textures, and colors. The persimmons add a wonderful dimension, and the brussels sprouts are so delicious that even those who dislike this vegetable will enjoy them. The flavored butter that is served with the rolls is another special touch. Adapt this recipe to complement any of the menus in this book. It is attractive served in butter crocks, and makes a lovely hostess gift.

Our entree is classically festive. The real twist here comes from the fresh ginger and pasilla chiles in the sauce. Both of these ingredients add surprise, excitement, and fabulous flavor. Remember this sauce when serving duck, turkey, or chicken.

Cornish game hens are delicious, but it is imperative that they not be overcooked. I prepare them in a Weber-type barbecue, with fabulous results. The wild rice dish that accompanies the entree is something you can get great mileage from during the holidays. It is a complex composition, full of interesting, earthy flavors and textures.

The complexity of the flavors in the entree and wild rice demand a simple, straightforward treatment for the vegetable. The beets could not be any more direct. They are so often ignored.

As for the dessert, it is light, but decadent. When my father, a dedicated dessert-lover, tasted it, he pronounced it my best ever. I think this will replace your standard pumpkin pie.

I'm sure it's already obvious to you, this is a wonderful Thanksgiving or Christmas menu. If you are set on turkey, simply substitute it for the Cornish game hens.

The look of the table for this party is just as eclectic and interesting as the menu. I use a very light gray cloth with black napkins, and arrange all sizes of artichokes, along with persimmons, in a huge glass bowl. I first dry the artichokes by either leaving them at room temperature for several days, or putting them in a very low oven until dry, then spray-paint some of them in high-gloss black and others in silver. Finally I intersperse baby's breath in the top of the bowl. White candles in round silver holders run down the center of the table, along with more silver baby artichokes. Gorgeous!

MENU

Caviar Pastries

Harvest Salad Platter with Gingered Mustard Vinaigrette

Sourdough rolls with Green Onion Lemon Butter

Cornish Game Hens with Cranberry Ginger Sauce

Barley and Wild Rice Pilaf

Beet Shreds

Pumpkin Cream Tart

FASTER & FLASHIER MENU

Caviar with Cream Cheese and Crackers

Tossed Salad with Kiwi and Persimmons

Cornish Game Hens with Cranberry Sauce (use canned and season it with ginger, sherry, and hot sauce)

Beets (canned)

Wild Rice (use packaged and seasoned)

Pumpkin Pie (purchased)

WINES

Champagne or Chardonnay

Pinot Noir

Late harvest Gewürztraminer or Champagne

Fast & Fabulous Timetable

Up to 6 Months in Advance and Frozen
Chutney Glaze • Cranberry Ginger Sauce

Up to 3 Months in Advance and Frozen
Pastry for Caviar Pastries • Green Onion Lemon Butter • Pumpkin Cream Tart • Caramel Whipped Cream

5 Days in Advance and Refrigerated
Gingered Mustard Vinaigrette • Chutney Glaze • Green Onion Lemon Butter

4 Days in Advance and Refrigerated
Cranberry Ginger Sauce • Buttered Bread Crumbs (freeze)

2 Days in Advance and Refrigerated
Prepare pastry for Caviar Pastries • Marinate Cornish game hens • Barley and Wild Rice • Beet Shreds through step 4 • Thaw frozen prepared-ahead foods

1 Day in Advance and Refrigerated
Harvest Salad • Pumpkin Cream Tart • Caramel Whipped Cream • Set Table

Party Day!
Assemble Caviar Pastries • Warm bread • Bake game hens and tart • Heat pilaf and beets

---

CAVIAR PASTRIES

One 1-pound package frozen
  puff pastry, thawed
1 pound Saint André cheese,
  at room temperature
Caviar, as much as your
  budget allows
Minced fresh chives or green
  onions
Finely grated lemon zest
Pansies, watercress, and/or
  dill sprigs for garnish

Yield: 60 to 80

This is the perfect little something to serve before an elegant dinner. It's a definite "champagne hors d'oeuvre," but would also make any martini proud!

1. Preheat the oven to 400°F.
2. Roll the pastry out to 1/8 inch thickness.
3. Cut into 2-inch circles, using a cookie cutter or wineglass.
4. Place the circles on a cookie sheet and pierce with a fork. Bake 15 to 20 minutes, until crisp and golden. They will be puffed and can be split in half as if they were beaten biscuits to create two pastries from one.
5. Top each cooled pastry circle with a generous amount of Saint André, a dollop of caviar, a sprinkling of chives or green onions, and lemon zest.

Fast: Can prepare through step 4 up to 2 days in advance and store in plastic bag(s) or freeze for up to 3 months. Thaw at room temperature for several hours.

Flashy: On a silver tray with a pansy and watercress or dill in the center.

Fabulous: With Brie instead of Saint André, or smoked mussels or smoked salmon instead of caviar.

HARVEST SALAD PLATTER

1 to 2 bunches watercress,
stems removed
16 to 24 baby brussels
sprouts, blanched until just
tender, about 4 to 7
minutes
4 red bell peppers, seeded,
roasted, and peeled (see
page 28)
2 fennel bulbs, thinly sliced
lengthwise and blanched 3
to 5 minutes, until just
tender.
4 kiwi, thinly sliced
2 to 4 Japanese persimmons,
thinly sliced
Gingered Mustard
Vinaigrette (recipe follows)

Serves 6 to 8

A beautiful and refreshing tribute to the season's produce. This salad
plays two roles in this menu, serving both as a salad course and a green
vegetable. A perfect choice for a Thanksgiving or Christmas dinner.

1. Make a bed of watercress leaves on a large platter, then attractively
    arrange all the remaining ingredients except the vinaigrette.
2. Drizzle the vinaigrette over the top. Serve with extra dressing on the
    side.

Fast: Can prepare up to 1 day in advance and refrigerate. Bring to room
temperature and add dressing before serving, though the fennel, peppers, and persimmons are delicious refrigerated in the dressing.

Fabulous: With sliced raw jicama, turnips, papaya, mango, hearts of
palm, and/or blanched or canned baby corn.

GINGERED MUSTARD VINAIGRETTE

2 to 5 tablespoons minced
fresh ginger
2 cloves garlic
2 to 4 tablespoons Dijon
mustard
3/4 cup grapeseed oil
1/4 cup walnut or sesame
oil
1/4 cup apple cider vinegar
Salt and freshly ground white
pepper to taste

Yield: about 1 1/4 cups

This is a light dressing with intriguing flavors. It makes a delightful cold
sauce for fish, chicken, and vegtables.

1. Combine all the ingredients in a food processor fitted with a metal
    blade or in a blender, or whisk together by hand. Taste and adjust
    the seasonings.

Fast: Can prepare up to 5 days in advance and refrigerate.

Fabulous: As a marinade for almost anything. For something special, try
it with shrimp.

GREEN ONION LEMON BUTTER

1/2 pound (2 sticks)
    unsalted butter
2 green onions, chopped, or
    to taste
Grated zest of 2 lemons
Fresh lemon juice to taste
Salt and freshly ground white
    pepper to taste

Yield: 1 cup

1. Combine all the ingredients in a food processor fitted with a metal
    blade or in a bowl with an electric mixer. Taste and adjust the
    seasonings.

Fast: Can prepare up to 5 days in advance and refrigerate, or freeze for
    up to 3 months. Thaw in the refrigerator for 2 days or at room tempera-
    ture for 4 to 8 hours.

Flashy: Serve in little butter crocks or in small white soufflé dishes.

Fabulous: With chopped shallots or garlic instead of green onions. With
    any fresh or dried herb. With about 1 tablespoon capers and 1 tea-
    spoon anchovy paste. Used instead of a sauce, on almost anything from
    fish to vegtables.

Further: Use leftovers as a seasoning in place of plain butter.

CHUTNEY GLAZE

1/4 pound (1 stick) unsalted
    butter
2 cloves garlic
1/4 cup Mango Chutney,
    homemade (see page 101)
    or purchased
1 tablespoon Dijon mustard

Yield: about 1 cup

A delicious basting sauce to use on anything from pork to turkey.

1. Melt the butter in a small saucepan over low heat.
2. Add the garlic and cook until it releases its flavor, about 5 minutes.
3. Stir in the remaining ingredients. Continue to cook over low while
    stirring until the chutney melts.

Fast: Can prepare up to 5 days in advance and refrigerate, or freeze for
    up to 6 months. Thaw in the refrigerator for 2 days or at room tempera-
    ture for 4 to 8 hours.

Fabulous: With honey or Chinese plum sauce instead of the chutney.

Further: Use leftovers on chicken, duck, or turkey.

CORNISH GAME HENS WITH CRANBERRY GINGER SAUCE

MARINADE:

4 cloves garlic

One 1-inch piece fresh ginger

4 to 8 green onions

Fresh or dried thyme to taste

2 to 4 dried pasilla chiles, rehydrated, stemmed, and seeded

Salt to taste

4 to 8 Cornish game hens, depending on the appetites of your guests, giblets removed, rinsed, patted dry, and brought to room temperature

2 onions, thinly sliced

Salt and freshly ground white pepper to taste

1/2 cup sherry

1/4 cup brandy

Chutney Glaze (recipe follows)

Cranberry Ginger Sauce (recipe follows)

Kale leaves for garnish

A great holiday entree.

1. Preheat oven to 400°F.
2. Puree all the marinade ingredients in a food processor fitted with a metal blade, or in a blender.
3. Place the hens in a large glass or ceramic pan. Pour the marinade over them and cover with plastic wrap. Let marinate in the refrigerator for 24 to 48 hours.
4. Remove the hens from the marinade and pat dry with paper towels.
5. Place the sliced onions in the bottom of a roasting pan and set the hens on top, breast-side down, and season the inside cavities with salt and pepper. Roast for 15 minutes, then turn the hens over, breast-side up, and reduce the temperature to 300°F.
6. Add the sherry and brandy to the pan and brush the hens with the chutney glaze. Continue to cook until just done, about 30 to 45 minutes. Baste frequently with the glaze.
7. Remove to a warm platter and tent with aluminum foil while removing the fat from the pan juices. Strain and add to the cranberry ginger sauce. Let simmer over medium heat. Cut the hens in half using kitchen shears. Set back on the platter. Serve with the sauce on the side.

Fast: Can marinate hens up to 2 days in advance and refrigerate.

Flashy: Serve on platter garnished with kale leaves.

CRANBERRY GINGER SAUCE

2 tablespoons unsalted butter

One 12-ounce package
  whole cranberries

1 bunch green onions,
  minced

1/4 to 1/2 cup chopped
  fresh ginger

6 tablespoons pasilla chiles,
  rehydrated, stemmed,
  seeded, and chopped

3 cups chicken broth,
  homemade or canned

1 cup sherry

1/2 to 1 cup Mango
  Chutney, homemade (see
  page 101) or purchased

1 teaspoon fennel seeds

Minced fresh or dried
  rosemary to taste

Salt and freshly ground white
  pepper to taste

1 tablespoon cornstarch

2 tablespoons water

Yield: about 5 cups

If you can't face another uninspired, overly sweet, gloppy cranberry sauce—this is for you!

1. Melt the butter in a saucepan and sauté the cranberries, green onions, and ginger over medium heat until tender.
2. Add the strained cooking juices from the game hens or about 1 cup chicken broth.
3. Add the remaining ingredients, except the cornstarch and water. Bring to a boil over high heat, then reduce heat to medium-low and simmer until the flavors are fully developed, about 10 to 15 minutes.
4. For added thickness, dissolve the cornstarch in the water, return the sauce to a boil, stir it in and cook until thickened.

Fast: Can prepare up to 4 days in advance and refrigerate, or freeze for up to 6 months. Thaw in the refrigerator for 2 days or at room temperature for 4 to 8 hours.

Flashy: Strain the sauce for a more elegant presentation and serve it separately.

Fabulous: Enriched with 1 cup heavy cream during step 3.

Further: Use leftover sauce with chicken, pork, or beef, or add to soups.

BARLEY AND WILD RICE PILAF

1 cup uncooked wild rice

4 tablespoons (1/2 stick)
  unsalted butter

1/4 to 1/2 pound pancetta,
  thinly sliced, then minced

2 leeks, washed and thinly
  sliced

1 bunch red chard (including
  stems), chopped

4 stalks celery, coarsely
  chopped

1 cup uncooked barley

1 bay leaf

1/2 cup sherry

7 cups chicken broth,
  homemade or canned

Salt and freshly ground white
  pepper to taste

Minced fresh or dried thyme
  to taste

1. Rinse the wild rice in a strainer under cold running water several times and remove any foreign particles.
2. Melt the butter in a large saucepan and sauté the pancetta, leeks, chard, and celery over low heat for 15 to 20 minutes.
3. Stir in the wild rice and barley and cook for several minutes, stirring.
4. Add the bay leaf, sherry, broth, salt, pepper, and thyme, and bring to a boil. Cover, reduce heat to low, and cook for about 40 minutes, or until the rice and barley are tender. If there is any unabsorbed liquid, simply boil until gone.

Fast: Can prepare up to 2 days in advance and refrigerate. Reheat in a microwave at high power for about 20 minutes or in a preheated 350°F oven, covered, for 15 to 30 minutes, adding more liquid if necessary.

Fabulous: With chopped walnuts, water chestnuts, and/or mushrooms.

Further: Add 4 cups broth, 1/4 to 1/2 cup sherry, and 1/4 cup heavy cream for a fabulous soup.

BEET SHREDS

2 pounds beets, stems and
leaves removed (but
reserved—see "Further")
2 tablespoons unsalted
butter, melted
Salt and freshly ground white
pepper to taste
Fresh lemon juice to taste
Freshly grated nutmeg to
taste
2 to 4 tablespoons sesame
seeds, toasted (see page
29), for garnish

A delicious but very neglected vegtable!

1. Place the beets in a large bowl, cover with plastic wrap, and microwave until tender, about 5 to 10 minutes.
2. Put the beets under cold running water, then peel.
3. Shred in a food processor fitted with a shredding disc, or by hand
   with a grater.
4. Transfer to a bowl, toss with the melted butter, and season with salt,
   pepper, lemon, and nutmeg.
5. Place in ovenproof baking dish, cover with foil, and warm in a
   preheated 350°F oven for about 15 minutes, or in the microwave.

Fast: Can prepare through step 4 up to 2 days in advance and refrigerate.

Flashy: Sprinkle sesame seeds over the beets for an attractive presentation.

Fabulous: With olive oil instead of butter or with 2 to 4 tablespoons sour
cream mixed in.

Further: Stir leftovers into salads or make a soup using the beet greens
and stems, minced, along with chicken broth.

PUMPKIN CREAM TART

WALNUT CRUST

1/2 pound (2 sticks)
   unsalted butter, cold, and
   cut into small pieces
2/3 cup packed light or dark
   brown sugar
2 teaspoons vanilla extract
1 1/2 cups all-purpose flour
2 cups walnut halves or
   pieces, toasted (see page
   29)
Freshly grated nutmeg to
   taste
1/4 cup ice water

PUMPKIN FILLING

1 1/2 to 2 cups canned
   pumpkin
8 ounces cream cheese
1/2 cup sour cream
2 tablespoons cornstarch
3/4 cup packed dark brown
   sugar or to taste
1 large egg
4 large egg yolks
2 teaspoons vanilla extract
2 tablespoons bourbon
Grated zest of 2 oranges
Pumpkin pie spice to taste
Marigolds, mint, and/or
   Caramel Whipped Cream
   (recipe follows) for garnish

Yield: 8 or more servings

This just might become your favorite version of pumpkin pie. It is light in texture, with an elegant flavor, and is easy to prepare.

1. Preheat the oven to 375°F.
2. To make the crust, cream the butter, sugar, and vanilla together in a food processor fitted with a metal blade or in a bowl using an electric mixer. Add the flour, walnuts, and nutmeg, and, using quick on-and-off motions, process until the mixture resembles a coarse meal or cut in using a pastry blender. Slowly add the water through the feed tube while processing, until the mixture forms a ball, or mix in with a wooden spoon.
3. With your hands, spread this mixture in a 9-inch springform pan, coating the sides and bottom evenly. Bake the empty shell for 15 minutes.
4. To make the filling, combine the pumpkin, cream cheese, sour cream, and cornstarch in a food processor fitted with a metal blade, then process in the remaining ingredients, except the garnish. Taste and adjust the flavors.
5. Pour the filling into the crust after it has cooled and bake until set, about 45 minutes.

Fast: Can fully prepare up to 1 day in advance and refrigerate, or freeze for up to 3 months. Can also fully assemble up to 1 day in advance and refrigerate, or freeze for up to 3 months. Add 30 minutes extra to baking time if frozen.

Flashy: Garnish with a dollop of caramel whipped cream and mint, and/or a marigold.

Fabulous: Prepared with chopped or sliced apples, peaches, or pears instead of pumpkin.

CARAMEL WHIPPED CREAM

1/3 cup packed light or dark
   brown sugar
2 tablespoons brandy
2 teaspoons vanilla extract
1 cup heavy cream
Freshly grated nutmeg to
   taste

Yield: about 1 1/2 cups

1. Melt the sugar with the brandy in a small, heavy saucepan over medium heat until the sugar dissolves completely. Increase the heat to medium-high and bring the syrup to a boil. Cover the pan with a tight-fitting lid for 1 to 2 minutes, until the bubbles are thick, swirling the pan frequently. When the syrup turns a light caramel color, remove the pan from the burner and swirl the pan until the syrup reaches a rich caramel color.
2. Hold the saucepan over a pan of cold water. Let cool several minutes, then stir in the vanilla and cream.
3. Return to the burner over medium heat and stir until the caramel dissolves. Season with the nutmeg.
4. Transfer to small bowl and chill in the freezer for 30 to 60 minutes.
5. Place in a food processor fitted with a metal blade and process until it holds soft peaks or whip to soft peaks with a mixer.

Fast: Can prepare up to 1 day in advance and refrigerate, or freeze for up to 3 months. Thaw in the refrigerator for 2 days, or at room temperature for about 1 hour.

Flashy: On mousses, cakes, pies.

Fabulous: With bourbon, rum, Grand Marnier, or Kahlua instead of brandy.

CASUAL FALL MENUS

• • • • • • • • • • • • • • • • • • • •

Pasilla Chile and Pork Ragout Dinner

Light a fire or turn on a football game and prepare to kick back and have fun. The recommended attire is anything uninhibited, such as warm-ups. Dress your table with the same spirit. For the centerpiece, create a seasonal still life using nuts in the shell and a variety of dried or fresh chiles, then intersperse bulky candle pillars. As an alternative to nuts, use a variety of dried beans or simply use a basket of onions and votive candles. The impact of these tablescapes comes from the use of items not normally considered decorative. This provides an element of surprise and creates an energy, otherwise known as atmosphere.

The menu itself offers the cook maximum convenience while at the same time providing a maximum amount of robust flavor. The evening begins with an hors d'oeuvre that could not be any more uninhibited in spirit. The fall salad is a swan song to summer, utilizing items that are in season now but are on their way out. The entree, Pasilla Chile and Pork Ragout, is a marvelous earthy stew. Southwestern Bulgur is designed to complement and contrast the ragout but more importantly, to catch the sauce. The menu concludes with an interesting version of Crème Brûlée, which soothes the palate and comforts the soul.

MENU

Chile con Queso with Chips

Escarole Salad with Avocado, Tangerines, and Olives

French Bread and Butter

Pasilla Chile and Pork Ragout

Southwestern Bulgur

Crème Brûlée with Walnuts and Sautéed Apples and Pears

FASTER & FLASHIER MENU

Warmed Salsa (purchased) with Grated Cheddar Cheese and Chips

Tossed Salad with Roasted Red Peppers

Pasilla Chile and Pork Ragout

Bulgur

Dessert (purchased)

WINES

Petite Sirah, assorted beers, and/or Champagne

Champagne

Fast & Fabulous Timetable

Up to 6 Months in Advance and Frozen
Tortilla Chips • Sautéed Apples and Pears

Up to 3 Months in Advance and Frozen
Chile con Queso • Pasilla Chile and Pork Ragout through step 6

5 Days in Advance and Refrigerated
Tortilla Chips • Cilantro Vinaigrette

4 Days in Advance and Refrigerated
Sautéed Apples and Pears

3 Days in Advance and Refrigerated
Chile con Queso

2 Days in Advance and Refrigerated
Pasilla Chile and Pork Ragout through step 6 • Southwestern Bulgur through step 2 • Thaw frozen prepared-ahead foods

1 Day in Advance and Refrigerated
Set Table • Crème Brûlée

Party Day!
Heat Chile con Queso • Escarole Salad with Avocado, Tangerines, and Olives • Warm bread • Finish Pasilla Chile and Pork Ragout • Finish Southwestern Bulgur

CHILE CON QUESO

2 cups green chiles, canned,
    deveined, seeded, and
    chopped
1 pound sharp cheddar
    cheese, grated
1 pound jack cheese, grated
1 cup heavy cream
4 cloves garlic, minced
1 to 2 bunches cilantro,
    minced
1 teaspoon ground cumin or
    to taste
1 teaspoon dried oregano or
    to taste
4 cups peeled, seeded, and
    chopped tomatoes, canned
    or fresh
One 8-ounce can pitted
    black olives, drained and
    halved or chopped
6 minced green onions or to
    taste
Tortilla chips, homemade
    (recipe follows) or
    purchased

Trust me, this is too good to describe, you simply must taste it!

1. Combine all the ingredients, except the chips, in a large saucepan
    over medium low heat or in the top of a double boiler over simmer-
    ing water. Stir until the cheeses melt. (This can also be done in a
    preheated 350° oven for about 35 minutes.)

Fast: Can prepare up to 3 days in advance and refrigerate, or freeze for
up to 3 months. Thaw in the refrigerator for 2 days or at room temperature for 8 hours. Reheat in the top of a double boiler for 15 to 20
minutes, or covered in a preheated 325°F oven for 20 to 30 minutes.

Flashy: Serve in a fondue pot, chafing dish, cast-iron skillet, or pottery
casserole along with the chips.

Fabulous: With minced clams and/or hot sauce added.

TORTILLA CHIPS

Flour or corn tortillas
Peanut, grapeseed, or olive
  oil
Salt to taste

These are delicious and a lot healthier than purchased chips.

1. Preheat the oven to 350°F.
2. Brush the oil of your choice on the tortillas and sprinkle with salt.
3. Stack them and cut into eighths.
4. Place on cookie sheets and bake until crisp, about 10 to 15 minutes.

Fast: Can prepare up to 5 days in advance and store in airtight jar(s) or plastic bag(s), or freeze for up to 6 months. Thaw at room temperature for several hours.

ESCAROLE SALAD WITH AVOCADO, TANGERINES, AND OLIVES

1 1/2 pounds tender escarole
  leaves, washed and dried
2 ripe avocados, pitted,
  peeled, sliced, and
  squirted with fresh lemon
  juice to prevent
  discoloration
2 to 3 tangerines, peeled,
  seeded, and thinly sliced
1/2 pound jicama or to
  taste, peeled and cut into
  thin matchstick pieces
4 to 8 green onions, minced
1 cup pitted black olives
Cilantro Vinaigrette (see
  page 122)

A beautiful composition of flavors, colors, and textures.

1. Place all the salad ingredients in a large bowl and toss with the desired amount of vinaigrette.

Fast: Can assemble up to 6 hours in advance and refrigerate. Dress and toss right before serving. To prepare in advance, put the avocados in the bottom of bowl and liberally squirt with lemon juice. Top with tangerines, then jicama, green onions, and olives. Add escarole leaves and cover with a few paper towels.

Flashy: Toss avocados, tangerines, and jicama separately with dressing. Toss escarole, olives, and onions together with dressing and arrange on salad plates. Surround with individually tossed ingredients in decorative manner.

Fabulous: With matchstick strips of celery root and thinly sliced mushrooms. Substitute romaine lettuce, spinach, or endive for the escarole.

PASILLA CHILE AND PORK RAGOUT

6 tablespoons peanut oil or
more as needed

3 onions, thinly sliced

1 pound mushrooms, halved
or quartered

4 to 8 cloves garlic, minced

3 tablespoons all-purpose
flour

3 pounds boneless pork leg,
cut into 1/2-inch cubes

Salt and freshly ground white
pepper to taste

3 ounces dried pasilla chile
pods, rehydrated,
stemmed, and seeded

2 cups tomatillos, husked

3/4 cup sherry

1 cup heavy cream

5 cups chicken or pork
broth, homemade or
canned

2 yams, peeled and thinly
sliced

1 cup sour cream

2 bunches fresh cilantro,
chopped

Dried oregano to taste

Black olives, thinly sliced
radishes and green onions,
and/or thin strips of
tortilla fried until crisp

Yield: 6 to 8 servings

This Southwestern stew abounds with earthy, lusty flavors.

1. Heat 3 to 4 tablespoons of the oil in a large skillet and slowly sauté
   the onions, mushrooms, and garlic over medium-low heat, until the
   mushrooms are tender and the onions are golden, about 20 to 30
   minutes. Stir from time to time. This can also be done in a preheated 350°F oven, baking for 30 to 40 minutes.
2. Place the flour in a plastic bag, along with the pork, and shake to
   coat well.
3. Heat the remaining oil in a large soup pot or casserole over medium-
   high heat and add some of the pork. Season with salt and pepper
   and brown. Do this in batches.
4. Cut the chiles into pieces and place in a food processor fitted with
   a metal blade or a blender. Add the tomatillos and puree.
5. Stir the puree into the pork along with the sherry, cream, broth,
   oregano and browned onion mixture. Add the yams.
6. Bring to a boil over high heat, then reduce the heat to low and
   simmer for about 30 minutes or until hot and the flavors are pleasing, or bake in a preheated 325°F oven in an ovenproof pot for
   about 40 minutes.
7. Combine the sour cream and cilantro.
8. Skim off any fat that rises to top of the stew, then stir in the sour
   cream mixture. Taste and season with salt, pepper, and oregano.

Fast: Can prepare through step 6 up to 2 days in advance and refrigerate
or freeze for up to 3 months. Thaw in the refrigerator for 2 days or at
room temperature for 8 hours.

Flashy: Garnish with black olives, thinly sliced radishes and green onions, and/or crisp fried thin strips of tortillas. Serve on a bed of
Southwestern Bulgur in large soup bowls.

Fabulous: Add diced eggplant or sliced okra, or beef, chicken, or monkfish instead of pork.

Further: Add more chicken, beef or pork broth (enough to create the
desired consistency), a touch of wine and possibly cream to create a
soup, Pasilla Chile and Yam Soup. Add cooked white, red, or black

beans or hominy and serve over a crisped tortilla with grated cheese and guacamole to create a tostada. Wrap in a flour tortilla and top with cheese and sour cream for a burrito.

SOUTHWESTERN BULGUR

3 cups chicken broth,
   homemade or canned
Finely grated zest of 2
   oranges
1/2 cup sherry
2 cups uncooked bulgur
1/4 cup minced green onions
1/4 cup minced fresh
   cilantro
2 to 4 tablespoons minced
   fresh mint
Salt and freshly ground white
   pepper to taste

Bulgur's earthiness complements the entree while the mint and other flavors provide a fresh contrast.

1. Bring the chicken broth, zest, and sherry to a boil over high heat.
2. Stir in the bulgur and reduce the heat to medium. Cover and cook until the water is absorbed and the bulgur is tender, about 15 minutes.
3. Stir in the green onions, cilantro, and mint. Season with salt and pepper.

Fast: Can prepare through step 2 up to 2 days in advance and refrigerate. Bring to room temperature and add a bit more chicken broth to keep it moist. Reheat in a microwave for about 15 minutes or a preheated 325°–350°F oven, covered, for 20 to 30 minutes.

Fabulous: With orzo or couscous instead of bulgur. With ground cumin or chili powder to taste.

Further: Cold as a salad with a vinaigrette, olives, sliced fennel bulb, and avocado.

CRÈME BRÛLÉE WITH WALNUTS AND
SAUTÉED APPLES AND PEARS

3/4 cup sugar

1/4 cup brandy

4 cups milk

2 cups heavy cream

6 large egg yolks, beaten

6 large whole eggs, beaten

2 teaspoons vanilla extract

Grated zest of 2 oranges

Freshly grated nutmeg to
 taste

Sautéed Apples and Pears
 (recipe follows)

1 cup walnuts, toasted (see
 page 29) and chopped

Brown sugar for topping

Whipped cream or Caramel
 Whipped Cream (see page
 164—optional)

This rich baked custard is a favorite of mine. The crunchy caramelized topping provides a wonderful contrast in flavor and texture, while the sautéed fruit lends a seasonal touch and balance to the custard's richness. Don't let all these steps fool you; it takes just a few minutes to prepare.

1. Preheat the oven to 325°F.
2. Heat the sugar with the brandy in a large, heavy saucepan over low heat until melted. Do not stir, rather, hold the pan by the handle and swirl it throughout this process.
3. Increase the heat to medium-high and cover the pan with a tight-fitting lid for 1 to 2 minutes, just until the mixture boils and has thick bubbles. Uncover, continue to swirl frequently, and cook until the syrup turns a light golden color. Remove the pan from the heat and continue to swirl until it turns a rich caramel color.
4. In the meantime, heat the milk and cream together in another saucepan.
5. Carefully stir the warm milk and cream mixture into the caramel.
6. Return to the burner and cook over low heat until the caramel dissolves, stirring from time to time.
7. Whisk some of the caramel mixture into the beaten yolks, then add the yolk mixture to the caramel mixture, whisking continuously. Add the vanilla, zest, and nutmeg.
8. Place the apple-pear mixture in a buttered dish or cups. Strain the custard through a fine mesh strainer on top.
9. Place the dish in a baking pan filled with hot water that reaches halfway up the sides of the custard.
10. Bake for 1 hour or more, until a tester inserted into the middle comes out clean. Do not overbake.
11. Cool to room temperature, then chill in the refrigerator.
12. Top the custard with a layer of walnuts, then a thin layer of brown sugar.
13. Set the custard in a baking pan filled with ice and place under a hot broiler until the sugar melts. Serve warm or cold.

Fast: Can prepare up to 1 day in advance and refrigerate.

Flashy: For added decadence, top with a dollop of plain whipped cream or caramel whipped cream. Instead of combining the sautéed apples and pears with the custard as directed in step 8, serve them warm over the crème brûlée.

Fabulous: Create a coconut crème brûlée by adding 1/2 cup of unsweetened shredded coconut to the custard at step 7.

SAUTÉED APPLES AND PEARS

2 Granny Smith or pippin apples, quartered, cored, and thinly sliced

4 firm pears, quartered, cored, and thinly sliced

Fresh lemon juice to taste

2 tablespoons unsalted butter

1 tablespoon orange marmalade

1 tablespoon apricot preserves

1/4 to 1/2 cup brandy

Freshly grated nutmeg to taste

Ground cinnamon to taste

1. Squirt the apple and pear slices with the lemon juice to prevent discoloring.
2. Heat the butter in a large, heavy skillet over medium heat.
3. Add the marmalade, preserves, and fruit, and sauté until the fruit is tender, stirring frequently, for about 15 minutes.
4. Add the brandy and season with the nutmeg and cinnamon. Cook until the brandy evaporates.

Fast: Can prepare up to 4 days in advance and refrigerate, or freeze for up to 6 months. Thaw in the refrigerator for 2 days or at room temperature for 8 hours. Can reheat in a microwave for about 10 minutes or preheated 300°F oven for 15 to 30 minutes.

Flashy: On ice cream or in crêpes. Serve warm or cold.

Fabulous: Flavored with apple pie or pumpkin pie spice seasonings instead of the cinnamon. To adapt this recipe in the summer use peaches, nectarines, apricots, and/or plums instead of apples and pears. With minced or sliced onions and garlic sautéed with the apples and seasoned with thyme and rosemary, as a condiment to serve with chicken, pork, or game.

Pasta Dinner

Here is a menu that conjures up images of small, friendly Italian or provencial French bistros where the food is bold and the atmosphere comfortable. From the cook's point of view, it is a joy, as this menu exhalts simplicity. It makes a great choice for a take-a-long dinner when going to the mountains or to a friend's home.

To create the right ambiance, concentrate on rustic charm. For this party, I use a rough-textured pink cotton bedspread from an import store. My napkins are black and handwoven, contributing a great deal of texture. This strong color contrast adds to the drama of the table.

I use a centerpiece made of three brass candlesticks with white candles on a round Mexican tin plate, flanked by three mini pumpkins. Two oversize Spanish goblets hold arrangements of wine-colored mums and sprigs of fresh mint, though you could substitute any fragrant herb for the mint. This combination of herbs with the mums is not simply a visual necessity, but also an aesthetic one, as the herbs mask the smell of the mums.

Mussels Vinaigrette and Pickled Cauliflower with three dipping sauces start the evening off. Both of these hors d'oeurves are very unusual and tasty, while not too filling. The dipping sauces for the cauliflower provide fun choices for your guests. This is one of my favorite ways to break the ice and get the party off to a flying start. The salad that follows is a celebration of seasonal flavors with a wonderful composition of textures, ranging from soft to crisp.

The entree is inspired by a French provincial vegetable stew, ratatouille. I have interjected Italian elements with the pancetta and roasted peppers. You can see that this is an eclectic Mediterranean dish with fabulous flavor. It is served on pasta with garlic bread.

A Cold Apricot Soufflé concludes this menu on a delightfully light, but satisfying note. This is a dessert that works well for any occasion.

MENU

Mussels Vinaigrette

Pickled Cauliflower with Three Sauces

Celery Root and Mushroom Salad with Pears

Pasta with Ratatouille Niçoise

Garlic/Herb Bread

Cold Apricot Soufflé

FASTER & FLASHIER MENU

Smoked Mussels (purchased)

Tossed Salad with Pears and Walnuts

Pasta with Ratatouille Niçoise

Dessert (purchased)

WINES

Champagne or Sauvignon Blanc

Merlot

Orange Muscat

Fast & Fabulous Timetable

Up to 6 Months in Advance and Frozen
Pasta Ratatouille through step 2 • Lemon Sherry Biscotti (see page 142) (optional)

Up to 3 Months in Advance and Frozen
Cold Apricot Soufflé • Brandied Chocolate Sauce (see page 141) (optional)

Up to 1 Month in Advance and Refrigerated
Pickled Cauliflower

5 Days in Advance and Refrigerated
Lemon Mustard Vinaigrette • Dijon Sauce • Curry Sauce • Garlic/herb butter for bread

3 Days in Advance and Refrigerated
Tapanade Sauce • Pasta Ratatouille through step 2

2 Days in Advance and Refrigerated
Soak mussels • Cold Apricot Soufflé • Thaw frozen prepared-ahead foods

1 Day in Advance and Refrigerated
Mussels Vinaigrette • Celery Root and Mushroom Salad with Pears • Assemble bread • Set Table

Party Day!
Arrange salad • Cook pasta • Heat ratatouille and warm bread

MUSSELS VINAIGRETTE

4 pounds mussels, scrubbed
  and debearded
1/4 cup cornmeal
1/2 cup dry vermouth
2 1/2 cups water
1/4 cup white wine vinegar
4 cloves garlic, minced
Fresh or dried tarragon to
  taste
1 bay leaf
Salt and freshly ground white
  pepper to taste
1 cup extra virgin olive oil
Fresh lemon juice to taste
Capers, rinsed and drained,
  to taste
1/2 cup minced green onions
1/2 cup minced celery
Sprigs fresh parsley for
  garnish
Lemon wedges for garnish

I am a registered mussel maniac. Caution, this could happen to you! If mussels are not your favorite, use shrimp instead.

1. Place the mussels in a large bowl with enough water to cover them. Add the cornmeal and cover with plastic wrap. Refrigerate for 6 hours or overnight.

2. In a large soup pot or saucepan combine the vermouth, water, vinegar, garlic, tarragon, and bay leaf. Bring to a boil, over high heat then simmer until the flavors develop, about 10 minutes.

3. Meanwhile, drain the mussels and rinse several times in cold water to remove the cornmeal.

4. Add the mussels to the simmering liquid and cook until the mussels open, about 5 minutes, over medium-high heat. Discard any that remain unopened.

5. Remove the mussels using a strainer or slotted spoon and place them in a bowl.

6. Raise the heat to high and reduce the cooking liquid to about 1/2 cup. Taste and season with salt and pepper.

7. Transfer the reduced liquid to a large bowl and slowly whisk in the oil, then the lemon juice. Taste and adjust the seasonings.

8. When the mussels are cool enough to handle, remove them from their shells and put them in a glass or ceramic dish. Cover with the vinaigrette and mix in the capers, green onions, and celery.

9. Cover with plastic wrap and refrigerate for up to 24 hours.

Fast: Can prepare up to 1 day in advance and refrigerate. Drain off the marinade before serving.

Flashy: Garnish with sprigs of parsley and wedges of lemon. Serve with toothpicks and thinly sliced baguette.

Fabulous: Substitute scallops, clams, or shrimp for the mussels, all cooked in the same manner as the mussels.

Further: Toss leftovers into salads or pastas.

PICKLED CAULIFLOWER WITH THREE SAUCES

1/4 cup salt

1 1/2 cups white vinegar or
to taste

2 heads cauliflower (about 2
pounds), cut into small
florets

Bay leaves

Black peppercorns

1 small dried red pepper or
to taste

3 cloves garlic or to taste

Several slices fresh ginger

Curry Sauce, Dijon Sauce,
and Tapanade Sauce
(recipes follow)

Yield: about 7 pints

An old family recipe I got from my Aunt Fanny, this always gets rave reviews.

1. To make the brine, mix the salt and vinegar with enough water so that it is not too salty or too sour.
2. Place the cauliflower in plastic containers or glass jars and cover with the brine. Add a bay leaf, several black peppercorns, a piece of the red pepper, a clove of garlic, and a slice of ginger to each container.
3. Cover the containers and leave at room temperature in a sunny spot for at least 3 days or until the flavors develop.

Fast: Can prepare up to 1 month in advance and refrigerate.

Flashy: With dijon sauce, curry sauce, and tapanade sauce.

Fabulous: With fresh or dried herbs, such as rosemary or fennel, added to the brine. Substitute sliced turnips, celery, carrots, or jicama, or green beans, for the cauliflower.

CURRY SAUCE

1/2 cup mayonnaise

1/2 cup sour cream

1 1/2 teaspoons curry
powder or to taste

1/4 teaspoon ground ginger
or to taste

1/4 cup minced fresh
cilantro or to taste

2 tablespoons pickled ginger

Fresh lemon juice to taste

Yield: about 2 1/4 cups

A bit of Indian mystique.

1. Combine all the ingredients. Taste and adjust the seasonings.

Fast: Can prepare up to 5 days in advance and refrigerate.

Flashy: Dunk Pita Chips (see page 277); raw cauliflower, jicama, celery, or mushrooms; cooked asparagus or artichoke leaves; or cooked seafood.

Fabulous: With lamb as an entree sauce, or on a seafood salad. With about 1 tablespoon of minced pickled or fresh ginger instead of the ground ginger.

DIJON SAUCE

1 cup mayonnaise
1 tablespoon Dijon mustard
    or to taste
1/4 cup sour cream
Fresh lemon juice to taste

Yield: about 1 cup

So simple, but so good!

1. Combine all the ingredients. Taste and adjust the seasonings.

Fast: Can prepare up to 5 days in advance and refrigerate.

Flashy: With cooked sausages, chicken, or any vegetable.

Fabulous: Replace the mustard with soy sauce to create a soy dunk. Add minced green onions or fresh parsley to either sauce.

TAPANADE SAUCE

One 7 1/2-ounce can tuna
1/2 cup pitted black olives
1/2 cup calamata olives,
    pitted
2 to 4 tablespoons minced
    green onions
1 teaspoon green peppercorns
3 tablespoons capers, rinsed
    and drained
3 cloves garlic
6 tablespoons fresh lime juice
    or to taste
1/2 teaspoon coarsely ground
    black pepper
1/2 cup chopped fresh
    parsley
2 to 3 tablespoons brandy
1 cup olive oil
One 6-ounce jar marinated
    artichoke hearts, drained
    and minced

Yield: about 3 cups

The classic Italian tuna-olive sauce.

1. Combine all the ingredients, except the olive oil and artichoke hearts, in a food processor fitted with a metal blade or in a blender.
2. Slowly add the olive oil through the feed tube while the machine is running.
3. Add the artichoke hearts and process with several quick on-and-off motions to chop them, using care not to destroy their texture.

Fast: Can prepare up to 3 days in advance and refrigerate.

Flashy: With any raw or cooked vegetable, or with crackers.

Fabulous: With cooked fresh or frozen shrimp or crab, or canned or fresh-cooked salmon instead of tuna, or any kind of olives.

CELERY ROOT AND MUSHROOM SALAD WITH PEARS

1 celery root (1 to 1 1/2
  pounds), peeled and
  grated
1 pound mushrooms, thinly
  sliced
1 bunch fresh parsley,
  minced
6 to 10 green onions, minced
4 ounces bleu cheese,
  crumbled (optional)
1/2 cup pine nuts, toasted
  (see page 29)
Lemon Mustard Vinaigrette
  (recipe follows)
2 pears, sliced and squirted
  with fresh lemon juice to
  prevent discoloration

1. Toss the celery root with the mushrooms in a large bowl, then toss in the remaining ingredients, except for the pears, along with the desired amount of dressing. Arrange the pears over the salad

Fast: Can prepare up to 1 day in advance and refrigerate.

Flashy: Place the celery root mixture on individual plates, surrounded by several slices of pears.

Fabulous: With thinly sliced celery or fennel, instead of grated celery root. With walnuts or pumpkin or sesame seeds instead of the pine nuts. With watercress leaves. Add wild rice and it becomes a luncheon entrée.

Further: Add leftovers to tossed salads.

LEMON MUSTARD VINAIGRETTE

Fresh lemon juice to taste
  (about 2/3 cup)
2 cups extra virgin olive oil
1 tablespoon Dijon mustard
  or to taste
1 tablespoon minced shallots
Salt and freshly ground white
  pepper to taste

Yield: approximately 2 cups

1. Combine all the ingredients in a food processor fitted with a metal blade or whisk together by hand. Taste and adjust the seasonings.

Fast: Can prepare up to 5 days in advance and refrigerate.

Fabulous: With several cloves minced garlic, or minced fresh dill, oregano, or basil added.

PASTA WITH RATATOUILLE NIÇOISE

*3 cups minced or thinly
   sliced onions*

*1/2 to 1 pound pancetta,
   sliced 1/4 inch thick and
   cut into 1/4-inch wide
   strips*

1/2 cup olive oil

*3 to 6 heads roasted (see
   page 27) garlic, removed
   from the peel*

*3 to 4 zucchini, cut into thin
   strips*

*1 large eggplant or several
   small eggplants, cut into
   thin strips*

*3 red bell peppers, roasted
   (see page 28), seeded, and
   chopped or sliced*

*3 yellow bell peppers,
   roasted, seeded, and
   chopped or sliced*

*1/2 cup Italian or calamata
   olives or to taste*

*Two 6-ounce jars marinated
   artichoke hearts, drained
   and minced*

1 bunch fresh parsley, minced

1 bunch fresh basil, minced

1 bay leaf

*Salt and freshly ground white
   pepper to taste*

*2 pounds pasta, fusilli, shells,
   rigatoni, or penne*

*1/2 cup grated mizithra
   cheese, or to taste*

1 cup grated mozzarella cheese

Yield: 8 to 12 servings

Ratatouille is a classic French provencial vegetable stew. I've taken liberties with it and created a dish that has a marvelous, lusty, Mediterranean quality. The omission of tomatoes and the addition of pancetta, roasted garlic, imported olives, and artichoke hearts makes this ratatouille memorable. Also, using roasted peppers instead of sautéed peppers further distinguishes this dish.

1. Sauté the onions and pancetta in 3 tablespoons of the olive oil over low heat until the pancetta is fully cooked and the onions are soft and golden, about 15 minutes.
2. Add the garlic, zucchini, eggplant, peppers, olives, artichoke hearts, parsley, basil, and bay leaf, along with more olive oil, if needed. Simmer, covered, until the vegetables reach the desired degree of tenderness, about 15 to 30 minutes.
3. Taste and season with salt and pepper.
4. Cook the pasta in large pot of salted boiling water until al dente. Drain and toss with the cheeses in a large bowl. Serve the ratatouille on top.

Fast: Can prepare through step 2 up to 3 days in advance and refrigerate or freeze for up to 6 months. Thaw in the refrigerator for 2 days or at room temperature for 8 hours.

Fabulous: With leeks instead of onions and ham instead of pancetta. With rosemary, oregano, and/or thyme (fresh or dried) to taste instead of basil. Served on beans or rice instead of pasta.

Further: Add chicken broth to create a soup. Mixed with ricotta and grated Parmesan and mozzarella cheese and used to fill crêpes or egg roll skins. Serve with a marinara sauce.

GARLIC-HERB BREAD

1/4 pound (1 stick) unsalted
    butter
1/2 cup olive oil
2 to 6 cloves garlic, minced
1/4 cup minced fresh parsley
1/4 cup minced green onions
1/4 cup minced fresh basil
    or to taste
Salt to taste
1 loaf sourdough bread,
    thinly sliced

1. In a large skillet, melt the butter with the olive oil.
2. Add the garlic, parsley, onions, basil, and salt, and sauté over low
    heat for a few minutes until the flavors develop to your liking.
3. Brush the herb mixture on the slices of bread that have been placed
    on an ungreased cookie sheet. Bake in a preheated 350°F oven, until
    hot, about 10 to 20 minutes.

Fast: Can prepare the butter mixture up to 5 days in advance and
    refrigerate. Completely assemble up to 1 day in advance, wrap in foil,
    and refrigerate. Heat before serving.

Fabulous: There is no end to the herbs and cheeses you can use in this
    recipe, so experiment and have fun. Some good choices are: feta,
    Parmesan, Gruyère, bleu cheese, rosemary, dill, and/or oregano. Use
    only olive oil for a delicious "zero" cholesterol alternative.

COLD APRICOT SOUFFLÉ

1 cup dried apricots
2 to 4 tablespoons apricot
  preserves
One 15-ounce container
  ricotta cheese
1/2 cup sour cream
2 teaspoons vanilla extract
3 tablespoons orange-flavored
  liqueur
Grated zest of 1 lemon
Fresh lemon juice to taste
Freshly grated nutmeg to
  taste
1 envelope unflavored gelatin
3 tablespoons brandy

1. Put the apricots in a small bowl and sprinkle with a small amount of water. Cover and microwave on high for 1 to 2 minutes to soften them, or place in a small saucepan over medium heat for about 10 minutes.
2. Combine the apricots with the preserves, cheese, sour cream, vanilla, liqueur, and zest in a food processor fitted with a metal blade or in a blender.
3. Season to taste with the lemon juice and nutmeg. Add sugar or more preserves if necessary.
4. Place the gelatin in a small bowl and mix in the brandy. Place it over a larger bowl of hot water and stir until dissolved or microwave on low power for about 1 minute.
5. Add the dissolved gelatin to the food processor or blender and combine thoroughly.
6. Oil a Pyrex loaf pan and line with plastic wrap. Transfer the mixture to the pan and refrigerate until set, about 3 hours.

Fast: Can prepare up to 2 days in advance and refrigerate or freeze for up to 3 months. Thaw in the refrigerator for 2 days.

Flashy: Serve a slice on individual dessert plates with some Brandied Chocolate Sauce (see page 141) and a piece of Lemon Sherry Biscotti (see page 142).

Fabulous: With about 1 cup of persimmon pulp or canned pumpkin instead of the apricots, with orange marmalade instead of apricot, if you choose. Can use almost any fruit, from cooked apples to fresh raspberries!

Black Bean Soup Dinner

Whether you are planning an après-ski dinner, or just want an effortless menu for any size group, you will love this menu. Serve it for friends on Halloween, after the ghosts and goblins are tucked away in their beds with bags of candy clutched to their bosoms. This menu is the epitome of a hearty, fun, and casual dinner party—designed to be served buffet style. Roasted Garlic Decadence From Hell awakens everyone's tastebuds, as well as spirits. Make sure you inform your guests of its tendency to be an aphrodisiac. The entree consists of a wonderful salad, delicious garlic bread, and the black bean soup, which is served with a huge array of condiments. Everyone gets into the act by helping themselves and embellishing their own soup. Remember ice-cream sundae parties? The social dynamics are similar. Brownies à la Mode, a dream come true for brownie lovers, conclude the menu. The dessert is elevated to adult status by drizzling liqueur over the ice cream. As for the brownies, after years of experimenting I have come up with something wonderful!

Dress your table in earthy tones and use fresh kitchen towels, or oversize napkins, in a complementary color. Scatter dried beans, nuts, and assorted dried and fresh peppers down the center of the table. Intersperse baby pumpkins and bulky pillar candles on upside-down terra-cotta pots. Several pottery pitchers filled with colorful bouquets of oregano cuttings, mixed with bougainvillea, help create a rustic look.

MENU

Roasted Garlic Decadence From Hell

Tossed Salad

Garlic-Oregano Bread

Southwestern-Style Black Bean Soup

Orange Walnut Brownies à la Mode

FASTER & FLASHIER MENU

Brie and Crackers

Tossed Salad

Sourdough Bread

Southwestern-Style Black Bean Soup (use canned cooked beans and a few accompaniments)

Brownies à la Mode (buy brownies)

WINES

Champagne

Zinfandel

Fast & Fabulous Timetable

Up to 6 Months in Advance and Frozen
Roasted Garlic Decadence From Hell • Southwestern-Style Black Bean
Soup

Up to 3 Months in Advance and Frozen
Orange Walnut Brownies

5 Days in Advance and Refrigerated
Roasted Garlic Decadence From Hell • Mustard-Thyme Vinaigrette

4 Days in Advance and Refrigerated
Orange Walnut Brownies

3 Days in Advance and Refrigerated
Southwestern-Style Black Bean Soup

2 Days in Advance and Refrigerated
Thaw frozen prepared-ahead foods

1 Day in Advance and Refrigerated
Accompaniments for soup • Garlic-Oregano Bread • Set Table

Party Day!
Toss salad • Warm bread and soup • Assemble dessert

ROASTED GARLIC DECADENCE FROM HELL

3 heads garlic or to taste
Olive oil
4 ounces feta cheese
1/4 pound (1 stick) unsalted
 butter
3 to 6 dried pasilla chiles,
 rehydrated, stemmed, and
 seeded
Fresh or dried rosemary to
 taste
2 to 4 tablespoons sherry
Salt and freshly ground white
 pepper to taste
Toasted (see page 29) pine
 nuts and roasted (see page
 27) garlic cloves for
 garnish

Yield: about 1 1/2 cups

A garlic lover's fantasy!

1. Cut one third off the top of the heads of garlic to expose the cloves. With your fingers, peel away several outer layers around the garlic.
2. Place the garlic in a baking dish and coat with some of the olive oil to prevent burning. Bake, covered, in a preheated 250° to 300°F oven until the garlic is soft and buttery, about 1 hour.
3. Squeeze the garlic out of their wrappers and into a food processor fitted with a metal blade. Squeeze out only as much garlic as is desired.
4. Process in the remaining ingredients, except the garnish, until a smooth paste is formed.
5. Pack into an oiled, plastic-lined bowl or mold. Chill until firm, about 2 hours

Fast: Can prepare up to 5 days in advance and refrigerate, or freeze for up to 6 months. Thaw in the refrigerator for 2 days or at room temperature for 4 to 8 hours. Store roasted garlic in the refrigerator in a jar filled with olive oil for up to 2 weeks, or freeze for up to 6 months.

Flashy: Unmold, top with pine nuts, and/or peeled roasted garlic cloves. Serve with thinly sliced baguette, crackers, or melbas.

Further: Toss leftovers into hot pasta or rice. Use to season cooked vegetables.

TOSSED SALAD WITH MUSTARD-THYME VINAIGRETTE

2 heads butter and/or
    romaine lettuce
1/2 to 1 cup pumpkin seeds,
    toasted (see page 29), or
    to taste
2 cups packed watercress
    leaves
Mustard-Thyme Vinaigrette
    (recipe follows)

1. Combine the first three ingredients in a large salad bowl.
2. Add the desired amount of dressing and toss.

Fast: Can prepare through step 1 up to 8 hours in advance and refrigerate. Toss before serving.

Fabulous: With any toasted nut or seed instead of the pumpkin seeds. With sliced pears or pieces of tangerine added.

MUSTARD-THYME VINAIGRETTE

2 cups peanut oil
2/3 cup red wine vinegar
2 teaspoons Dijon mustard
    or to taste
1 teaspoon dried thyme or to
    taste
2 shallots
2 cloves garlic
Salt and freshly ground white
    pepper to taste

Yield: about 3 cups

1. Combine all the ingredients together in a food processor fitted with a metal blade or in a blender.
2. Taste and adjust the seasonings.

Fast: Can prepare up to 5 days in advance and refrigerate.

Fabulous: With any kind of oil, vinegar, and/or herb.

SOUTHWESTERN-STYLE BLACK BEAN SOUP

1/4 cup olive oil

1/2 to 1 pound smoked
   ham, minced

3 to 4 onions, chopped

1/4 cup minced fresh parsley

1 to 2 carrots, chopped

6 to 12 cloves garlic, minced

1 pound dried black beans,
   soaked overnight in a
   large pot filled with cold
   water

8 to 12 cups chicken broth,
   homemade or canned

2 to 4 corn tortillas, torn up

2 cups dry red wine

2 bay leaves

1/2 teaspoon hot pepper
   sauce or to taste

1 teaspoon dried oregano or
   to taste

1 tablespoon ground cumin
   or to taste

Salt and freshly ground white
   pepper to taste

1 to 2 bunches fresh cilantro,
   minced

I realize that it sounds a bit bizarre to tear up tortillas and throw them into the soup. Just trust me. It adds a touch of magic!

1. Heat the oil in a large soup pot and sauté the ham, onions, parsley, carrots, and garlic over medium-low to medium heat, until the onions and carrots are tender.
2. Drain the beans and rinse well. Add the beans, chicken broth, tortillas, wine, and all the seasonings, except the cilantro, to the soup pot. Bring to a boil over high heat, then reduce the heat to medium-high. Add more liquid if needed or if a thinner consistency is wanted. Reduce the heat to medium and let simmer gently until the beans are tender and the flavors have developed to your liking. This will take at least 30 minutes, but the soup can be simmered for several hours—the flavors will just get better.
3. Puree the soup or leave as is and stir in the cilantro.
4. Taste and adjust the seasonings.
5. Serve soup surrounded by bowls of accompaniments, so your guests can select their own additions.

Fast: Can prepare soup up to 3 days in advance and refrigerate, or freeze for up to 6 months and thaw in the refrigerator for 2 days or at room temperature for 8 hours. Can prepare accompaniments up to 1 day in advance and refrigerate.

Fabulous: For added complexity, lace the soup with approximately 1/2 cup merlot just before serving.

ACCOMPANIMENTS (amounts are left to your discretion)

Chopped green onions

Minced fresh cilantro

Grated sharp cheddar cheese

Quartered lemon or lime

Deveined, seeded, and chopped
   canned green chiles

Cooked rice

Chopped black olives

Chopped fresh tomato

Grated jack cheese

Sour cream

Avocado slices, sprinkled with lemon
   juice to avoid discoloration

GARLIC-OREGANO BREAD

2 cups extra virgin olive oil

2 to 6 cloves garlic, minced

1/4 cup minced fresh parsley

1/4 cup minced green onions

Salt to taste

Dried oregano to taste

1 loaf sourdough bread,
    thinly sliced

1. Heat the olive oil in a skillet.
2. Add the garlic, parsley, onions, and seasonings, and sauté over low heat for a few minutes, until the flavors develop to your liking.
3. Brush the mixture onto the slices of bread and heat in the oven.

Fast: Can prepare butter mixture up to 1 day in advance and refrigerate. Can completely assemble up to 1 day in advance, wrap in foil, and refrigerate.

Fabulous: With any herb. Experiment and have fun! All sorts of cheeses can be used to top Garlic-Oregano Bread. Some good choices are: feta, Parmesan, Gruyère, or bleu.

ORANGE WALNUT BROWNIES À LA MODE

4 ounces semisweet
    chocolate, broken into
    pieces
2 ounces bittersweet
    chocolate, broken into
    pieces
2 ounces unsweetened
    chocolate, broken into
    pieces
1/4 pound (1 stick) unsalted
    butter
8 ounces cream cheese, at
    room temperature
2 extra large eggs
1 to 1 1/2 cups sugar
1 1/2 teaspoons vanilla
    extract
2 tablespoons orange-flavored
    liqueur, plus more for
    topping
2/3 cup all-purpose flour
Grated zest of 1 to 2
    oranges
1 cup walnut pieces, toasted
    (see page 29)
French vanilla ice cream

Yield: about 16 brownies

At long last, I have come up with brownies-from-heaven!

1. Preheat the oven to 350°F and butter a 9- by 12-inch baking pan.
2. Place the chocolates in a bowl with the butter and melt in the microwave on low power for about 4 minutes, or place in the top of a double boiler over simmering water until melted.
3. Combine the cream cheese, eggs, and sugar in a food processor fitted with a metal blade, or cream together in a large bowl.
4. Process or stir in the melted chocolate mixture.
5. Process or stir in the vanilla, liqueur, and flour until just blended.
6. Add zest and walnuts, using several quick on-and-off motions so as not to destroy texture, if using a processor.
7. Transfer to the baking dish. Bake for about 35 minutes, until a tester inserted into the middle comes out clean. Cool for about 30 minutes before removing from pan.
8. Place a brownie or two in large wine goblets, top with ice cream, and a drizzle of liqueur.

Fast: Can prepare brownies up to 4 days in advance and refrigerate or freeze for up to 3 months. Thaw in the refrigerator for 2 days or at room temperature for 4 to 8 hours.

Fabulous: With any kind of liqueur. For an added touch of decadence, also top with Brandied Chocolate Sauce (see page 141) and raspberries!

Eggplant and Lamb Shank Antipasto Dinner

Have you ever tasted an hors d'oeuvre that you felt should be transformed into an entree? I created this menu as the result of such an inspiration. While teaching a class at a wonderful bookstore in Carmel, California, we tasted my antipasto, which is normally served at room temperature or chilled, while it was still warm. Because of its wonderful rustic quality, I thought it would make a perfect match for lamb shanks. Since antipastos usually consist of numerous items, I wanted to reflect that by serving the entree with a selection of starches. You and your guests can choose any or all of rice, pasta, lentils, polenta, couscous, or beans to complement the eggplant and lamb. They can also pick Parmesan or feta cheese to sprinkle over their antipasto.

Offering choices is always a good way to break the ice at parties, as it forces your guests to get involved and stimulates conversation. This menu is a snap to prepare and as a bonus, is also very healthy. I know this sounds too good to be true, but just wait until you taste it.

Our party opens with a fun, flavorful, and fabulous Sun-Dried Tomato and Roasted Garlic Salsa, served with Garlic Crouton Rounds. Again, the preparation couldn't be simpler, nor the flavors better. From this taste fantasy, we move on to an escarole salad with Sesame-Mustard Vinaigrette. Escarole is one of my very favorite salad greens. It has substantial texture and a slightly astringent flavor. If you can't find it, or don't care for it, use your favorite green. Spinach is a good substitute. The dressing is so delicious that you will find all sorts of uses for it. Try it on a shredded cabbage, cold pasta, rice, or potato salad. As a marinade, it is wonderful with chicken, pork, or lamb. As a cold sauce, drizzle it over cooked vegetables, grilled or broiled chicken, pork, lamb, or seafood.

When it is time for the entree, serve it buffet style. I like to have the antipasto in a Spanish earthenware cazuela, or a wok—something equally simple and functional. As for the side dishes, they too should reflect this quality. Use pottery, blue-and-white spatterware enamel, or cast-iron skillets. Use a textured cotton bedspread in a festive color, such as lavender. Tie colorful striped napkins with rope. For centerpieces on the buffet and dinner table use a combination of natural baskets and terra-cotta pots, perhaps spraying some of them black. Arrange breadsticks, baguettes, rolls, and round loaves with purple statice, bay leaves, and bamboo cuttings in them and, for an added touch, spray-paint some of the bread gloss black, or pick an accent color of your choice. Sounds bizzare, but it's visually dramatic! Instead of candlesticks, for another interesting twist, use black candles in Spanish grape pattern glass bottles, or any other unusual empty glass bottles.

MENU

Sun-Dried Tomato and Roasted Garlic Salsa

Garlic Crouton Rounds

Watercress, Escarole, and Persimmon Salad with Sesame-Mustard Vinaigrette

Pita Toast

Warm Eggplant and Lamb Shank Antipasto with Side Dishes

Pumpkin-Date Bread with Vanilla-Nutmeg Sauce

FASTER & FLASHIER MENU

Tossed Salad with Sesame-Mustard Vinaigrette

Warm Eggplant and Ham Antipasto with Pasta

Dessert (purchased)

WINES

Chardonnay or Champagne

Merlot

Late harvest Chardonnay or Champagne

Fast & Fabulous Timetable

Up to 6 Months in Advance and Frozen
   Sun-Dried Tomato and Roasted Garlic Salsa • Garlic Crouton Rounds
   • Warm Eggplant and Lamb Shank Antipasto • Pita Toast • Vanilla-
   Nutmeg Sauce

Up to 3 Months in Advance and Frozen
   Pumpkin-Date Bread

5 Days in Advance and Refrigerated
   Sun-Dried Tomato and Roasted Garlic Salsa • Garlic Crouton Rounds
   • Sesame-Mustard Vinaigrette • Pumpkin-Date Bread

3 Days in Advance and Refrigerated
   Warm Eggplant and Lamb Shank Antipasto • Vanilla-Nutmeg Sauce

2 Days in Advance and Refrigerated
   Side dishes for antipasto • Thaw frozen prepared-ahead foods

1 Day in Advance and Refrigerated
   Pita Toast • Set Table • Prep salad

Party Day!
   Assemble salad and refrigerate • Warm lamb, side dishes, and bread

SUN-DRIED TOMATO AND ROASTED GARLIC SALSA

2 cups sun-dried tomatoes,
   minced
1 to 2 heads roasted (see
   page 27) garlic removed
   from the peel
3 to 6 dried pasilla chiles,
   rehydrated, stemmed,
   seeded, and minced
4 green onions, minced
1/4 cup minced fresh parsley
1/4 cup pine nuts, toasted
   (see page 29)
One 6-ounce jar marinated
   artichokes, drained and
   minced
1 cup extra virgin olive oil
3/4 cup crumbled feta
   cheese
Fresh or dried rosemary to
   taste
Coarsely ground black
   pepper to taste
Hot pepper sauce to taste
Fresh lemon or lime juice to
   taste

Yield: about 4 cups

A guaranteed hit!

1.   Combine all the ingredients in a large bowl. Taste and adjust the
     seasonings. Serve chilled or at room temperature.

Fast: Can prepare up to 5 days in advance and refrigerate, or freeze up
   to 6 months and thaw in the refrigerator for 2 days or at room temperature for 8 hours.

Flashy: Serve with Garlic Crouton Rounds (recipe follows).

Fabulous: With chopped calamata olives. Over beans or pasta. As a pizza
   topping. On grilled fish, lamb, or beef. As an omelette filling.

GARLIC CROUTON ROUNDS

1 loaf sourdough bread,
  sliced
4 cloves garlic or to taste
1 cup olive oil
Salt to taste

Yield: about 40 rounds

Serve alone or with any topping.

1. Preheat the oven to 350°F.
2. Cut the bread into 2-inch rounds or squares. (I use a wineglass.)
3. Puree the olive oil and garlic in a food processor fitted with a metal blade or in a blender. Season with salt.
4. Brush the bread with the garlic oil and place on an ungreased cookie sheet. Bake until crisp, about 15 minutes.

Fast: Can prepare up to 5 days in advance and store in airtight jar(s) or plastic bag(s), or freeze for up to 6 months. Thaw at room temperature for at least 1 hour.

Fabulous: Made in a smaller size and used as croutons in salads. Prepared with thin slices of baguette to create melbas (also referred to as crostini) With any fresh or dried herb and/or freshly grated Parmesan cheese.

WATERCRESS, ESCAROLE, AND PERSIMMON SALAD WITH SESAME-MUSTARD VINAIGRETTE

2 bunches watercress,
  stemmed
1 head escarole, torn into
  bite-size pieces
1/2 cup sesame seeds,
  toasted (see page 29)
2 to 4 Japanese persimmons,
  peeled and sliced
Sesame-Mustard Vinaigrette
  (recipe follows)

1. Combine the watercress, escarole, and sesame seeds in a large salad bowl.
2. Toss with the persimmons and the desired amount of dressing.

Fast: Can assemble (without persimmons) up to 6 hours in advance, cover with a damp paper towel and refrigerate. Add the persimmons and toss before serving.

Fabulous: With crumbled feta cheese. With pickled ginger.

SESAME-MUSTARD VINAIGRETTE

1/4 cup sesame oil
1 cup olive oil
1/3 cup rice vinegar or more
2 teaspoons Dijon mustard
1 to 2 cloves garlic
1 teaspoon salt
Freshly ground white pepper
   to taste

Yield: about 1 1/2 cups

1. Combine all the ingredients in a food processor fitted with a metal blade or in a blender. Taste and adjust the seasonings.

Fast: Can prepare up to 5 days in advance and refrigerate.

Fabulous: As a marinade and/or sauce for: asparagus, chicken, pork, or fish.

PITA TOAST

Pita bread, each split into 2
   rounds
1 cup olive oil
3 to 6 cloves garlic
2 to 4 tablespoons minced
   fresh parsley
Salt to taste
Fresh or dried herbs to taste

These crisp rounds make a lovely change from bread or rolls.

1. Preheat the oven to 350°F. Place the split pitas on an ungreased cookie sheet.
2. Place the olive oil in a food processor fitted with a metal blade, or in a blender. Puree in the garlic, parsley, salt, and herbs. Taste and adjust the seasonings.
3. Brush the garlic oil on the pitas and bake until crisp, 10 to 15 minutes. Enjoy hot or at room temperature.

Fast: Can assemble up to 1 day in advance and refrigerate, or fully prepare up to 5 days in advance and store in airtight jar(s) or plastic bag(s) at room temperature or freeze for up to 6 months. Thaw at room temperature for at least 1 hour. Can reheat in a preheated 350° oven for about 5 minutes.

Fabulous: As a base for pizza.

WARM EGGPLANT AND LAMB SHANK ANTIPASTO

2 eggplants, cut into
1/2-inch wide strips
Salt to taste
8 to 16 lamb shanks
(depending upon whether
if you want to serve 1 or
2 apiece)
2 to 4 tablespoons olive oil,
plus more for coating
4 to 10 cloves garlic, minced
2 onions, thinly sliced
1 bunch celery, with leaves,
cut into 1-inch lengths
1 cup minced fresh parsley
Two 6-ounce jars marinated
artichoke hearts (reserve
the liquid)
1 cup calamata or Italian
olives
2 teaspoons fennel seeds
2 teaspoons mustard seeds
2 bay leaves
1/4 cup packed light or dark
brown sugar
One 6-ounce can tomato
paste
1 1/2 cups sherry wine
vinegar
2 cups chicken broth,
homemade or canned
Freshly ground white and
black pepper to taste
Rosemary, oregano,
marjoram, thyme, and/or
basil to taste

Yield: 8 plus servings

Rustic exotica!

1. Place the eggplant in a colander in the sink. Toss with a generous amount of salt and allow to sit for at least 1 hour to draw off the bitter juices.
2. Meanwhile, blot the lamb dry using paper towels. Brown in a large skillet with the olive oil over medium to medium-high heat. Do this in several batches—do not crowd. Remove to a large casserole or earthenware baking dish.
3. Add the garlic and onions to the skillet and sauté until tender and golden.
4. Stir in the celery, parsley, artichoke hearts, olives, fennel and mustard seeds, bay leaves, brown sugar, tomato paste, vinegar, broth, and seasonings. Bring to a boil over high heat.
5. Return the lamb to the skillet and simmer over low to medium-low heat until the lamb is tender, about 30 minutes.
6. Preheat the oven to 350° to 400°F.
7. Meanwhile, rinse the eggplant and blot with paper towels.
8. Place the eggplant in a bowl and toss with the reserved artichoke marinade, along with enough olive oil to coat the eggplant.
9. Transfer to a baking dish and bake until tender, about 20 to 30 minutes.
10. Combine the eggplant with the lamb mixture.

Fast: Can fully prepare up to 3 days in advance and refrigerate, or freeze for up to 6 months. Thaw in the refrigerator for 2 days or at room temperature for 8 hours. Can prepare side dishes up to 2 days in advance and reheat.

Flashy: Serve buffet style, surrounded by bowls of any or all of the suggested side dishes, and with crumbled feta cheese and/or freshly grated Parmesan.

Rice, cracked wheat, lentils, polenta, couscous, beans, and/or pasta (tossed with olive oil to prevent sticking)
Crumbled feta cheese
Freshly grated Parmesean cheese

Fabulous: With short ribs or chicken instead of lamb.

Further: Add tomato juice to leftovers and you have a soup to die for!

PUMPKIN-DATE BREAD WITH VANILLA-NUTMEG SAUCE

1 1/2 to 2 cups well-packed, chopped pitted dates
2 cups cake flour
1/2 to 3/4 cup packed light or dark brown sugar
1/2 teaspoon salt
1 tablespoon baking powder
1 cup buttermilk
1 cup canned pumpkin
Freshly grated nutmeg to taste
Grated zest of 1 to 2 lemons
1/4 teaspoon ground cinnamon
2 large eggs
2 teaspoons vanilla extract
4 ounces cream cheese, at room temperature
3 tablespoons unsalted butter, melted
1 cup pecan halves, toasted (see page 29)
Vanilla-Nutmeg Sauce (recipe follows)

Yield: one 9-by-5-inch loaf

Homey and nurturing!

1. Preheat the oven to 350°F and butter a five-cup 9- by 5-inch bread pan.
2. Combine the first five ingredients in a food processor fitted with a metal blade or in a large bowl.
3. Process or beat in in the remaining ingredients, except the pecans, until well combined, but not overprocessed.
4. Add the pecans and process with several quick on-and-off motions, so as not to destroy texture, or mix in.
5. Pour the batter into the pan and bake in the center of the oven for 1 1/4 hours or until a tester inserted into the middle of the bread comes out clean.
6. Cool for 10 minutes, then remove from the pan and cool completely.

Fast: Can prepare up to 5 days in advance, wrap in plastic, and refrigerate or freeze for up to 3 months. Thaw at room temperature for about 8 hours.

Flashy: Serve with French vanilla ice cream or vanilla-nutmeg sauce. For an added touch, serve warmed or even toasted.

VANILLA-NUTMEG SAUCE

1/2 vanilla bean, cut
  lengthwise
1/4 cup packed light brown
  sugar
1/2 cup brandy
Freshly grated nutmeg to
  taste
1 3/4 cups heavy cream

Yield: about 2 cups

You can make all sorts of plain-Jane desserts glamorous with this sauce!

1. Place the vanilla bean, brown sugar, and brandy in a saucepan. Bring to a boil over high heat and grate in the nutmeg. Cook, stirring frequently, until reduced by half.
2. Stir in the cream and continue to cook over high heat until the flavor and consistency are pleasing.

Fast: Can prepare up to 3 days in advance and refrigerate, or freeze for up to 6 months. Thaw in the refrigerator for 2 days or at room temperature for about 3 hours.

Flashy: On crêpes, fresh fruit, and/or pound cake. Serve hot or cold.

Fabulous: With rum, bourbon, or tequilla instead of the brandy.

CHAPTER 6

Winter Dinner Parties

WINTER DINNER PARTIES AT A GLANCE

The Setting

ELEGANT
- Glitz blitz—dazzling and glittery to provide an upbeat counterpoint to the season's weather

CASUAL
- Warm, homey, and comforting to provide a cheerful nurturing atmosphere

Party Props

ELEGANT
- Colors are opulent and sophisticated: silver, gold, pearl, red, hunter green, black, and white
- Silver, china, crystal, pewter, and copper serving pieces—all of your best!
- Mirror squares on tables to reflect food, candles, and/or flowers
- Formal tablecloths and napkins
- Flowers in champagne flutes, crystal vases, antique copper or brass pots/vases
- Masses of candlesticks, candelabra, or votives
- Glitter, confetti, tinsel, garlands, shiny ribbons and bows, Christmas balls, pine cones, and/or dried artichokes (sprayed and/or glittered in gold, silver, green, red, and/or black)

CASUAL

- Colors are rich and earthy: red, green, white, brown, rust, and pumpkin
- Pottery, ceramic, copper, and pewter serving pieces
- Handwoven, textured print, or solid-colored tablecloths
- Can substitute import-store cotton bedspreads or buy fabric with the appropriate feel for tablecloths
- Napkins can be large and oversized. Can match the cloth or be in contrasting colors and/or prints
- Flowers in baskets, pitchers, teapots, wine bottles, crocks, or terra-cotta flowerpots, as is, or sprayed in colors to complement your table, or covered in fabric or wrapping paper, with bows.
- Lots of candles in pottery or ceramic candle holders or use bricks, wood platters or blocks, or old trays as candle bases. Can also use terra-cotta flowerpots turned upside-down as candle holders, sprayed in colors to complement your table, or covered in fabric or wrapping paper, with bows.
- Tinsel, cotton ribbons and bows, pine cones, homey Christmas decorations

Cuisine

ELEGANT

- Richer, more complex, and heartier than any other time of the year
- Slow-cooked foods that fill the air with warmth and marvelous aromas
- Soups, more complex sauces, and baked goods

CASUAL

- All of the above, plus
- heartier, less refined dishes, with fewer items on a menu

Foods for Decorating

- Nuts in the shell, spray-painted in gold, silver, or black, or left natural
- Uncooked fresh vegetables: salad savoy, onions, heads of garlic, winter squashes, stalks of brussels sprouts, pumpkins, artichokes, gourds, beans, dried pasta—try spraying them gold, silver, or black, or leave them natural.
- Fresh fruits: cranberries, apples, oranges, pomegranates, persimmons, pears, etc.

ELEGANT WINTER MENUS

. . . .

Roast Tenderloin Dinner

Velvety red wines and succulent, full-flavored beef dishes are natural choices for elegant winter dinner parties. They possess magical properties that make the season's harshness not only bearable, but almost welcome. This dinner party menu truly is a fitting reward for slogging through winter's cold.

Roast tenderloin is a sheer luxury in itself, but when studded with slivers of garlic, covered with Dijon mustard, and wrapped with Italian bacon it achieves an even loftier gastronomical position. Instead of a complex sauce, it is adorned with a colorful dollop of Roasted Red Pepper and Shallot Butter and flanked by a brandy-flavored mixture of mushrooms that could easily be used to sauce the beef. Crusty, chèvre-flavored mashed potato sausages, along with a flavorful broccoli dish complete the entree composition. Both side dishes are rich and exciting, but do not overshadow the beef.

Coming up with an hors d'oeuvre, salad, and dessert for this menu was a challenge. I wanted an hors d'oeuvre equal to the entree without being too filling. Smoked Salmon Mousse is the solution. It will get the evening started with just the right amount of razzle-dazzle and it can be prepared in advance. As for the salad, I wanted it to be unusual and seasonal. My salad of Fennel Slivers and Endive with Pears and Papaya is all of that, and more. Finally, I placed a similar criterion on the dessert, and decided on a Caramel Mousse. It is rich and elegant while being light enough to follow a large meal. Simply stated, to die for!

To create a tablescape that reflects a bit of Old World charm mixed with an upscale contemporary feel, use a stately hunter green cloth, along with crisp white napkins decoratively arranged in the wine goblets. For an added touch of elegance, use copper service plates. Adorn the center of the table with copper pots filled with white camellias along with white candles in brass candlesticks. To create even more opulence, consider spraying fava beans gold, and scattering them down the center of the table. These elements create a rich, charming look and a perfect backdrop for a fabulous menu.

MENU

Smoked Salmon Mousse

Bagel Chips

Salad of Fennel Slivers and Endive with Pears and Papaya

Sliced Baguette with Butter

Roast Tenderloin of Beef with Pancetta and Roasted Red Pepper and Shallot Butter

Mushroom Melange

Broccoli with Pine Nuts and Garlic-Dill Sauce

Sesame Potato Sausages

Caramel Mousse

Caramel-Pecan Sticks

FASTER & FLASHIER MENU

Smoked Salmon and Chèvre Served with Water Crackers or Belgian Endive

Tossed Salad with Fennel and Pears

Roast Tenderloin of Beef with Pancetta and Roasted Red Pepper and Shallot Butter

Boiled Red Potatoes with Sesame Seeds

French Vanilla Ice Cream with Raspberries (fresh or thawed, frozen) and Raspberry Liqueur

Butter Cookies (purchased)

WINES

Fumé Blanc or Champagne

Cabernet Sauvignon

Fast & Fabulous Timetable

Up to 6 Months in Advance and Frozen
Bagel Chips • Marinade • Roasted Red Pepper and Shallot Butter • Caramel-Pecan Sticks

Up to 3 Months in Advance and Frozen
Smoked Salmon Mousse • Mushroom Melange • Garlic-Dill Sauce •
Sesame Potato Sausages • Caramel Mousse

Up to 1 Week in Advance and Refrigerated
Bagel Chips

5 Days in Advance and Refrigerated
Tarragon-Sherry Vinaigrette

4 Days in Advance and Refrigerated
Roasted Red Pepper and Shallot Butter • Garlic-Dill Sauce • Marinade

3 Days in Advance and Refrigerated
Smoked Salmon Mousse • Caramel-Pecan Sticks

2 Days in Advance and Refrigerated
Mushroom Melange • Caramel Mousse • Set table • Thaw frozen
prepared-ahead foods

1 Day in Advance and Refrigerated
Salad of Fennel Slivers through step 3 • Tenderloin through step 4 •
Broccoli through step 2 • Sesame Potato Sausages • Potato Skins
through step 2 • Boiled Red Potatoes with Sesame Seeds

Party Day!
Toss salad • Warm bread • Roast the tenderloin • Heat the potatoes
• Finish the broccoli

SMOKED SALMON MOUSSE

3 tablespoons dry vermouth

1 envelope unflavored gelatin

3 1/2 ounces smoked salmon
(lox)

1 tablespoon minced shallots
or to taste

3 tablespoons fresh lemon
juice or to taste

1/4 cup minced red or green
onion

1/4 cup chopped fresh dill or
1 tablespoon dried

Grated zest of 1 to 2 lemons

Salt and freshly ground white
pepper to taste

3 cups heavy cream

Smoked salmon, capers,
sprigs of fresh dill, and/or
minced green or red onion
for garnish

Yield: about 4 1/2 cups

Light and elegant!

1. Oil a 5-cup mold.
2. Place the vermouth in a small bowl. Stir in the gelatin and dissolve
   it over a larger bowl of hot water or in a microwave for about 30
   seconds on low power. Allow it to cool slightly.
3. Puree the salmon and shallots, along with the gelatin mixture, in a
   food processor fitted with a metal blade, or in a blender.
4. Add the lemon juice, onions, dill, zest, salt, and pepper. Process just
   until combined. Taste and adjust the seasonings.
5. Add the cream and process *very* briefly, or it will curdle.
6. Transfer to the prepared mold and chill until firm, about 1 1/2
   hours in the refrigerator or 45 minutes in the freezer.
7. Unmold and enjoy!

Fast: Can prepare up to 3 days in advance and refrigerate, or freeze for
up to 3 months. Thaw in the refrigerator for 2 days.

Flashy: Serve with Bagel Chips (recipe follows) or thin squares of pumpernickel. To garnish, roll a slice of smoked salmon into a rose and
place on top of the mousse. Sprinkle capers and sprigs of dill and/or
minced green onions on top and around the base.

Fabulous: With prosciutto, smoked trout, or cooked turkey instead of
the smoked salmon.

Further: Toss leftovers into freshly cooked pasta, rice, couscous, or
bulgur.

BAGEL CHIPS

2 cups olive, grapeseed, or
   peanut oil
8 cloves garlic, smashed, or
   to taste
Fresh or dried dill to taste
Salt to taste
1 dozen bagels, cut into thin,
   vertical slices

Yield: about 18 dozen

You will love these and want to keep them on hand for nibbling. I discovered them years before they were packaged commercially, when I had a glut of bagels. These are much healthier than those available in stores.

1. Preheat the oven to 350°F.
2. Puree all the ingredients, except the bagels, in a food processor fitted with a metal blade or in a blender. Taste and adjust the seasonings.
3. Place the bagel slices on an ungreased cookie sheet and brush with the flavored oil.
4. Bake for about 20 minutes or until crisp. Watch carefully to prevent burning.

Fast: Can prepare up to 1 week in advance and store in airtight jar(s) or plastic bag(s), or freeze for up to 6 months. Thaw at room temperature for at least 1 hour.

Fabulous: Seasoned with any herb, depending on what the chips are to be served with.

SALAD OF FENNEL SLIVERS AND ENDIVE WITH PEARS AND PAPAYA

1 pound small fennel bulbs, tops cut off and reserved (for the beef tenderloin)

Tarragon-Sherry Vinaigrette (recipe follows)

Salt and freshly ground white pepper to taste

1 pear, halved, cored, and squirted with fresh lemon juice

1 papaya, peeled, halved, and seeded

1 bunch green onions, minced

1 head curly endive, torn into bite-size pieces

Remember this salad when hunting for an interesting luncheon entree. Simply add chicken, seafood, or fish and you have a magnificent main dish.

1. Cut fennel bulbs in half and slice into long, thin, vertical slices.
2. Place the fennel in a large salad bowl and toss with the desired amount of dressing. Season, then cover with plastic wrap and refrigerate.
3. Slice the pear and papaya into long, thin slices. Put in a glass or ceramic pan and cover with dressing and green onions.
4. Add the curly endive to the fennel and toss together with more vinaigrette.

Fast: Can prepare through step 3 up to 1 day in advance and refrigerate.

Flashy: To serve, arrange some of the tossed fennel mixture on individual salad plates or on a large platter. Surround with the sliced fruit.

Fabulous: With chicken, shrimp, or crab tossed into the fennel mixture. With any toasted nut or seed.

TARRAGON-SHERRY VINAIGRETTE

1 teaspoon dried tarragon or to taste

6 cornichons

2 cups extra virgin olive oil

1/3 cup fresh lemon juice

1/3 cup sherry wine vinegar

1 tablespoon Dijon mustard

Salt and freshly ground black pepper to taste

Yield: about 2 2/3 cups

If I were stranded on a desert island, this is the dressing I would want!

1. Combine all ingredients in a food processor fitted with a metal blade, or in a blender.
2. Taste and adjust the seasonings.

Fast: Can prepare up to 5 days in advance and refrigerate.

Flashy: On any salad, hot or cold vegetable, or as a marinade for fish, seafood, poultry, or vegetables.

Fabulous: With any fresh or dried herb instead of the tarragon. With tarragon wine vinegar instead of sherry wine vinegar.

ROAST TENDERLOIN OF BEEF WITH PANCETTA AND ROASTED RED PEPPER AND SHALLOT BUTTER

One 4-pound beef tenderloin
Marinade (optional—recipe
   follows)
4 cloves garlic, cut into
   slivers
1/4 cup Dijon mustard
Freshly ground black pepper
   to taste
Fresh or dried thyme to taste
Fresh or dried rosemary to
   taste
1/2 pound pancetta, sliced
   1/8 inch thick
1/2 cup brandy
Mushroom Melange (see
   page 207)
Watercress and reserved
   fennel leaves (from the
   salad) for garnish
Roasted Red Pepper and
   Shallot Butter (recipe
   follows)

This recipe provides a fresh and flamboyant rendition of this luxurious cut of beef.

1. Place the meat in a nonreactive pan and cover with the marinade. Cover with plastic wrap and refrigerate for up to 2 days, turning the meat daily.
2. Preheat the oven to 450°F.
3. Remove the beef from the marinade and blot it dry using paper towels.
4. Make small slits in the beef with a knife and insert the garlic slivers.
5. Spread the mustard over the beef and season with the pepper and herbs. Wrap with the pancetta and secure with toothpicks.
6. Place the meat in a baking pan and bake until an instant-read thermometer registers 120°F for rare, about 1 hour.
7. Remove the meat to a platter and tent with aluminum foil to keep warm. Let sit for about 15 minutes. Meanwhile, pour the cooking juices into a bowl and defat using ice cubes (see page 22).
8. Return the juices and the brandy to the pan and cook over high heat until the liquid is reduced to almost a glaze.
9. Stir this reduction into the mushroom melange, adjust the seasonings, and serve.

Fast: Can prepare the tenderloin through step 4 up to 1 day in advance and refrigerate. Bring it to room temperature before cooking.

Flashy: Garnish with sprigs of watercress and/or fennel leaves. Top each slice of tenderloin with a dollop of the butter mixture and place Mushroom Melange on the side.

Further: Use cold leftovers in salads or in sandwiches.

MARINADE

1 white onion, cut up
4 to 8 cloves garlic
2 tablespoons chopped fresh
  rosemary
1 to 2 tablespoons chopped
  fresh thyme
2 tablespoons brandy
1/2 cup Madeira
1 cup olive oil
Freshly ground black pepper
  to taste

I have been accused of marinating everything but old socks. It is not necessary, but it does provide another dimension in flavor.

1. Combine all the ingredients in a food processor fitted with a metal blade or in a blender.

Fast: Can prepare up to 4 days in advance and refrigerate, or freeze for up to 6 months. Thaw in the refrigerator for 2 days or at room temperature for about 8 hours.

Flashy: On pork, poultry, or lamb.

Fabulous: With juice of 1 to 2 lemons, 1/4 cup Dijon mustard, and/or 1/2 cup red or white wine added.

Further: When done marinating, remove the meat and freeze the marinade for reuse later.

ROASTED RED PEPPER AND SHALLOT BUTTER

3 large red bell peppers,
  roasted (see page 28),
  seeded, and skinned
6 to 8 shallots, roasted (see
  page 28)
1/2 pound (2 sticks)
  unsalted butter, cut up
  and at room temperature
1 tablespoon green
  peppercorns
Salt and freshly ground white
  pepper to taste

This compound butter provides lovely flavor and color for any roasted or grilled pork, lamb, or beef dish.

1. Combine all the ingredients in a food processor fitted with a metal blade, or in a bowl with an electric mixer. Taste and adjust the seasonings.
2. Transfer to a bowl, cover with plastic wrap, and chill for at least 1 hour before using.

Fast: Can prepare up to 4 days in advance and refrigerate, or freeze for up to 6 months. Thaw in the refrigerator for 2 days or at room temperature for 4 to 8 hours.

Flashy: Serve a dollop on each slice of roast tenderloin.

Fabulous: With minced sun-dried tomatoes and seasoned with any fresh or dried herb.

Further: Use leftovers on pasta, fish, lamb, chicken, or vegetables.

MUSHROOM MELANGE

4 tablespoons (1/2 stick)
  unsalted butter
2/3 cup minced shallots
3 to 4 ounces dried shiitake
  mushrooms, rehydrated,
  stemmed, and thinly sliced
1 1/2 to 2 pounds
  mushrooms, thinly sliced
1/4 cup minced fresh parsley
Salt and freshly ground white
  pepper to taste
Fresh or dried rosemary to
  taste
Fresh or dried thyme to taste
3 cups dry red wine
3 cups beef broth, homemade
  or canned
2 teaspoons tomato paste
1/2 cup heavy cream
2 teaspoons cornstarch
2 teaspoons water

If you are a mushroom maniac, this dish will put you into a state of ecstasy.

1. Melt the butter in a large skillet and sauté the shallots over low to medium-low heat until tender, but not brown.
2. Stir in the mushrooms and parsley and sauté until the domestic mushrooms lose their liquid. Season to taste with salt, pepper, rosemary, and thyme.
3. Increase the heat to medium-high and add the wine, broth, and tomato paste. Bring to a boil and cook until the mixture is reduced by about half.
4. Stir in the cream and let come to a boil again. Dissolve the cornstarch in the water, then add to the pan. Simmer over medium heat for a few minutes until the flavor and consistency are pleasing. Stir in the reduction from deglazing the roasting pan that the tenderloin was cooked in.

Fast: Can prepare up to 2 days in advance and refrigerate or freeze for up to 3 months. Thaw in the refrigerator for 2 days or at room temperature for about 4 hours.

Fabulous: With chopped crisp-fried pancetta mixed in.

Further: Use leftovers in risotto, pilaf, pasta, or soups.

BROCCOLI WITH PINE NUTS AND GARLIC-DILL SAUCE

2 large heads broccoli,
   broken into florets
1/2 cup pine nuts, toasted
   (see page 29)
Garlic-Dill Sauce (recipe
   follows)

A delicious dish.

1. Cut florets into small pieces.
2. Bring a large pot of salted water to a boil and blanch the florets. When they turn deeper green and are not quite tender, remove them with a strainer and immediately plunge them into a bowl of ice water. Remove and drain when florets are cold.
3. Place the florets in a glass or ceramic pan and cover with the pine nuts and the desired amount of sauce.
4. Before serving, heat in a microwave on low power for about 10 minutes or in a preheated 350°F oven for about 15 minutes. (Can also heat in a sauté pan on top of the stove.)

Fast: Can prepare through step 2 up to 1 day in advance and refrigerate.

Fabulous: With any nut, from cashews to Brazil nuts.

Further: Stir leftovers into chicken broth for a delicious soup, or toss into freshly cooked pasta.

GARLIC-DILL SAUCE

2 tablespoons unsalted butter
3 to 8 cloves garlic, minced
1 tablespoon minced shallots
Stems from 1 bunch fresh
    dill, minced
2 tablespoons all-purpose
    flour
1 teaspoon anchovy paste
1/2 cup dry vermouth
1 3/4 cups chicken broth,
    homemade or canned
1/2 cup minced fresh dill
Salt and freshly ground white
    pepper to taste
Fresh lemon juice to taste

Yield: about 2 1/4 cups

Another scrumptious and versatile sauce for your repertoire.

1. Melt the butter in medium-size saucepan over medium-low heat and sauté the garlic, shallots, and dill stems briefly; do not brown.
2. Whisk in the flour and anchovy paste and cook over low heat for several minutes, continuing to whisk.
3. Turn the heat to high, whisk in the vermouth and broth, and bring to a boil while whisking.
4. Reduce the heat to medium-low and simmer for about 5 minutes.
5. Strain the sauce through a fine mesh strainer into another saucepan. Add the minced dill, salt, pepper, and lemon juice. Simmer until flavors are pleasing, about 5 minutes.

Fast: Can prepare up to 4 days in advance and refrigerate or freeze for up to 3 months. Thaw in the refrigerator for 2 days or at room temperature for about 8 hours.

Flashy: On anything from pasta to fish.

Fabulous: Seasoned with any fresh or dried herb. With 1/4 cup freshly grated Parmesan, and/or 1 cup grated mozzarella or jack cheese and 1/4 cup heavy cream added at step 5.

SESAME POTATO SAUSAGES

3 pounds baking potatoes,
  scrubbed
2 large eggs, separated
4 ounces chèvre cheese, at
  room temperature
4 tablespoons (1/2 stick)
  unsalted butter
1 to 2 tablespoons minced
  shallots
Salt and freshly ground white
  pepper to taste
2 cups dried sourdough
  bread crumbs
1 cup sesame seeds, toasted
  (see page 29)
2 tablespoons water
1 cup all-purpose flour
Peanut or olive oil as needed

Yield: about 25 two-inch sausages

These potatoes are a real show-stopper! They have a crisp crust and soft interior. Give them a try with sweet potatoes for Thanksgiving. As a bonus, if you prepare them as directed, you'll be able to use the skins for Potato Skins (recipe follows) . . . such a deal!

1. Preheat the oven to 400°F, then bake the potatoes until soft, about 35 to 45 minutes.
2. When cool enough to handle, cut in half, scoop out the pulp, and mash with a fork or use a potato ricer.
3. Combine the still-warm mashed potatoes with the egg yolks, chèvre, butter, shallots, salt, and pepper.
4. Place in a pastry bag fitted with the largest plain tip and squeeze out into sausage shapes. You can also do this by hand by flouring your hands and rolling small amounts of the mixture into sausage shapes.
5. Combine the bread crumbs and sesame seeds in a medium-size bowl and lightly beat the egg whites with the water in another.
6. Roll the sausages in the flour, dip in the egg whites, and roll in the crumbs. Then place on an oiled cookie sheet and drizzle lightly with oil.
7. Set in the oven until brown and crusty, about 30 minutes.

Fast: Can prepare through step 3 up to 1 day in advance and refrigerate, or flash freeze for up to 3 months. Do not thaw. Cook frozen adding about 10 minutes to the cooking time.

Fabulous: Substitute herbed cream cheese for the chèvre. Season with any herb and/or minced ham, proscuitto, and/or sun-dried tomatoes. Add 1/2 cup freshly grated Parmesan cheese and/or some cornmeal to the crumb mixture. Substitute baked sweet potatoes instead of the potatoes.

POTATO SKINS

Reserved potato skins, pulp removed

Olive or peanut oil

Salt to taste

Beware, they are addictive! Unlike the more common variety, these are baked not fried—eliminating the guilt!

1. Preheat the oven to 350° to 400°F.
2. Cut each potato skin half in half, brush with oil, and sprinkle with salt.
3. Place on an ungreased cookie sheet and bake until crisp, about 20 minutes

Fast: Can prepare through step 2 up to 1 day in advance and refrigerate. Can also prepare fully up to 1 day in advance and reheat before serving.

Flashy: Serve plain, with guacamole, or with any dunk imaginable.

Fabulous: Top with grated cheddar or jack cheese, minced herbs, browned onions, crumbled bacon, and/or minced chiles.

BOILED RED POTATOES WITH SESAME SEEDS

2 pounds red potatoes, whole or halved

4 tablespoons (1/2 stick) unsalted butter or 1/4 cup extra virgin olive oil

2 to 4 tablespoons minced fresh parsley

Salt and freshly ground white pepper to taste

1. Bring a half inch of salted water to a boil in a large pot.
2. Add the potatoes and cook over medium heat, covered, shaking the pot frequently, until tender, about 20 minutes.
3. Increase the heat to high and cook away any moisture. Toss in the remaining ingredients, combine, and serve.

Fast: Can prepare up to 1 day in advance, leaving the potatoes slightly undercooked, and refrigerate. Bring to room temperature, then place in a preheated 350°F oven for 20 to 30 minutes.

Fabulous: Seasoned with any fresh herb instead of parsley.

CARAMEL MOUSSE

10 large eggs, separated, at
    room temperature (see
    page 23)
Pinch of cream of tartar
3 1/3 cups heavy cream
2 teaspoons vanilla extract
2 cups sugar
1 cup dark rum
2 envelopes unflavored
    gelatin
1/2 to 1 cup shaved
    bittersweet chocolate and
    Caramel-Pecan Sticks
    (recipe follows) for garnish

Yield: up to 12 servings

What flavor! What texture! A perfect conclusion to a big meal.

1. Whip the egg whites with the cream of tartar, using an electric mixer or in a food processor fitted with a metal blade, until they hold stiff peaks. Transfer to a large bowl and place in the freezer.
2. Whip the cream with the vanilla until it holds soft peaks. Transfer this to the bowl containing the egg whites, and fold it in, then return it to the freezer.
3. Combine the sugar plus half of the rum in a heavy saucepan. Cook over medium-low heat until the sugar dissolves while holding the pan by the handle and swirling it frequently. Increase the heat to medium-high and cover with a tight-fitting lid for 1 to 2 minutes, until the mixture boils and has thick bubbles, then uncover and cook until it turns a light golden caramel color, swirling the pan frequently. Remove the pan from the heat and continue to swirl until the syrup turns a rich, deep caramel color. Place the pan over a pan of cold water until it cools slightly, to prevent it from turning too dark. Do not let it harden. At this point, if necessary, the pan can be placed over very low heat to maintain a liquid consistency. As a word of caution, never let your skin come in contact with hot caramel. It burns you instantly.
4. Place the egg yolks in a food processor fitted with a metal blade and process until light and lemon-colored, or beat with an electric mixer.
5. Next, process in the cooled caramel while the machine or mixer is running. Transfer the mixture to a large, heavy saucepan and place over medium-low heat until it thickens a bit more, whisking constantly, about 10 minutes.
6. Place the gelatin and remaining rum in a small bowl. Mix well and dissolve over a larger bowl of hot water or in the microwave for about 30 seconds on low power.
7. Slowly process in the dissolved gelatin through the feed tube while the machine is running.
8. Transfer the mixture to a large bowl and place in the freezer to chill for about 10 minutes. Thoroughly fold in a third of the egg whites, then fold in the rest.
9. Refrigerate until set, at least 2 hours.

Fast: Can prepare up to 2 days in advance and refrigerate, or freeze for about 3 months. Thaw in the refrigerator for 2 days.

Flashy: Serve in stemmed goblets and garnish with a sprinkling of shaved chocolate and with a caramel-pecan stick.

Fabulous: With slices of cooked or raw apple or pear.

CARAMEL-PECAN STICKS

1 cup all-purpose flour
1 cup rolled oats, plus extra
  for rolling dough
1/4 to 1/2 cup packed dark
  or light brown sugar
1/8 teaspoon salt
1/4 pound (1 stick) unsalted
  butter, cold and cut into
  small pieces
Freshly grated nutmeg to
  taste
2 teaspoons vanilla extract
2 large eggs
2/3 cup heavy cream
Grated zest of 2 oranges
1 1/2 cups pecan halves,
  toasted (see page 29)
1 1/2 cups granulated sugar
1/2 cup bourbon or water

Yield: about 24

Crunchy crisp, you can't eat just one!

1. Preheat the oven to 400°F.
2. Combine the flour, oatmeal, sugar, and salt in a food processor fitted with a metal blade.
3. Process in the butter with quick on-and-off motions, until the dough forms a coarse meal.
4. Process in the nutmeg and vanilla. Lightly beat together the eggs and cream, then process into the mixture until almost thoroughly combined.
5. Add the zest and pecans and process with several quick on-and-off motions, so as not to destroy their texture. To prepare using an electric mixer, cream the butter with the brown sugar, salt, and zest. Beat in the eggs, cream, vanilla, and nutmeg until well blended. Next add the flour, oatmeal, and pecans and stir until thoroughly mixed.
6. Remove the dough to a flat surface, using oatmeal instead of flour to work the dough. Flatten to a thickness of no more than 1/2 inch. Cut into strips about 1/2-inch wide, then, with your hands, roll each strip into a thinner log shape. Cut each log into 3-inch-long lengths.
7. Place the sticks on an aluminum foil–lined cookie sheet. Bake for about 20 to 25 minutes.
8. While the sticks are baking, prepare the caramel by placing the sugar and bourbon in a small saucepan over medium-low heat until the sugar dissolves, while holding the pan by the handle and swirling frequently. Increase the heat to medium-high and cover with a tight-fitting lid for 1 to 2 minutes, until the mixture boils and has

thick bubbles, then uncover and cook until it turns a light golden caramel color, swirling the pan frequently. Remove the pan from the heat and continue to swirl until the syrup turns a rich, deep caramel color. Place the saucepan over a pan of cold water until it cools slightly; this will prevent it from turning too dark. Do not let it harden. If necessary, the saucepan can be placed over very low heat to maintain a liquid consistency. A word of caution: never let your skin come in contact with hot caramel—it burns instantly.

9. Transfer the sticks to an oiled cookie sheet, then dip them in the caramel or spoon it over them. Let harden.

Fast: Can prepare up to 3 days in advance and store in an airtight container, or flash freeze for up to 6 months. Thaw at room temperature for at least 1 hour.

Fabulous: Prepared with any nut instead of pecans.

Pork Loin with Brandied Onion-Applesauce Dinner

This dinner party menu is an absolute lifesaver during the holidays. It has a big, important, traditional feel without being labor-intensive. Every dish, down to the salad, is designed to be prepared or assembled at least a day in advance.

The evening begins with Crab and Artichoke Stuffed Mushrooms, something special to get the evening off on the right footing. It is rich, but not overpowering. The salad, a contemporary version of an old classic, Celery Victor, will spark everyone's interest. In case you are unfamiliar with this salad, it consists of celery hearts poached in broth with an anchovy-flavored vinaigrette. The entree, a roast pork loin, is infused with garlic and marinated, producing a succulent and flavorful dish. Using balsamic vinegar in the marinade seems to magically assist the seasonings in permeating the pork. Serving the two fruit condiments, Prunes in Port and Apples, Onions, and Pancetta, is reminiscent of a charming, old-fashioned dining style. Simply prepared new potatoes and colorful green beans complete the entree. The potatoes continue the traditional theme, but the green beans bring contrast and a touch of real excitement. Speaking of excitement, just wait until you serve your guests dessert! If you like bittersweet chocolate, you'll love this; if not, use semisweet to make it a bit sweeter.

As for the tablescaping, this is definitely the time of the year for fun. One possibility is to use a black cloth and matching napkins. Then, get your cans of gold and silver spray paint involved. Acorn squash, painted silver, looks fabulous placed in the center of the table. White pillar candles are striking in upside-down terra-cotta pots, sprayed black, silver, and gold. Use all three colors to create an abstract look or just pick one color for a simpler look. I know this sounds outrageous but baby's breath, along with fusilli, sprayed gold, scattered directly on the table provide another wonderful touch. I guarantee that this will create a fabulous and festive table and party.

MENU

Crab and Artichoke Stuffed Mushrooms

Hearts of Celery and Shrimp Salad

Sliced Baguette and Butter

Pork Loin with Brandied Onion-Applesauce

Apples, Onions, and Pancetta

Prunes in Port

Herbed Red Potatoes

Green Beans with Sun-Dried Tomato Salsa

Chocolate-Apricot Ecstasy with Walnuts

FASTER & FLASHIER MENU

Mini Quiche (purchased, frozen)

Tossed Salad with Shrimp

Pork Loin with Brandied Applesauce (use beef gravy from a jar and add applesauce, brandy, and seasonings)

Prunes in Port

Herbed Red Potatoes

Green Beans with Sun-Dried Tomatoes (use frozen green beans and season with olive oil, minced garlic, and chopped sun-dried tomatoes)

Dessert (purchased)

WINES

Semillon or Champagne

Merlot

Fast & Fabulous Timetable

Up to 6 Months in Advance and Frozen
Brandied Onion-Applesauce • Apples, Onions, and Pancetta • Prunes in Port • Green Beans through Step 2 • Chocolate-Apricot Ecstasy with Walnuts • Chocolate Ganache Glaze

Up to 3 Months in Advance and Frozen
Filling for Crab and Artichoke Stuffed Mushrooms

5 Days in Advance and Refrigerated
Prunes in Port • Fennel-Parmesan Vinaigrette

3 Days in Advance and Refrigerated
Marinate pork loin • Brandied Onion-Applesauce • Apples, Onions, and Pancetta

2 Days in Advance and Refrigerated
Chocolate-Apricot Ecstasy with Walnuts • Chocolate Ganache Glaze • Hearts of Celery and Shrimp Salad • Sun-Dried Tomato Salsa • Thaw frozen prepared-ahead foods

1 Day in Advance and Refrigerated
Crab and Artichoke Stuffed Mushrooms • Boil potatoes • Marinate shrimp • Green beans through step 2 • Set table

Party Day!
Assemble salad • Warm bread • Heat mushrooms • Roast pork loin • Finish potatoes, green beans, and dessert • Heat Apples, Onions, and Pancetta

CRAB AND ARTICHOKE STUFFED MUSHROOMS

16 large mushrooms, stems
  removed and reserved

Salt and freshly ground white
  pepper to taste

2 tablespoons unsalted butter

2 to 6 tablespoons minced
  onion

3 tablespoons minced fresh
  parsley

1 to 2 cloves garlic, minced

1 tablespoon all-purpose flour

1/2 cup heavy cream

2 teaspoons Madeira or to
  taste

1/2 cup crabmeat

One 6-ounce jar marinated
  artichoke hearts or
  bottoms, drained and
  minced

1/4 cup grated Gruyère
  cheese

3 tablespoons fresh lemon
  juice or to taste

1 teaspoon Dijon mustard

Freshly grated nutmeg to
  taste

Brut champagne

Freshly grated Parmesan
  cheese to taste

3 tablespoons unsalted
  butter, melted

A luscious combination of flavors!

1. Preheat the oven to 375°F.
2. Brush mushroom caps with melted butter and season with salt and pepper.
3. Mince the stems and sauté in the 2 tablespoons of butter with the onions, parsley, and garlic over medium heat. Cook until the liquid given off by the mushrooms evaporates, about 10 minutes.
4. Stir in the flour and cook for 1 minute, without browning.
5. Remove the pan from the burner and whisk in the cream and Madeira. Return the pan to the burner and add the crab, artichokes, Gruyère, lemon juice, mustard, and nutmeg. Cook over medium-low heat until the cheese melts and the flavors develop. Taste and adjust the seasonings.
6. Fill the mushroom caps with the crab mixture and place in a baking dish with 1 to 2 inches of champagne; make sure the champagne doesn't come high enough to touch the stuffing. Top the mushrooms with Parmesan cheese and melted butter. Bake until hot, about 15 to 20 minutes.

Fast: Can assemble up to 1 day in advance, and refrigerate. Bake before serving. Can only freeze the filling for up to 3 months. Thaw in the refrigerator for 2 days or at room temperature for about 4 hours.

Fabulous: Substitute minced spinach, broccoli, or asparagus for the artichoke hearts, or any minced seafood for the crab. Use filling as an entree in crêpes or on pasta, rice, or couscous.

HEARTS OF CELERY AND SHRIMP SALAD

4 bunches celery, each bunch
  cut into halves lengthwise
2 cups chicken broth,
  homemade or canned
1 bay leaf
6 tablespoons minced fresh
  parsley
2 cloves garlic, minced
Fennel-Parmesan Vinaigrette
  (see page 241)
16 strips roasted red bell
  pepper (see page 28—or
  purchased)
3/4 to 1 pound cooked baby
  shrimp
1/4 to 1/2 cup minced
  green onion
1/4 to 1/2 cup minced fresh
  dill
Salt and freshly ground white
  pepper to taste
Flowering kale or red lettuce
  leaves for garnish

Yield: 8 or more servings

This is my updated version of an old classic, Celery Victor, which was created by chef Victor Hirtzler of the St. Francis Hotel in San Francisco during the early 1900s. It is a change-of-pace salad that can easily be served as a luncheon entree.

1. Remove the tough outer stalks from the celery and discard. Trim off the bottom leafy portion so it is 4 to 6 inches long. Save the leaves.
2. Place the celery and trimmed leafy portions in a large enameled or stainless steel skillet. Add the broth, bay leaf, half the parsley, and the garlic.
3. Bring to a boil over high heat, cover the skillet, and reduce the heat to low. Simmer for about 15 minutes.
4. Remove the celery halves to a deep platter or glass or ceramic pan. Pour the vinaigrette over the celery and place several red pepper strips over each celery heart. Cover with plastic wrap, cool to room temperature, then chill.
5. In a bowl, combine the shrimp with some vinaigrette, the green onions, and dill. Taste and adjust the seasonings, cover with plastic wrap, and chill.

Fast: Can prepare through step 4 up to 2 days in advance and refrigerate. Can prepare the shrimp mixture up to 1 day in advance and refrigerate. Store the mixtures separately.

Flashy: Arrange flowering kale or red lettuce leaves on salad plates and center a celery heart and some shrimp salad on them.

Fabulous: With crab, lobster, or salmon instead of the shrimp. With equal amounts of mayonnaise and vinaigrette mixed together to dress the shrimp.

PORK LOIN WITH BRANDIED ONION-APPLESAUCE

One 6-pound boneless pork
   loin
Several cloves garlic, cut into
   slivers

MARINADE
1 cup balsamic vinegar
1 cup olive oil
1/4 cup Dijon mustard
Fresh or dried sage, thyme,
   and rosemary to taste
1 teaspoon fennel seeds

2 onions, sliced thinly
1/4 pound pancetta, thinly
   sliced
Salt and freshly ground black
   pepper to taste
1/4 to 1/2 cup brandy
Sprigs fresh parsley,
   watercress, and/or
   rosemary
Brandied Onion-Applesauce
   (recipe follows)
Apples, Onions, and
   Pancetta (see page 221)
Prunes in Port (see page
   221)

1. Cut several slashes in the pork using a sharp knife; insert the garlic slivers.
2. Combine the ingredients for the marinade.
3. Place the pork in a glass or ceramic pan and pour the marinade over it. Cover with plastic wrap and allow it to marinate, in the refrigerator, for at least 24 hours. Turn the roast over at least once during that time.
4. Bring it to room temperature before cooking. Remove it from the marinade, and blot dry with paper towels. Place thinly sliced onions in the bottom of the baking pan. Set the pork on top, season with salt and pepper and drape with the thin slices of pancetta. Bake in a 325°F oven until it reaches an internal temperature of 160°F, about 20 to 25 minutes per pound.
5. Transfer the pork to another pan or platter, and tent with aluminum foil to keep warm.
6. To deglaze the pan, discard all of the remaining fat in the pan and stir in the brandy, using a wooden spoon or a wire whisk. Cook over high heat, stirring or whisking vigorously to dissolve the brown bits that cling to the bottom of the pan, until the liquid has cooked down into a rich, almost syrupy liquid, about 4 to 5 minutes. Strain the juices through a fine mesh strainer into the brandied onion-applesauce.
7. Slice the pork and drizzle some of the sauce over the pork. Serve the remaining sauce on the side, separately.

Fast: Can marinate for up to 3 days in advance and refrigerate. Cook before serving.

Flashy: Serve on a platter with a mound of Apples, Onions, and Pancetta, and garnish with sprigs of parsley, watercress, and/or rosemary. Serve the Prunes in Port separately in a bowl.

Further: Make a sauce or use leftover sauce, if you are lucky enough to have any, and heat up leftover pork in it along with sautéed mushrooms and the Apples, Onions, and Pancetta.

BRANDIED ONION-APPLESAUCE

4 tablespoons (1/2 stick)
   unsalted butter
2 onions, minced
1 teaspoon fennel seeds
1 teaspoon dried rosemary
1 bay leaf
2 cups unsweetened
   applesauce
3/4 cup sherry
1/4 cup brandy
2 1/2 cups chicken broth,
   homemade or canned
1/4 cup balsamic vinegar
Salt and freshly ground white
   pepper to taste

The essence of wintery flavors.

1. Melt the butter in a saucepan over medium-high to high heat and sauté the onions until brown, stirring from time to time, for about 20 minutes.
2. Add the fennel seeds, rosemary, and bay leaf, then stir in the applesauce, sherry, and brandy and simmer over medium heat until the flavors develop and the liquid reduces by half, about 10 minutes.
3. Stir in the chicken broth and simmer until the flavors develop to your liking, about 10 minutes more.
4. Stir in the strained deglazing juices from the pork, along with the balsamic vinegar for added depth in flavor. It is not essential to add the deglazing juices, but it is delicious if you do.
5. Taste and season with the salt and pepper.

Fast: Can prepare through step 3 up to 3 days in advance and refrigerate, or freeze for up to 6 months. Can fully prepare, if you aren't using the deglazing juices. Thaw in the refrigerator for 2 days or at room temperature for about 4 hours.

Flashy: For a more elegant presentation, strain through a fine mesh strainer before serving.

Fabulous: With leeks instead of onions, with 2 ounces shiitake mushrooms, sautéed, and 1/4 pound pancetta, chopped and sautéed, added after the sauce has been strained.

APPLES, ONIONS, AND PANCETTA

3 tablespoons unsalted butter

1/4 pound pancetta, thinly sliced

2 to 3 onions, thinly sliced

3 Granny Smith apples, peeled, cored, and thinly sliced

1 teaspoon fennel seeds

1 teaspoon dried rosemary

1/2 cup sherry

Salt and freshly ground white pepper to taste

Ground cinnamon to taste

A mixture you will want to keep in your freezer.

1. Melt the butter in a large skillet over medium heat and sauté the pancetta for 2 to 3 minutes.

2. Add the onions, apples, fennel seeds, and rosemary. Sauté until the onions are golden about 10 to 15 minutes.

3. Stir in the sherry and cook until reduced by half. Season with salt, pepper, and cinnamon.

Fast: Can prepare up to 3 days in advance and refrigerate, or freeze for up to 6 months. Thaw in the refrigerator for 2 days or at room temperature for about 8 hours. Reheat before serving.

Flashy: With pork, chicken, or turkey.

Further: Stir leftovers into risotto. Add chicken broth and a splash of cream sherry for a great soup.

PRUNES IN PORT

2 cups pitted prunes

4 cups port

Freshly grated nutmeg to taste

Ground cinnamon to taste

Drunken prunes!

1. Put the prunes and port in a large saucepan and simmer for about 20 minutes over medium heat.

2. Season with nutmeg and cinnamon.

Fast: Can prepare up to 5 days in advance and refrigerate, or freeze for up to 6 months. Thaw in the refrigerator for 2 days or at room temperature for about 8 hours.

Flashy: With any grilled or roasted beef, pork, or fowl.

Fabulous: With dried figs or apricots instead of prunes, but increase the cooking time to 30 minutes.

HERBED RED POTATOES

2 pounds baby red potatoes,
   halved
3 tablespoons unsalted butter
2 shallots, minced
1/4 cup minced fresh parsley
2 tablespoons minced fresh
   rosemary
Salt and freshly ground white
   pepper to taste
1/4 cup sesame seeds,
   toasted (see page 29)

1. Place the potatoes in a large saucepan with boiling salted water. Cook until tender, about 8 minutes, over medium heat.
2. Meanwhile, in large skillet, melt the butter over medium-low heat and sauté the shallots, parsley, and rosemary until the shallots are tender.
3. Drain the potatoes and add them to the skillet. Season with salt and pepper, increase the heat to medium-high, and cook for 10 to 15 minutes, tossing to coat them with the herb mixture. Remove from the heat and toss with the sesame seeds.

Fast: Can boil potatoes and toss with remaining ingredients up to 1 day in advance and refrigerate. Bring to room temperature and complete before serving.

Fabulous: With extra virgin olive oil instead of butter.

GREEN BEANS WITH SUN-DRIED TOMATO SALSA

2 pounds green beans, stems
   removed
1 cup Sun-Dried Tomato
   and Roasted Garlic Salsa
   (see page 191) or to taste
Olive oil, if needed
Fresh lemon juice to taste
Salt and freshly ground white
   pepper to taste
Freshly grated nutmeg to
   taste

This dish brings great color and flavor to your dinner plate.

1. Bring a large pot of salted water to a boil. Add the green beans and cook until they reach desired tenderness, about 4 minutes for crisp.
2. Remove and place in colander under cold running water. This will stop the cooking process and lock in the color. Refrigerate.
3. Bring to room temperature, combine with the salsa, olive oil, if necessary, and lemon juice, and season with salt and pepper, Heat in a large skillet or wok over medium to medium-high heat, or in the microwave, for about 5 minutes.

Fast: Can prepare through step 2 up to 1 day in advance and refrigerate covered, or freeze for up to 6 months. Thaw in the refrigerator for 2 days or at room temperature for about 4 hours.

CHOCOLATE-APRICOT ECSTASY WITH WALNUTS

1/4 pound (1 stick) unsalted
butter, cut up

4 ounces bittersweet
chocolate, broken into
pieces

Grated zest of 1 to 2
oranges

3 large eggs, at room
temperature

Pinch of salt

Freshly grated nutmeg to
taste

1/2 cup walnuts, toasted
(see page 29)

1/2 cup dried apricots,
chopped

Chocolate Ganache Glaze
(recipe follows) and
walnut halves for garnish

This dessert is well worth the caloric splurge! It is a good idea to make a double recipe and put one in your freezer.

1. Preheat the oven to 425°F. Butter a 7- by 9-inch Teflon-coated or other nonstick cake pan. Line the bottom with a round of buttered aluminum foil or wax paper.
2. Combine the butter, chocolate, and zest, and melt over simmering water in a double boiler or in a microwave on low power.
3. Meanwhile, place the eggs, salt, and nutmeg in a food processor fitted with a metal blade and process well, or combine in a bowl with an electric mixer.
4. Slowly add several tablespoons of the melted chocolate mixture through the feed tube while processing or beat in with an electric mixer.
5. Add the remaining chocolate mixture and process just long enough to combine or briefly beat in with an electric mixer.
6. Add the walnuts and apricots to the prepared pan and pour the batter on top.
7. Place the pan in a larger roasting pan filled with hot water reaching two-thirds up the sides of the cake pan.
8. Bake for 5 minutes, then cover with buttered aluminum foil and bake another 15 minutes.
9. Remove the pan from the oven and cool for 45 minutes, while still in the pan of hot water. Remove from the larger pan and refrigerate for about 3 hours or until firm.

Fast: Can prepare up to 2 days in advance and refrigerate or freeze for up to 6 months and thaw in the refrigerator for 2 days or at room temperature for about 8 hours.

Flashy: Frost the cake with the ganache and top with the walnut halves. Chill in the refrigerator for at least 1 hour or freeze for about 30 minutes.

Fabulous: With dried prunes, or fresh peaches or pears instead of the apricots. Served on a pool of Vanilla-Nutmeg Sauce (see page 196) or a raspberry variation of Boysenberry Sauce (page 116).

CHOCOLATE GANACHE GLAZE

2/3 cup heavy cream
12 ounces semisweet
 chocolate chips
Pinch of salt
1 tablespoon orange-flavored
 liqueur
1 tablespoon brandy
1 tablespoon unsalted butter

Yield: about 2 cups

1. Bring the cream to a boil in a saucepan.
2. Chop the chocolate in a food processor fitted with a metal blade or by hand using a knife, then transfer to a blender.
3. Add the hot cream through the feed tube while processing, or to the blender. Then add remaining ingredients and process until combined.

Fast: Can prepare up to 4 days in advance and refrigerate or freeze for up to 6 months. Thaw in the refrigerator for 2 days or at room temperature for about 4 hours.

Fabulous: With different kinds of chocolate and liqueurs.

Roast Duck Dinner

When in the mood for total indulgence, in other words, pulling out all the stops, this is the menu. It is extravagant, opulent, and exotic, both in spirit and flavor. The menu is a colorful composition of foods that are traditionally served at elegant winter dinners, handled in a contemporary, eclectic manner. A caviar mousse and champagne start this special evening off and set the tone. The salad that follows is another showstopper with a distinct Mediterranean influence. The vegetable dish combines Chinese ingredients with classic French preparation, resulting in a refreshing note to the meal. The wild rice dish also combines several ingredients common to Chinese cooking—green onions and water chestnuts—with a middle-Eastern grain—bulgur—to create something full of both texture and an absolutely wonderful flavor.

The beautifully colored and delicious Champagne Kiwi Sorbet provides a welcome chance for your guests to cleanse their palates and take a break while you carve the ducks. The duck breaks with tradition and uses lemon rather than orange as a flavoring for the sauce. Furthermore, the sauce is rich and zesty, not typically sweet. An amazing amount of garlic, along with cabernet sauvignon, lemon zest, and green peppercorns come together to create a rich, intensely flavored duck dish that is extremely well balanced.

The same adjectives can be used to describe the dessert. It ends the meal on the exact note that it began.

As for the table, an opulent look is called for. A cloth in a pale pink or gray or possibly one with an ornate design all are good choices. For contrast, I like to use dark napkins, arranged in the wineglasses. Votive candles in small glass holders are effective scattered down the center of the table. Rather than flowers, consider purple heads of salad savoy, placed in small glass bowls, to provide bursts of dramatic color. For a final touch, sprinkle hot pink and silver confetti down the center of the table. Both the table and menu make this party a memorable celebration.

MENU

Caviar Mousse with Bagel Chips

Warm Goat Cheese Salad with Raspberry Vinaigrette

Sliced Baguette and Butter

Champagne Kiwi Sorbet

Herb and Garlic Roast Duck with Citrus-Peppercorn Sauce

Wild Rice Pilaf

Chinese Pea Pods with Shiitake Mushrooms and Carrot Shreds

Almond Mocha Ecstasy with Mocha Custard Sauce

FASTER & FLASHIER MENU

Tossed Salad with Goat Cheese and Raspberry Vinaigrette

Herb and Garlic Roast Chicken with Citrus-Peppercorn Sauce (prepared with canned chicken broth instead of homemade stock)

Chinese Pea Pods with Shiitake Mushrooms and Carrot Shreds

Rice with Pecans and Water Chestnuts (toss sliced water chestnuts and chopped pecans into plain cooked rice)

Dessert (purchased)

WINES

Champagne or Sauvignon Blanc

Pinot Noir

Late harvest Zinfandel, or Cabernet Sauvignon

Fast & Fabulous Timetable

Up to 6 Months in Advance and Frozen
   Caviar Mousse • Bagel Chips • Citrus-Peppercorn Sauce through step
   2 • Duck stock • Mocha-Custard Sauce

Up to 3 Months in Advance and Frozen
   Wild Rice Pilaf • Almond Mocha Ecstasy

5 Days in Advance and Refrigerated
   Raspberry Vinaigrette

4 Days in Advance and Refrigerated
   Mocha-Custard Sauce • Mocha Almond Ecstasy

3 Days in Advance and Refrigerated
   Champagne Kiwi Sorbet (freeze) • Duck stock • Citrus-Peppercorn
   Sauce through step 2 • Mix together all the seasonings for the vegetables

2 Days in Advance and Refrigerated
   Caviar Mousse • Cheese balls for salad through step 4 • Wild Rice Pilaf
   • Thaw frozen prepared-ahead foods

1 Day in Advance and Refrigerated
   Roast duck through step 7 • Prep salad greens • Blanch pea pods and
   carrots • Set table

Party Day!
   Finish salad, wild rice • Warm bread • Roast ducks • Finish vegetables

CAVIAR MOUSSE

3/4 cup sour cream

1/4 cup minced fresh dill

1 shallot, chopped

3 large hard-cooked eggs, peeled and chopped

1/4 cup cream cheese

1/4 cup fresh lemon juice or to taste

1/4 teaspoon freshly ground white pepper

1 1/2 teaspoons salt or to taste

1/2 teaspoon prepared white horseradish or to taste

1 1/2 envelopes unflavored gelatin

2 tablespoons gin

3 ounces black caviar or to taste, put in a fine strainer and rinsed

Sour cream, more caviar, minced green onions, minced hard-cooked eggs, and grated lemon zest for garnish

Yield: 10 servings

Relax, you need not blow your budget. Inexpensive caviar is just fine for this scrumptuous hors d'oeuvre.

1. Combine first nine ingredients in a food processor fitted with a metal blade, or in a blender.
2. In a small bowl, sprinkle the gelatin over the gin and let soften for 5 minutes. Set the bowl in a larger bowl of hot water and stir until the gelatin dissolves.
3. Add the gelatin to the food processor through the feed tube while the machine is running or to the blender.
4. Fold in the caviar. Taste and adjust the seasonings.
5. Transfer the mousse to a 2-cup oiled mold and refrigerate for 3 hours or more until set. For faster results, chill in the freezer until set. Unmold.

Fast: Can prepare up to 2 days in advance and refrigerate, or freeze for up to 6 months. Thaw in the refrigerator for 2 days.

Flashy: Serve with squares of pumpernickel bread and/or Bagel Chips (see page 203) and thinly sliced cucumbers. Garnish with sour cream on the top. Sprinkle with minced green onions, grated lemon zest, more caviar, and minced hard-boiled eggs.

Fabulous: With salmon caviar instead of black.

WARM GOAT CHEESE SALAD WITH
RASPBERRY VINAIGRETTE

4 cups bite-size escarole pieces

4 Belgian endive, pulled apart

1 to 2 bunches watercress, stemmed

8 ounces chèvre cheese

One 15-ounce jar roasted red peppers

24 calamata olives

Olive oil as needed

Freshly ground black pepper to taste

Raspberry Vinaigrette (recipe follows)

This type of a salad is very chic, and as soon as you taste it you will understand why.

1. Place the greens in a large salad bowl.
2. Form the cheese into sixteen small balls, about 1 inch wide, using your hands.
3. Wrap a roasted red pepper around each cheese ball.
4. Place the balls in a glass or ceramic pan, scatter with the olives, and cover with olive oil. Grind black pepper over the top, cover with plastic wrap, and let marinate at room temperature for at least 1 hour or up to 36 hours refrigerated.
5. Toss the greens with the desired amount of dressing when heating the cheese.
6. When ready to serve, place the pan with the cheese balls in the microwave for about 30 seconds, or until warm, or in a preheated 350°F oven for about 15 minutes.
7. Put the greens on salad plates and top each with two cheese balls and some olives.

Fast: Can prepare cheese balls through step 4 up to 36 hours in advance and refrigerate. Can prep greens up to 1 day in advance and refrigerate, covered with damp paper towels. Toss before serving.

Fabulous: With toasted walnuts, pine nuts, or pumpkin seeds tossed in.

RASPBERRY VINAIGRETTE

2/3 cup raspberry vinegar

2 cups extra virgin olive oil

2 tablespoons minced shallots

Salt and freshly ground white pepper to taste

Red wine vinegar to taste

Fresh or dried dill to taste

Yield: about 2 2/3 cups

1. Combine all the ingredients in a food processor fitted with a metal blade or in a blender. Taste and adjust the seasonings.

Fast: Can prepare up to 5 days in advance and refrigerate.

Fabulous: On cooked green vegetables, such as broccoli, asparagus, or chard. On pasta, rice, or seafood salads.

CHAMPAGNE KIWI SORBET

1 cup sugar

1/2 vanilla bean

1 cup water

16 kiwi, peeled and cut up

2 cups brut champagne

2 teaspoons fresh lemon juice
or to taste

3 large egg whites, whipped
until they hold soft peaks
(see page 23)

Fresh mint leaves and/or
kiwi slices for garnish

Yield: 8 to 12 servings

Add a sorbet to any of the elegant menus. It provides a lovely touch. Use this recipe with almost any fruit according to the season and menu.

1. Bring the sugar, vanilla bean, and water to a boil in a small saucepan, stirring often. Remove from the heat; let stand, covered, until cooled to room temperature. Remove the vanilla bean, wash, dry, and store in a jar of sugar. This will result in a vanilla-flavored sugar.

2. Puree the kiwi in a food processor fitted with a metal blade, or in a blender. You should have about 4 cups of puree. Combine the puree, sugar syrup, and champagne in medium-size bowl; stir until thoroughly blended. Stir in the lemon juice.

3. Place the bowl, covered with plastic wrap, in the freezer. When the mixture is slushy, about one hour, return to the food processor or blender and process briefly. Return to the bowl and fold in the egg whites. Cover with plastic wrap and freeze until frozen, about 3 hours.

Fast: Can prepare up to 3 days in advance and freeze. If frozen for longer periods of time, return to the food processor, fitted with a metal blade, or blender and process before serving.

Flashy: Served in stemmed glasses, garnished with fresh mint leaves and/or kiwi slices.

Fabulous: With almost any fruit in season.

HERB AND GARLIC ROAST DUCK WITH CITRUS-PEPPERCORN SAUCE

Two or three 6-pound ducks (allow at least 1 pound per person)

2 or 3 heads garlic (1 head per duck), peeled (see step 5)

Salt and freshly ground white pepper to taste

Several lemons, washed and cut into halves or quarters

2 or 3 celery stalks

Minced fresh or dried rosemary and thyme to taste

4 to 6 green onions, root end removed

2 onions, sliced

Citrus-Peppercorn Sauce (recipe follows)

Watercress leaves, orange or lemon slices, and/or baby corn (canned) for garnish

This is truly an exotic dish that will delight your guests.

Despite its appearance, the preparation is amazingly easy. If you wish, prepare this recipe with chicken instead of duck.

1. Preheat the oven to 450°F.
2. Remove the bag of giblets, neck, and heart from inside the ducks and reserve for stock.
3. Cut off the wing tips and reserve for stock.
4. Wash and dry the ducks. Remove all the extra fat from the duck and prick the skin all over with a fork. This will allow the fat to run off and produce a crisp skin.
5. To peel the garlic faster, separate into cloves, place in a saucepan of boiling water, and blanch for about 1 minute, then put in a colander under running cold water until cool enough to handle. Squeeze the garlic out of its skin. Bring a saucepan of salted water to a boil and add the peeled garlic. Blanch for 1 more minute. Drain and repeat.
6. Season inside of each duck with salt and pepper. Add the garlic cloves, along with several lemon quarters, a piece of celery, the rosemary, thyme, and several green onions.
7. Place the ducks and sliced onions in a large roasting pan. Season the skin with salt and pepper.
8. Place in the oven and reduce the heat to 350°F. It will require about 20 minutes per pound, about 2 hours for a 6-pound duck. For crispier skin, raise the temperature to 425°F for the last 20 to 30 minutes. Watch carefully to prevent burning. The duck is medium-rare when the juices from the thigh are a light rose color; it's well done when the juices are pale yellow. A well-done duck will be dry.
9. When done, transfer to a platter and return to the oven with the heat turned off and the door ajar. Prepare the sauce using the drippings in the roasting pan.
10. Carve and enjoy!

Fast: Can prepare through step 7 up to 1 day in advance. Bring to room temperature and cook before serving.

Flashy: Serve on a large platter garnished with sprigs of watercress, baby corn, and slices of lemon or orange. Serve the sauce in a bowl on the side.

Further: Remove leftover duck from bones and add to pasta, risotto, soups, or salads.

CITRUS-PEPPERCORN SAUCE

6 tablespoons sugar

1/2 cup balsamic vinegar

2 to 4 tablespoons minced fresh ginger

4 cups Duck Stock (recipe follows) or chicken broth, homemade or canned

1/3 cup dry red wine

Orange liqueur to taste

1 teaspoon dried thyme or to taste

1 tablespoon green peppercorns or to taste

Grated zest of 4 to 8 lemons

Fresh lemon juice to taste

1/4 cup cornstarch dissolved in 1/4 cup dry red wine

1 cup Madeira

Salt and freshly ground white pepper to taste

5 tablespoons unsalted butter, at room temperature

Yield: about 4 cups

This is a rich and intense sauce that is a nice break from the ubiquitous orange sauce.

1. Place the sugar and vinegar in a heavy saucepan over medium-low heat until the sugar is dissolved. Raise the heat to medium-high and cook until the sugar is caramel-colored. Remove from the heat and stir in the ginger and 1 cup of the duck stock. Return to the burner and simmer over medium heat, stirring to dissolve the caramel.
2. Stir in the remaining stock, the red wine, liqueur, thyme, peppercorns, zest, and lemon juice. Bring to a boil over high heat and stir in the dissolved cornstarch. Continue boiling until thickened, about 5 minutes.
3. To deglaze the pan, skim off as much fat as possible from the roasting pan. Stir in the Madeira, using a wooden spoon or whisk, and stir or whisk over high heat to dissolve the brown bits on the bottom of the pan. Cook until the liquid reduces to a syrupy consistency, about 4 to 5 minutes.
4. Stir the juices into the sauce.
5. Taste and adjust the seasonings. Add a bit more Madeira and swirl in the butter. Hold over low heat while the duck is being carved and enjoy!

Fast: Can prepare through step 2 up to 3 days in advance and refrigerate, or freeze for up to 6 months. Thaw in the refrigerator for 2 days or at room temperature for about 8 hours.

Fabulous: Substitute grapefruit, orange, or tangerine zest for the lemon zest. With 1 cup cooked, sweetened cranberries, Chinese plum sauce, dried apricots, and/or prunes added. Add 5 to 10 minutes to the cooking time if using dried fruits.

DUCK STOCK

Reserved wing tips, giblets,
   and neck
1 onion, chopped
1/2 to 1 carrot, chopped
1 cup dry red wine
1 to 2 stalks celery (with
   leaves), chopped
4 cloves garlic, smashed and
   peeled
4 to 8 parsley stems,
   chopped
1 bay leaf
4 to 8 black peppercorns
1 teaspoon dried thyme

Yield: about 6 cups

Duck stock is liquid gold, well worth the extra preparation time. To speed things along a bit, you may use canned chicken broth instead of water.

1. Add the duck parts, onion, and carrot to a large saucepan and cook over medium heat until nicely browned. Pour off the excess fat.
2. Add all the remaining ingredients, along with enough water to cover them by 1 inch, and bring to a boil over high heat. Reduce the temperature to low and simmer, covered, for about 4 hours, occasionally skimming the surface with a fine mesh strainer to remove the scum that will form.
3. Strain the stock into a large bowl and discard the duck and vegetables. Cool to room temperature, cover with plastic wrap, and refrigerate to solidify the fat.
4. Remove and discard the fat.

Fast: Can prepare stock up to 3 days in advance and refrigerate, or freeze for up to 6 months. Thaw in the refrigerator for 2 days or at room temperature for about 8 hours.

Further: Use leftover stock in soups or to create wonderful sauces for beef, pork, lamb, or poultry.

WILD RICE PILAF

1 cup uncooked wild rice

6 tablespoons (3/4 stick)
   unsalted butter

1 bunch green onions,
   minced

2 shallots, minced

2 cloves garlic, minced

1/2 pound smoked ham,
   minced

1/4 cup minced fresh parsley

1/2 pound small mushrooms,
   halved

1/2 cup dry or sweet sherry

Salt and freshly ground white
   pepper to taste

Dried thyme to taste

1 cup uncooked bulgur

7 3/4 cups boiling chicken
   broth, homemade or
   canned

1 bay leaf

One 8-ounce can water
   chestnuts, drained and
   sliced

Minced green onions and 1
   cup pecan halves, toasted
   (see page 29), for garnish

I could make a meal of this alone!

1. Rinse the rice several times in cold water and remove any foreign particles. Drain well.

2. Melt 4 tablespoons of the butter in a large skillet over medium heat and sauté the green onions, shallots, and garlic with the ham until the shallots and onions are tender.

3. Add the parsley and mushrooms and sauté over medium-high heat for several minutes.

4. Stir in the sherry, season with salt, pepper, and thyme, and cook over high heat until the sherry is almost completely evaporated.

5. Meanwhile, melt the remaining butter in a 2-quart saucepan over medium heat and sauté the rice and bulgur until coated with the butter.

6. Stir in the boiling broth, along with the mushroom mixture and bay leaf. Bring to a boil over high heat, then reduce the heat to medium-low, cover, and cook until the rice is tender, about 40 minutes. Stir in the water chestnuts.

7. Transfer the rice to a serving bowl.

Fast: Can prepare up to 2 days in advance and refrigerate, or freeze for up to 3 months and thaw in the refrigerator for 2 days or at room temperature for about 8 hours. Reheat before serving.

Flashy: Garnish with a sprinkling of green onions and pecans.

Fabulous: With any nut instead of the pecans.

CHINESE PEA PODS WITH SHIITAKE MUSHROOMS AND CARROT SHREDS

4 carrots, peeled and
julienned
1 1/2 to 2 pounds pea pods,
stringed
2 tablespoons unsalted butter
2 tablespoons peanut oil
2 tablespoons sesame oil
1/4 cup sesame seeds,
toasted (see page 29)
2 tablespoons minced pickled
ginger
1 clove garlic, minced
1 large shallot, minced
8 dried shiitake mushrooms,
rehydrated, stemmed, and
thinly sliced
Salt and freshly ground white
pepper to taste
Pinch of sugar

Besides being delicious, this vegetable provides lovely color.

1. Bring a large pot of salted water to a boil and blanch the carrots, then the pea pods, until just tender, about 5 minutes for the carrots and 30 to 60 seconds for the pea pods. Remove each, place under cold running water to stop the cooking process, and drain well.

2. In a large skillet or wok, heat the butter, oils, sesame seeds, ginger, garlic, shallot, mushrooms, salt, pepper, and sugar over medium heat. Add the vegetables and sauté until hot.

Fast: Can blanch pea pods and carrots up to 1 day in advance and refrigerate. Bring to room temperature before finishing. Mix together the rest of the ingredients up to 3 days in advance and refrigerate.

ALMOND MOCHA ECSTASY

Butter and unsweetened
  cocoa powder for the cake
  pan
1/4 pound (1 stick) unsalted
  butter, cut up
4 ounces bittersweet
  chocolate, broken into
  pieces
3 large eggs
7 ounces almond paste
2 teaspoons vanilla extract
1/4 cup coffee liqueur
1 tablespoon cornstarch
2 tablespoons freshly ground
  coffee
Whipped cream and
  strawberries or shaved
  chocolate, for garnish
Mocha-Custard Sauce
  (recipe follows)

Yield: 8 or more servings

So rich, but so divine! You will be amazed by how effortless this is to prepare, even for the noncook.

1. Butter and lightly dust with cocoa powder a 7- to 9-inch Teflon-coated or other nonstick cake pan.
2. Preheat the oven to 325°F.
3. Combine the butter and chocolate, and melt in a microwave, or over simmering water in a double boiler.
4. Combine the eggs, almond paste, vanilla, liqueur, cornstarch, and coffee in a food processor fitted with a metal blade, or in a bowl with an electric mixer.
5. Slowly add the melted chocolate mixture through the feed tube while processing, or while beating with the electric mixer.
6. Transfer to the prepared cake pan and place in a larger pan filled with hot water that reaches halfway up the sides of cake pan. Bake for about 40 minutes, or until a tester inserted into the middle comes out clean.
7. Cool to room temperature, then refrigerate at least 2 hours before unmolding.

Fast: Can prepare up to 4 days in advance and refrigerate, or freeze for up to 3 months. Thaw in the refrigerator for 2 days or at room temperature for about 8 hours.

Flashy: Top with whipped cream and shaved chocolate or strawberries. Serve each slice on a puddle of Mocha-Custard Sauce for that added touch of decadence.

Fabulous: Prepare a double recipe and freeze the extra one.

MOCHA-CUSTARD SAUCE

6 large egg yolks (see page 23)

1/2 cup packed light or dark brown sugar

1/4 teaspoon salt

1/2 cup crème de cacao or other coffee-flavored liqueur

2 tablespoons bourbon

1 1/2 cups milk

1 to 2 ounces semisweet chocolate, cut up

1 teaspoon finely ground Italian or French roast coffee beans or to taste

2 teaspoons vanilla extract

Freshly grated nutmeg to taste

Yield: about 3 cups

Divine!

1. Combine the yolks, sugar, salt, liqueur, and bourbon in a food processor fitted with a metal blade, or in a bowl with an electric mixer, until the mixture is lemon-colored.
2. Heat the milk and chocolate over simmering water in a double boiler with the ground coffee until the chocolate melts.
3. Whisk the yolk mixture into the milk. Continue to cook over just simmering water until the custard thickens, about 5 to 10 minutes.
4. Fill a large bowl with ice and place a smaller bowl on top. Strain the custard into the smaller bowl and whisk frequently until cool. Stir in the vanilla and nutmeg.

Fast: Can prepare up to 4 days in advance and refrigerate, or freeze for up to 6 months. Thaw in the refrigerator for 2 days or at room temperature for about 4 hours.

Flashy: Serve under Almond Mocha Ecstasy, or on crêpes, soufflés, or pound cake.

Fabulous: Replace the bourbon with any liqueur (rum, brandy, Scotch).

Pork Chop Elegance

This dinner party gets off to a grand start with two of my favorite hors d'oeuvres, Chèvre and Lox Torta and Florentine Croustades. They are scrumptious! They represent pure luxury and magnificent indulgence at its best.

The salad that follows is refreshing, combining toasty pecans with sweet tangerines to create flavor magic. The dressing, Fennel-Parmesan Vinaigrette, offers another flavor fantasy.

Speaking of surprises, we do not normally associate pork chops with elegance, but the two need not be mutually exclusive. Good pork, as far as I am concerned, is just as delicate as veal. So, instead of the predictable homey treatment, we handle them with an upscale approach, paired with a wonderful Green Peppercorn and Shiitake Sauce. The Barley and Orzo Pilaf will help you to savor every last drop of this sauce. Winter squash, served in an artichoke bottom, completes the color composition of the dinner plate, while also providing a bit of visual excitement. Our party concludes with a stately Poached Fruit Trifle.

The entire menu has a hint of traditional elegance running through it. To reflect this, you might use a black cloth. Floral chintz napkins with a black background and pink flowers along with pink camellias arranged in a crystal vase help to complete the look for this special table. Matching pink candles in round silver holders, and silver Mylar streamers scattered down the center of the table, provide the final touch.

MENU

Florentine Croustades

Chèvre and Lox Torta

Tossed Greens with Pecans and Tangerines

Sliced Baguette and Butter

Pork Chops with Green Peppercorn and Shiitake Sauce

Barley and Orzo Pilaf

Winter Squash in Artichoke Bottoms

Poached Fruit Trifle

FASTER & FLASHIER

Mini Quiche (purchased, frozen)

Tossed Greens with Pecans and Tangerines

Sliced Baguette and Butter

Pork Chops with Green Peppercorn and Shiitake Sauce

Buttered Orzo with Parsley

Baked Winter Squash with Balsamic Vinegar

Fruit Trifle (use frozen fruit and fruit-flavored yogurt instead of the custard)

WINES

Gewürztraminer or Champagne

Petite Sirah or Pinot Noir

Champagne

Fast & Fabulous Timetable

Up to 6 Months in Advance and Frozen
Croustades • Green Peppercorn and Shiitake Sauce through step 6 • Fruit and sauce for trifle

Up to 3 Months in Advance and Frozen
Florentine Croustade filling • Chèvre and Lox Torta • Brandied Whipped Cream

Up to 1 Week in Advance and Refrigerated
Croustades

5 Days in Advance and Refrigerated
Chèvre and Lox Torta • Fennel-Parmesan Vinaigrette

3 Days in Advance and Refrigerated
Florentine Croustade filling • Green Peppercorn and Shiitake Sauce through step 6 • Prepare fruit and sauce for trifle

2 Days in Advance and Refrigerated
Thaw frozen prepared-ahead foods • Marinate pork chops

1 Day in Advance and Refrigerated
Prep salad greens • Pork chops through step 5 • Barley and Orzo Pilaf • Winter Squash in Artichoke Bottoms through step 3 • Brandied Whipped Cream • Set table

Party Day!
Assemble croustades and hold at room temperature • Heat croustades • Toss salad • Warm bread • Bake pork, finish sauce • Heat artichoke bottoms and pilaf • Assemble trifle

FLORENTINE CROUSTADES

2 tablespoons unsalted butter

1 onion, minced

2 cloves garlic, minced

6 ounces mushrooms, minced
and squeezed in tea towel
to remove all excess
moisture

2 tablespoons all-purpose
flour

1/4 cup medium-dry sherry

3/4 cup heavy cream

One 8-ounce package frozen
spinach, thawed, squeezed
in tea towel to remove all
excess moisture, and
chopped

Salt and freshly ground white
pepper to taste

Dried thyme to taste

Freshly grated nutmeg to
taste

Croustades (see page 146)

1/2 to 1 cup grated Gruyère
cheese

Yield: fills about 60 croustades

Next time you want to prepare creamed spinach, use this filling.

1. Preheat the oven to 350°F.
2. Melt the butter in a saucepan over medium heat and sauté the onion, garlic, and mushrooms until the onions are tender.
3. Stir in the flour and cook 1 minute, without browning.
4. Mix in the sherry and cook for a minute more.
5. Remove the pan from the burner and stir in the cream. Return to the burner and add the spinach, salt, pepper, thyme, and nutmeg. Cook until the flavors develop and the mixture thickens.
6. Fill the croustades, place them on an ungreased cookie sheet, and top with the Gruyère. Bake until hot and bubbly about 10 minutes.

Fast: Can assemble up to 3 hours in advance, hold at room temperature, and bake just before serving. Can prepare filling up to 3 days in advance and refrigerate, or freeze for up to 3 months. Thaw in the refrigerator for 2 days or at room temperature for about 4 hours.

Fabulous: Add 1/2 cup minced ham or prosciutto to the filling. Instead of spinach, substitute chopped broccoli, chard, or asparagus.

CHÈVRE AND LOX TORTA

1/2 pound (2 sticks)
    unsalted butter, cut into
    pieces
8 ounces cream cheese
12 ounces chèvre cheese
1 shallot, chopped
2 to 4 tablespoons fresh
    lemon juice
Grated zest of 2 lemons
Freshly ground white pepper
    to taste
3/4 pound lox, or as much
    as your budget allows
1 cup minced green onions
2 bunches fresh dill, minced

Yield: about 4 cups

Sheer bliss!

1. Combine the first 7 ingredients in a food processor fitted with a metal blade or cream together in a large bowl. Taste and adjust the flavors.
2. Oil a 4- to 5-cup straight-sided mold, bowl, or container, or use a pâté terrine. Line with plastic wrap.
3. Layer in all the ingredients. I usually start with the lox, green onion, and dill, then the cheese mixture. Repeat until the container is full.
4. Fold plastic wrap over the top, press gently to compress the layers, and chill until firm, at least 1 hour.
5. Unmold and enjoy!

Fast: Can prepare up to 5 days in advance and refrigerate, or freeze for up to 3 months. Thaw in the refrigerator for 2 days.

Flashy: Serve on a platter with Bagel Chips (see page 203), crackers, and/or breads.

Fabulous: With all the layered ingredients mixed into the cheese and then molded.

Further: Toss leftovers into hot pasta or rice, or use instead of a sauce on fish.

TOSSED GREENS WITH PECANS AND TANGERINES

1 head romaine leaves

1 bunch spinach leaves, stemmed

1 head butter lettuce

1/2 to 1 cup pecan halves, toasted (see page 29)

4 to 6 tangerines, peeled, white pith removed, and divided into segments or thinly sliced

Fennel-Parmesan Vinaigrette (recipe follows)

Simply marvelous!

1. Combine all the ingredients in a large salad bowl and toss with the desired amount of dressing.

Fast: Can prep and mix together the greens, pecans, and tangerines up to 1 day in advance and refrigerate. Dress before serving.

Fabulous: With cooked shrimp or crab or sliced avocado or fennel bulb tossed in. With walnuts, almonds, pine nuts, or pumpkin seeds instead of the pecans.

FENNEL-PARMESAN VINAIGRETTE

2 to 4 tablespoons fennel seeds

4 1/2 teaspoons anchovy paste

4 to 6 cloves garlic

2 cups extra virgin olive oil

2/3 cup balsamic vinegar

2 teaspoons Szechuan peppercorns

2 teaspoons green peppercorns

1/2 cup freshly grated Parmesan cheese

Yield: about 2 2/3 cups

A very distinctive dressing.

1. Combine all the ingredients in a food processor fitted with a metal blade or in a blender.
2. Taste and adjust the seasonings.

Fast: Can prepare up to 5 days in advance and refrigerate.

Fabulous: With sherry wine vinegar instead of balsamic. With minced fresh rosemary or cilantro instead of fennel seeds.

PORK CHOPS WITH GREEN PEPPERCORN AND SHIITAKE SAUCE

8 boneless pork sirloin chops,
    at least 1 inch thick

MARINADE
2 cups buttermilk
1 cup olive oil
3 to 8 cloves garlic, smashed
    or chopped
1 to 2 tablespoons green
    peppercorns, crushed
Grated zest of 2 lemons
Juice from 1 to 2 lemons
1 to 3 tablespoons minced
    fresh ginger

Peanut, canola, or grapeseed
    oil as needed
Green Peppercorn and
    Shiitake Sauce (recipe
    follows)
Flowering kale leaves and/or
    minced fresh parsley for
    garnish

This is an uptown pork chop.

1. Place the pork in a glass or ceramic pan.
2. Combine all the marinade ingredients, then pour over the pork. Cover with plastic wrap, and let marinate at room temperature for 2 hours, or up to 48 hours refrigerated.
3. Remove the pork from the marinade and blot dry with paper towels.
4. Preheat the oven to 350°F.
5. Heat enough oil to coat the bottom of a large, heavy skillet over high heat and quickly brown the pork on each side. Do this in batches, adding more oil as needed. Overcrowding will prevent proper browning.
6. Transfer the browned pork to an ovenproof pan, top with the sauce, and bake until cooked through, about 20 to 30 minutes. Properly cooked pork has a slight trace of pink to it.
7. Place the meat on a warm serving platter and finish the sauce.

Fast: Can prepare through step 5 up to 1 day in advance and refrigerate.

Flashy: Garnish with flowering kale leaves and sprinkle minced parsley over the top.

Fabulous: With a combination of any dried and fresh mushrooms. With pink or Szechuan peppercorns combined with or instead of the green peppercorns.

Further: Cut leftover pork into thin slices and warm in leftover sauce. Serve over risotto, bow-tie pasta, or couscous.

GREEN PEPPERCORN AND SHIITAKE SAUCE

4 tablespoons (1/2 stick)
    unsalted butter
6 to 10 shallots, thinly sliced
1 tablespoon minced or
    thinly sliced fresh ginger
2 tablespoons green
    peppercorns or to taste,
    crushed in the palm of
    your hand
1/2 pound button
    mushrooms, halved, or
    medium-size mushrooms,
    quartered
2 to 3 ounces dried shiitake
    mushrooms
2 cups chicken broth,
    homemade or canned
1/2 cup Madeira
1 bay leaf
1/4 cup minced prosciutto
Finely grated zest of 1 lemon
1 tablespoon cornstarch
    dissolved in 2 tablespoons
    Madeira
1/2 to 1 cup heavy cream

Yield: about 3 cups

This is an unbelievably delicious sauce—full of interesting flavor nuances. Use it to enhance anything from pasta to chicken breasts. I suggest you make a double batch so guests can have more, or to keep on hand in the freezer.

1. Melt the butter in a large saucepan over medium to medium-high heat and sauté the shallots, ginger, peppercorns, and button mushrooms until the shallots are golden.
2. In a covered bowl, rehydrate the shiitake mushrooms in the chicken broth by microwaving for about 4 minutes on low power or this can also be done in a saucepan over low heat.
3. Thinly slice the mushrooms when cool enough to handle and add to the other saucepan.
4. Strain (use a gold coffee filter or a fine sieve) the grit out of the chicken broth and add to the saucepan.
5. Bring the mixture to a boil, then add the Madeira, bay leaf, and prosciutto.
6. Stir the dissolved cornstarch mixture and zest into the boiling sauce. Continue to cook, while stirring, for about 30 to 60 seconds.
7. After the pork chops finish cooking, transfer the sauce to a saucepan. Whisk in the cream and bring to a boil. Cook, whisking, until the sauce reduces enough to coat the back of a spoon. Taste and adjust the seasonings. Serve on the side.

Fast: Can prepare through step 6 up to 3 days in advance and refrigerate or freeze for up to 6 months. Thaw in the refrigerator for 2 days or at room temperature for about 8 hours.

Fabulous: On rice, couscous, wild rice, barley, pasta, chicken, or beef. With pink and/or Szechuan peppercorns with or instead of the green peppercorns.

BARLEY AND ORZO PILAF

4 tablespoons (1/2 stick)
   unsalted butter
4 shallots, minced
2 cups quick-cooking barley
1/2 cup sherry
5 1/2 cups chicken broth,
   homemade or canned
1 bay leaf or several fresh
   sage leaves
Freshly grated Parmesan
   cheese to taste
1 cup orzo, cooked al dente
   according to package
   instructions
Salt and freshly ground white
   pepper to taste

This dish has an interesting texture and is a good alternative to rice. As an added bonus it is high in fiber. If you have not yet tried the new quick-cooking barley, you will be pleasantly surprised.

1. Melt the butter in a saucepan over medium to medium-low heat and sauté the shallots until tender.
2. Stir in the barley until coated with the butter.
3. Add the sherry, broth, and bay leaf. Bring to a boil, cover, and cook over low heat for about 10 minutes.
4. Stir in the orzo and Parmesan cheese. Taste and adjust the seasonings.

Fast: Can fully prepare up to 1 day in advance and refrigerate. Bring to room temperature and reheat in a preheated 350°F oven for about 30 minutes or in a microwave for 10 to 20 minutes, adding more broth if necessary. Or can prepare through step 3 up to 1 day in advance and refrigerate. Finish cooking before serving.

Fabulous: With sliced mushrooms, leeks, and/or marinated artichokes mixed in at step 4.

Further: Use leftovers in salads and soups.

WINTER SQUASH IN ARTICHOKE BOTTOMS

1 1/2 pounds winter squash
(butternut, banana,
hubbard, acorn), halved
and seeded

1/4 cup balsamic vinegar or
to taste

1/4 cup orange-flavored
liqueur

1 shallot, chopped

1 to 2 teaspoons dried
marjoram

4 tablespoons (1/2 stick)
unsalted butter

1/4 cup cream cheese

2 to 4 tablespoons poppy
seeds

2 tablespoons packed light or
dark brown sugar or to
taste

Salt and freshly ground white
pepper to taste

Freshly grated nutmeg to
taste

16 artichoke bottoms, cooked
(fresh, frozen, or in jars)

A lovely way to serve a pureed vegtable.

1. Sprinkle the squash with the balsamic vinegar and place on a microwaveable or ovenproof plate. Cover with plastic wrap and microwave until very tender, about 8 minutes, or place in a preheated 375°F oven for about 40 minutes.

2. Scoop the squash out and place in a food processor fitted with a metal blade or a bowl. Add the remaining ingredients, except the artichoke bottoms, and process well or combine with an electric mixer. Taste and adjust the seasonings.

3. Fill the artichoke bottoms with the mixture, using a spoon or pastry bag.

4. Heat before serving in a preheated 350°F oven for about 10 minutes, or covered with plastic wrap in a microwave until hot about 5 minutes over high power.

Fast: Can prepare through step 3 up to 1 day in advance and refrigerate.

Fabulous: With dried thyme or sage instead of marjoram. Served without the artichokes. With sesame instead of poppy seeds. Prepared with carrots or sweet potatoes instead of squash.

Further: Add chicken broth to the leftover squash for a fantastic soup.

POACHED FRUIT TRIFLE

POACHED FRUIT

2 cups water

1/4 cup liqueur (Tuaca, Benedictine, or Grand Marnier)

2 cups cream or regular sherry

1 vanilla bean, split lengthwise

1 cup sugar or to taste

Grated zest of 1 orange

Grated zest of 1 lemon

1 cup dried apricots

Freshly grated nutmeg to taste

2 tart green apples, peeled, cored, sliced, and squirted with lemon juice

4 to 5 ripe, but firm pears, squirted with lemon juice

CUSTARD

Strained poaching liquid from fruit

1 cup heavy cream

1/4 cup brandy

3 large egg yolks

1 tablespoon cornstarch

1 teaspoon vanilla extract

Freshly grated nutmeg to taste

1 tablespoon unsalted butter

1 tablespoon Poire Williams or other pear-flavored liqueur

Here is a delicious and versatile dessert recipe. Adapt it to any fruit in season. Looks long and complicated, but it's a snap!

1. To poach the fruit, place the first 10 ingredients into a large saucepan and bring to a boil over high heat. Reduce the heat to medium-low and simmer for about 20 minutes.
2. Peel, core, and slice the pears and add them to the poaching liquid. Reduce the heat to low and cook gently for 10 to 15 minutes.
3. Cool to room temperature. Strain the fruit from the sauce, reserve, and return the sauce to the saucepan.
4. To prepare the custard, bring the poaching liquid and cream to a boil over medium-high to high heat. Cook until reduced by about half and the pears are just tender, then add the brandy and continue to simmer over medium to medium-high heat.
5. Meanwhile, place the egg yolks and cornstarch in a food processor fitted with a metal blade, or in a blender. Add one or two ladles of the hot poaching liquid to the food processor through the feed tube while the machine is running and process well.
6. Turn the heat down to low and make sure the liquid is not boiling. Whisk the egg yolk mixture back into the saucepan. Cook, whisking constantly, until thickened enough for the custard to coat the back of a spoon about 10 minutes.
7. Whisk in the vanilla, nutmeg, butter, and liqueur.
8. Transfer to a metal or plastic bowl, cover with plastic wrap, and chill in the freezer for about 30 minutes.
9. To assemble, layer in the ingredients in a large glass bowl or special trifle bowl. Start with the poundcake, then the fruit and custard. Repeat until the bowl is filled.
10. Garnish each serving with a dollop of Brandied Whipped Cream, Brandied Chocolate Sauce, Raspberry Sauce, and/or pansies.

Fast: Can prepare fruit and sauce up to 3 days in advance and refrigerate, or freeze for up to 6 months. Thaw in the refrigerator for 2 days or at room temperature for about 4 hours. Can assemble trifle 6 hours in advance, cover with plastic wrap, and chill.

Flashy: Top a purchased or homemade shortcake or puff pastry, or fill

ASSEMBLY
Poundcake (purchased)
Brandied Whipped Cream
*   (recipe follows)*
Brandied Chocolate Sauce
*   (see page 141)*
Raspberry Variation of
*   Boysenberry Sauce (see*
*   page 116)*
Pansies for garnish

a crêpe with some of the custard, then the fruit. Can also serve without a base, in goblets.

Fabulous: With butter cookies or shortbread instead of poundcake.

BRANDIED WHIPPED CREAM

2 cups heavy cream
1/4 cup brandy
1/4 cup packed light or dark
*   brown sugar*
2 teaspoons vanilla extract
2 pinches of cream of tartar
Freshly grated nutmeg to
*   taste*

Yield: about 4 cups

This is definitely the stuff fantasies are made of.

1. Process the cream in a food processor fitted with a metal blade, or in a bowl with an electric mixer until it begins to thicken.
2. Add the brandy, brown sugar, vanilla, and cream of tartar and process until it holds firm peaks.
3. Taste and adjust the flavors. Transfer to a bowl or container, cover, and chill.

Fast: Can prepare up to 1 day in advance and refrigerate, or freeze for up to 3 months. Thaw in the refrigerator for 2 days.

Flashy: Garnish with a sprinkling of grated nutmeg over the top.

Fabulous: Flavored with almost any kind of spirits instead of the brandy.

Gingered Mango-Scallop Dinner

When you find yourself longing for spring's arrival and have exploited winter's charms to the fullest, this is the dinner party for you. It embodies spring's flirtatious spirit and sensuality, while still paying a bit of respect to winter. It is a way to coax the new season's arrival and help to celebrate the the culmination of present season.

We start this party off with Caviar Filled Shells. It is another one of those recipe that lets even the noncook shine. Besides, it is good enough to be illegal. The Hearts of Palm and Shrimp Salad is another magnificent flavor match.

Exotic-but-easy is the thematic thread running through this menu. The entree, Scallops in Mango-Ginger Sauce definitely falls into that category. Curried Rice and Sautéed Celery with Capers and Almonds are served with the entree. Both delicious, they act as nice complements. Celery is a vegetable that is overlooked. It is light, refreshing, and has a delightful crunch when prepared in this manner. In the winter, when many vegetables begin to look lackluster, it is a great choice.

For dessert, we serve a Chocolate Orange Paté. What a winning recipe this is—it is so elegant, yet takes only a few minutes to assemble, and can even be frozen.

As for the tablescape, I use a chintz cloth in a cabbage rose pattern and matching napkins. Instead of flower arrangements, I use small blooming hydrangeas in mauve pots. White votive candles in clear glass holders can be scattered down the table, making the whole table feel just like spring!

MENU

Caviar Filled Shells

Hearts of Palm and Shrimp Salad

Baguette with Lemon-Dill Butter

Scallops in Mango-Ginger Sauce

Curried Rice

Sautéed Celery with Capers and Almonds

Chocolate Orange Paté

FASTER & FLASHIER

Caviar and Saint André Cheese with Water Crackers

Hearts of Palm and Shrimp Salad

Scallops in a Mango-Ginger Sauce

Rice Seasoned with Curry Powder

Peas with Dill (frozen)

Dessert (purchased)

WINES

Champagne, Chardonnay, or Sauvignon Blanc

Chardonnay

Tawny Port

Fast & Fabulous Timetable

Up to 6 Months in Advance and Frozen
   Chocolate Orange Paté

Up to 3 Months in Advance and Frozen
   Mango-Ginger Sauce

Up to 1 Month in Advance and Frozen
   Vanilla Sauce

5 Days in Advance and Refrigerated
   Chocolate Orange Paté

3 Days in Advance and Refrigerated
   Mango-Ginger Sauce • Vanilla Sauce

2 Days in Advance and Refrigerated
   Blanch celery • Thaw frozen prepared-ahead foods

1 Day in Advance and Refrigerated
   Caviar Filled Shells • Salad through step 2 • Scallops through step 2
   • Curried Rice through step 2 • Set table

Party Day!
   Assemble salad • Warm bread • Finish scallops • Curried Rice • Heat
   celery and sauce

CAVIAR FILLED SHELLS

24 to 32 large pasta shells
Salt to taste
Olive oil
1 pound Saint André cheese,
    at room temperature
3 1/2 ounces black or
    golden caviar
2 to 3 hard-cooked eggs,
    mashed
1/4 cup minced fresh chives
Finely grated zest of 2
    lemons
Fried Chinese cellophane
    noodles or finely shredded
    red cabbage for garnish

I'm convinced this is too good and too easy to be legal!

1. Cook the pasta al dente in large pot of salted water. Drain well and toss in 2 tablespoons of olive oil. Let cool to room temperature.
2. Fill the shells with Saint André and top with caviar, a sprinkling of egg, and/or chives, and a piece of lemon zest.

Fast: Can prepare up to 1 day in advance and refrigerate.

Flashy: Served on a bed of fried Chinese cellophane noodles or finely shredded red cabbage.

Fabulous: Substitute chopped toasted (see page 29) almonds or pine nuts, or chopped smoked trout for the caviar.

HEARTS OF PALM AND SHRIMP SALAD

16 hearts of palm, sliced into
    thin rounds
2 cups cooked baby shrimp
2 to 4 bunches watercress,
    stemmed
1/2 cup minced fresh parsley
Two 5-ounce cans water
    chestnuts, drained and
    chopped
8 green onions, minced
1/2 cup capers, rinsed and
    drained
Tarragon Vinaigrette (see
    page 47)
Salt and freshly ground white
    pepper to taste
Butter lettuce leaves to line
    salad plates
Avocado slices, about 4 per
    person (squirt liberally
    with fresh lemon juice to
    prevent discoloring)
Johnny-jump-ups for garnish

A world-class salad!

1. Toss together the first seven ingredients in a large bowl.
2. Add the desired amount of vinaigrette and toss. Taste and adjust the seasonings.
3. Line the salad plates with the lettuce leaves, then top with some of the shrimp salad and surround with avocado slices.

Fast: Can prepare through step 2 up to 1 day in advance and refrigerate. Can assemble up to 4 hours in advance.

Flashy: Garnish with Johnny-jump-ups or any other nontoxic flower and/or fresh herb sprigs.

Fabulous: With cooked lobster, tuna, crab, or chicken instead of the shrimp.

SCALLOPS IN MANGO-GINGER SAUCE

2 to 3 pounds bay scallops,
  or sea scallops, sliced
Milk to cover
4 tablespoons (1/2 stick)
  unsalted butter
2 tablespoons grapeseed or
  peanut oil
2 shallots, minced
2 tablespoons minced fresh
  ginger
Flour
Salt and freshly ground white
  pepper to taste
Mango-Ginger Sauce (recipe
  follows)
Mango, papaya, and/or
  persimmon slices for
  garnish
Minced fresh cilantro or
  sprigs for garnish

1. Rinse scallops and put in bowl. Add milk to cover the scallops and refrigerate for at least 1 hour to remove any bitterness.
2. Melt the butter with the oil in a large skillet over medium-low heat and sauté the shallots and ginger for a few minutes, until tender.
3. Drain the scallops, and rinse. Lightly coat with flour and quickly sauté in the pan with the shallots and ginger. You may need to do this in several batches so as not to overcrowd them. Cook just until they start to turn opaque and begin to firm up. It will take a matter of seconds per side.
4. Combine the scallops with the warm mango-ginger sauce and cook for a minute—enjoy!

Fast: Can prepare through step 3 up to 1 day in advance and refrigerate. Bring to room temperature, heat the sauce, add the scallops, and gently warm until hot. This should take only a few minutes.

Flashy: Serve on rice and garnish with several slices of fruit and minced cilantro.

Fabulous: With swordfish, pork, or turkey, instead of the scallops, cut into small scallops or chunks and sautéed as directed. Served on couscous or pasta instead of rice.

MANGO-GINGER SAUCE

4 tablespoons (1/2 stick)
   unsalted butter

6 to 8 cloves garlic

4 to 8 leeks, white part only,
   sliced into long thin slices

2 teaspoons fennel seeds

One 1-inch piece fresh ginger
   or to taste, peeled and
   minced or pureed

1/2 cup prepared
   mango-ginger chutney

1/2 cup sherry

1 cup chicken broth,
   homemade or canned

1 teaspoon ground coriander

1 cup heavy cream

1/2 cup chopped fresh
   cilantro

1/2 cup walnuts, toasted
   (see page 29) and
   chopped

Salt and freshly ground white
   pepper to taste

Don't let the less than beautiful color upset you. The flavor more than compensates for it.

1. Melt the butter in a large saucepan over medium-low heat and sauté the garlic, leeks, fennel seeds, and ginger until softened, about 5 minutes.

2. Stir in the chutney, sherry, broth, and coriander. Bring to a boil over medium-high to high heat and cook until reduced by about a third.

3. Stir in the cream and bring back to a boil. Cook until reduced slightly and the flavors are pleasing.

4. Stir in the cilantro and walnuts. Season to taste and cook until the sauce thickens.

Fast: Can prepare up to 3 days in advance and refrigerate, or freeze for up to 3 months. Thaw in the refrigerator for 2 days or at room temperature for about 4 hours.

CURRIED RICE

4 tablespoons (1/2 stick)
  unsalted butter
1 onion, thinly sliced
1 tablespoon minced fresh
  ginger or to taste
1/2 to 1 red jalapeño
  pepper, seeded, deveined,
  and chopped
Grated zest of 1 lemon (or
  minced lemon grass if you
  can get it)
1 teaspoon curry powder or
  to taste
2 cups uncooked long grain
  white rice
4 cups chicken broth,
  homemade or canned

This is out of this world!

1. Melt the butter in a large saucepan over medium-low heat and sauté the onion, ginger, jalapeño, and zest until the onion is tender.
2. Stir in the curry powder and rice. Stir for a few minutes to coat the rice.
3. Add the chicken broth. Bring to a boil over high heat, cover with a lid, reduce the heat to low, and cook for 20 minutes. Fluff with a fork.

Fast: Can prepare through step 2 up to 1 day in advance and refrigerate. Bring to room temperature and finish cooking before serving.

Flashy: With fish, lamb, or seafood.

Fabulous: With a pinch of saffron and/or 1/2 cup unsweetened shredded coconut. With couscous instead of rice.

Further: Use leftovers in salads.

SAUTÉED CELERY WITH CAPERS AND ALMONDS

16 stalks celery
6 tablespoons (3/4 stick)
  unsalted butter
1/4 cup capers, rinsed and
  drained
1/2 cup slivered almonds,
  toasted (see page 29)
3/4 tablespoon minced fresh
  parsley
2 tablespoons chopped
  shallots
Salt and freshly ground white
  pepper to taste
Fresh lemon juice to taste

1. Place the celery in a large pot of boiling salted water. Cook until barely tender, about 4 to 5 minutes. Remove to a colander set under cold running water until the celery is cool to the touch. Drain well. Cut the celery into 2-inch pieces.
2. Heat the butter in a large frying pan over medium heat and sauté the celery, capers, almonds, parsley, and shallots until hot, about 7 minutes.
3. Taste and season with the salt, pepper, and lemon juice.

Fast: Can blanch the celery up to 2 days in advance and refrigerate. Allow it to come to room temperature before proceeding with the recipe.

Fabulous: Substitute olive oil for the butter. Serve either hot or at room temperature.

CHOCOLATE ORANGE PATÉ

5 large egg yolks (see page 23)

1 1/3 cups unsweetened cocoa powder

2 to 4 tablespoons Scotch, brandy, bourbon, or rum

1 1/2 to 1 3/4 cups confectioners' sugar

6 to 8 ounces good quality bittersweet chocolate, chopped

1/4 pound (1 stick) unsalted butter, cut up

Freshly grated nutmeg to taste

2 cups heavy cream

1 teaspoon vanilla extract

Finely grated zest of 2 oranges

Raspberries and/or any other berry, fresh or frozen

Sprigs fresh mint and Vanilla Sauce (recipe follows) for garnish

Guaranteed to leave you speechless.

1. Whip the yolks with the cocoa, Scotch, and sugar in a food processor fitted with a metal blade or with an electric mixer.
2. Combine the chocolate with the butter and melt in a microwave or over simmering water on top of a double boiler.
3. Add the chocolate mixture to the egg mixture and combine well.
4. Add the nutmeg, cream, vanilla, and zest and mix just until combined.
5. Pour the mixture into an oiled and plastic-wrap lined 2 1/2-quart tureen or soufflé dish. Cover with plastic wrap and refrigerate until set, about 4 hours.
6. Unmold, slice, and serve.

Fast: Can prepare up to 5 days in advance and refrigerate or freeze for up to 6 months. Thaw in the refrigerator for 2 days.

Flashy: Serve with fresh or thawed frozen raspberries, or fresh mint sprigs, and vanilla sauce.

Fabulous: With toasted pecans or almonds mixed into the paté.

NOTE: Because of the recent problem with eggs containing salmonella, it is important to buy eggs that have been refrigerated. Do not use eggs that you have had for more than 5 weeks and *always* keep them refrigerated.

VANILLA SAUCE

1 pint premium quality
    vanilla ice cream
1/4 cup orange-flavored
    liqueur
Finely minced zest of 2
    oranges

Yield: about 2 1/4 cups

1. Place the ice cream in a bowl and allow to soften for about 20 minutes at room temperature.
2. Mix in the liqueur and zest.

Fast: Can prepare up to 3 days in advance and refrigerate or up to 1 month and freeze. Let sit at room temperature for about 40 to 60 minutes before serving.

Flashy: With any kind of cake, pie, tart, or mousse.

Fabulous: With any type of liqueur.

CASUAL WINTER MENUS
· · · · · · · · · · · · · · · · · · · ·

Seafood Cannelloni Dinner

There's no need to stop entertaining after the holidays are over, but there is a need to do so without a lot of fuss. The correct prescription is casual, relaxed menus. The food should not be very heavy, since most people are recuperating from mountains of holiday mashed potatoes and stuffing. This is not to say that the menu should not be satisfying and somewhat indulgent. After all, it is cold and dreary and the need to brighten our spirits and nurture our souls is prevalent.

This menu is based on seafood, making it light, but rich in flavor. To characterize it as simply "casual" would be incorrect. It is "casually elegant." It need not be reserved for après-holiday parties. It is just as welcome during the holiday entertaining season.

The dinner party begins with a magnificently flavored cheese mixture. This is followed by a salad based on the combination of astringent greens with a classically simple red wine vinaigrette. It is cleansing and refreshing. The entree is a delightful mix of spinach, scallops, and cheeses wrapped in an egg roll wrapper. Egg roll wrappers are a great way to avoid making crêpes or pasta without sacrificing any quality. The cannelloni is served with peas seasoned with pancetta and pine nuts. This unique vegetable dish is full of interesting and delicious flavors and textures.

For the look of your table, think in terms of comfort and contrast—contrast to the weather. The goal is to create an environment that projects a bright, positive spirit. For this party, a bold black-and-white checked cloth with black dinner plates makes a striking seasonal statement. Instead of a more predictable flower arrangement, try potted primroses in baskets spray-painted glossy black—they will create instant spring fever among your guests. For a more manicured look put sphagnum moss all around the edges of the baskets. Place these baskets down the center of the table. In the middle, a large, square, terra-cotta saucer filled with white pillar candles looks sensational.

MENU

Potted Camembert

Escarole, Endive, and Watercress Salad with Red Wine Vinaigrette

French Rolls and Butter

Seafood Cannelloni

Peas with Pancetta and Pine Nuts

Dilled Couscous and Bulgur

Almond-Pear Cake

FASTER & FLASHIER

Camembert and Crackers

Tossed Salad with Red Wine Vinaigrette

French Rolls and Butter

Seafood Cannelloni (use frozen spinach or chard, and prepared marinara sauce)

Dessert (purchased)

WINES

Champagne (Extra Dry)

Chardonnay

Late harvest Riesling

Fast & Fabulous Timetable

Up to 6 Months in Advance and Frozen
Potted Camembert • Tomato-Cream Sauce

Up to 3 Months in Advance and Frozen
Cannelloni through step 10 • Almond-Pear Cake • Brandied Chocolate Sauce

5 Days in Advance and Refrigerated
Potted Camembert • Red Wine Vinaigrette

3 Days in Advance and Refrigerated
White Wine Sauce

2 Days in Advance and Refrigerated
Tomato-Cream Sauce • Dilled Couscous and Bulgur • Thaw frozen prepared-ahead foods

1 Day in Advance and Refrigerated
Prep salad greens • Cannelloni through step 10 • Peas with Pancetta and Pine Nuts through step 1 • Almond-Pear Cake • Set Table

Party Day!
Toss salad • Warm bread • Bake cannelloni • Heat peas and couscous

POTTED CAMEMBERT

1/2 pound Camembert
1/4 pound (1 stick) unsalted
  butter
1 to 2 tablespoons brandy or
  bourbon
1/2 to 1 shallot, chopped
Freshly ground white pepper
  to taste
Fresh sprigs rosemary and
  toasted (see page 29)
  sliced almonds for garnish

Yield: about 1 1/2 cups

This is a great way to use up all of those dribs and drabs of camembert or Brie. Store them in the freezer until you have collected enough.

1. Combine the cheese, butter, brandy, and shallot in a food processor fitted with a metal blade and process until smooth, or cream together in a large bowl. Taste and adjust the seasonings.
2. Pack in a crock or serving bowl and chill until firm, at least 1 hour.

Fast: Can prepare up to 5 days in advance and refrigerate, or freeze for up to 6 months. Thaw in the refrigerator for 1 day or at room temperature for about 4 hours.

Flashy: Garnish with rosemary and almonds and serve with Bagel Chips (page 203), thinly sliced baguettes, or crackers. Serve as is or unmold.

Fabulous: Substitute Brie for camembert. Topped with green, black, and/or pink peppercorns.

Further: Toss into hot pasta or place a dollop on grilled steak.

ESCAROLE, ENDIVE, AND WATERCRESS SALAD WITH RED WINE VINAIGRETTE

1 head escarole, torn into bite-size pieces

2 to 4 Belgian endive, thinly sliced

1 bunch watercress, stemmed

6 to 8 green onions, thinly sliced

Red Wine Vinaigrette (recipe follows)

Salt and freshly ground black pepper to taste

A simple and cleansing salad that will be equally appreciated with a casual or more formal menu.

1. Place the escarole, endive, watercress, and onions in a large salad bowl and toss.
2. Add the desired amount of dressing, toss well, taste, and season with salt and pepper.

Fast: Can wash and prepare all salad greens up to 1 day in advance and refrigerate.

Flashy: On chilled salad plates.

Fabulous: With crumbled bleu cheese, sliced pears (squirted with lemon juice to avoid discoloration) or tangerines, sliced fennel bulb, mushrooms, celery root, and/or toasted nuts mixed in.

RED WINE VINAIGRETTE

1/2 cup good quality red wine vinegar

2 cups extra virgin or pure olive oil

2 cloves garlic or to taste

Salt and freshly ground white and black pepper to taste

Minced fresh or dried herbs to taste

Yield: about 2 1/2 cups

A classic!

1. Place the vinegar, oil, and garlic in a food processor fitted with a metal blade, or in a blender and process well.
2. Taste and season with salt, pepper, and herbs.

Fast: Can prepare up to 5 days in advance and refrigerate.

Flashy: On anything from seafood to salad greens.

Fabulous: With different oils, 2 tablespoons minced fresh herbs, or more, of your choice, 1 to 2 tablespoons prepared mustard, or 1 teaspoon, or more, dried mustard.

SEAFOOD CANNELLONI

4 tablespoons (1/2 stick)
  unsalted butter
1/4 cup olive oil
1 onion, chopped
2 to 4 cloves garlic, chopped
1/4 cup minced fresh parsley
1/2 pound mushrooms,
  thinly sliced
1/4 cup dry vermouth
1 pound scallops, soaked in
  milk, refrigerated, for at
  least 1 hour to prevent
  bitterness
1 pound shrimp, shelled and
  deveined
1/2 cup plus extra freshly
  grated Parmesan cheese
1/2 cup ricotta cheese
1 cup crumbled feta cheese
1 large egg
Two 10-ounce packages
  frozen spinach, thawed
  and squeezed to remove
  excess moisture
Salt and freshly ground white
  pepper to taste
Freshly grated nutmeg to
  taste
Dried Italian herbs to taste
Tomato-Cream Sauce
  (recipe follows)
2 packages egg roll wrappers
  (freeze the leftovers for
  later use)
Minced fresh parsley for
  garnish

Yield: about 30 cannelloni

An interesting and lighter variation of the classic cannelloni.

You will be amazed by how well the egg roll wrappers work. Since this recipe makes so many, you will be able to stock your freezer at the same time as you prepare for the party.

1. Melt half the butter with half the olive oil in a large skillet over low to medium-low heat and sauté the onion, garlic, and parsley until tender. Do not brown.
2. Add the mushrooms and vermouth and cook until all the liquid, including that released from the mushrooms, is evaporated.
3. Cut the scallops and shrimp into small dice. Rinse and drain in a colander. Melt the remaining butter and olive oil in another large skillet over high heat and sauté them very rapidly for about 4 minutes. Do not cook fully. Remove from the heat and reserve.
4. Combine 1/2 cup of the Parmesan with the ricotta, feta, and egg in a food processor fitted with a metal blade or in a bowl with a wooden spoon.
5. Process or mix in the spinach and season with salt, pepper, nutmeg, and herbs.
6. Add the cooked mushroom mixture and mix in or process in with several quick on-and-off motions, so as not to destroy the texture.
7. Stir in the scallops and shrimp. Taste and adjust the seasonings.
8. Coat a shallow baking dish with some of the tomato-cream sauce and preheat the oven to 350°F.
9. Place several tablespoons of the filling in the middle of an egg roll wrapper and fold like an envelope or a crêpe. Moisten the edges lightly with water and seal. Place sealed-side down in the baking dish and repeat until all the filling is used.
10. Coat with the remaining sauce and sprinkle extra Parmesan cheese on top.
11. Bake until hot and bubbly, about 30 minutes.

Fast: Can prepare through step 10 up to 1 day in advance and refrigerate, or freeze for up to 3 months. Thaw in the refrigerator for 2 days or at room temperature for about 4 hours.

Flashy: Garnish with a sprinkling of minced parsley.

Fabulous: With your own crêpes, if you have time, or using flour tortillas instead of the egg roll wrappers. With crab, monkfish, or chicken instead of, or with, the scallops and shrimp. With sliced shiitake and/or oyster mushrooms added. With about 1 cup of cubed jicama mixed in for texture.

Further: Use extra filling to stuff pasta shells, or as an hors d'oeuvre in Croustades (see page 146), mushrooms, or Won Ton Cups (see page 47).

TOMATO-CREAM SAUCE

4 tablespoons (1/2 stick)
    unsalted butter
2 to 4 cloves garlic, crushed
    or minced
2 to 4 shallots, minced
1/4 cup minced fresh parsley
1/4 cup all-purpose flour
1/2 cup brandy
1 cup dry vermouth
2 cups chicken broth,
    homemade or canned
2 cups bottled clam juice or
    homemade fish stock
1 bay leaf
Grated zest of 1 lemon
1/2 to 1 teaspoon dried
    thyme
1/2 to 1 teaspoon dried
    tarragon
1/2 cup tomato paste
1 cup heavy cream
Salt and freshly ground white
    pepper to taste
Freshly grated nutmeg to
    taste

Yield: about 5 cups

A delicious sauce for any fish or seafood.

1. In a large saucepan, melt the butter over low to medium-low heat and sauté the garlic, shallots, and parsley until tender.
2. Whisk in the flour and cook for several minutes.
3. Add the brandy, vermouth, broth, and clam juice, along with the bay leaf, zest, thyme, and tarragon. Bring to a boil and simmer over medium to medium-high heat until flavors are pleasing, about 5 to 10 minutes.
4. Add the tomato paste, cream, salt, pepper, and nutmeg. Continue reducing until the sauce attains a pleasing consistency, about 5 minutes.

Fast: Can prepare up to 2 days in advance and refrigerate, or freeze for up to 6 months. Thaw in the refrigerator for 2 days or at room temperature for about 4 hours.

Fabulous: On anything from fish to seafood pasta.

PEAS WITH PANCETTA AND PINE NUTS

1/4 cup olive oil

4 ounces pancetta, cut into thin strips

2 to 4 shallots, minced

2 pounds frozen baby peas, thawed

Salt and freshly ground white pepper to taste

Freshly grated nutmeg to taste

1/4 cup pine nuts, toasted (see page 29)

One of the few convenience foods I use are frozen peas. Often, they are better than fresh ones and there is no waste.

1. Heat the olive oil in a large skillet over low to medium-low heat and sauté the pancetta and shallots until the pancetta has browned.

2. Stir in the peas, season with salt, pepper, and nutmeg and cook over medium-high to high heat just until the peas are hot, about 5 minutes, stirring frequently. The peas can also be cooked in a preheated 350°F oven for about 10 minutes, or in a microwave according to the package instructions.

3. Add the pine nuts and serve.

Fast: Can prepare through step 1 up to 1 day in advance and refrigerate.

Fabulous: Seasoned with thyme or marjoram and freshly grated Parmesan cheese. With fresh string beans instead of peas.

Further: Toss leftovers into pasta, rice, or soup.

DILLED COUSCOUS AND BULGUR

4 tablespoons (1/2 stick) unsalted butter

2 shallots, minced

1/2 cup minced fresh dill

1 cup uncooked couscous

1 cup uncooked bulgur

1/2 cup sherry

4 cups chicken broth, homemade or canned

Salt and freshly ground white pepper to taste

This is a wonderful side dish. It is quick to prepare and has great flavor and texture, as well as being healthful.

1. Melt the butter in a large saucepan over low to medium-low heat and sauté the shallots until tender. Do not brown.

2. Add the dill, couscous, and bulgur, stirring to coat with the butter and shallots, and sauté for a minute.

3. Stir in the remaining ingredients and bring to a boil. Cover with a lid, turn the heat off, and let sit for about 10 minutes.

Fast: Can prepare completely, or just through step 2, up to 2 days in advance and refrigerate. Reheat in the microwave at high power for about 10 minutes or over simmering water in a double boiler, adding more liquid if necessary.

Fabulous: With any herb instead of dill.

ALMOND-PEAR CAKE

7 ounces almond paste

Grated zest of 2 lemons

1/2 cup packed light or dark
brown sugar

1/4 pound (1 stick) unsalted
butter, cut into 8 pieces

2 tablespoons kirsch

Freshly grated nutmeg to
taste

3 large eggs

1/4 teaspoon baking powder

1/4 cup cake flour

1 red bosc pear, cut into 8
slices and squirted with
lemon juice

1/2 cup almonds, toasted
(see page 29) and
chopped

Brandied Chocolate Sauce
(see page 141)

Yield: one 8-inch cake

This recipe was inspired by Narsai David's Almond Cake. I fell in love with it, and think you'll understand why when you taste it. It is unbelievably simple to prepare, yet rich and indulgent.

1. Preheat the oven to 350°F. Butter and flour an 8-inch cake pan.
2. Combine the almond paste, zest, sugar, and butter in a food processor fitted with a metal blade or cream together in a bowl with an electric mixer.
3. Process or beat in the kirsch, nutmeg, eggs, and baking powder.
4. Add the cake flour and process or beat in just until combined; do not overprocess.
5. Line the cake pan with the pear slices, arranged in a concentric circle.
6. Pour the cake batter on top of the pears.
7. Sprinkle the almonds over the top and bake for 40 to 50 minutes, or until a tester inserted in the center comes out clean.
8. Let cool, then invert onto a serving platter.

Fast: Can prepare up to 1 day in advance and refrigerate, or freeze for up to 3 months. Thaw in the refrigerator for 1 day or at room temperature for about 4 hours.

Flashy: To serve, place some brandied chocolate sauce on each dessert plate and top with a slice of the cake. For an extra special touch, top each slice of cake with a dollop of kirsch-flavored whipped cream (see Brandied Whipped Cream, page 247, and substitute kirsch).

Fabulous: Beyond a doubt!

Braised Lamb Dinner

This menu is stylishly simple and soul satisfying. It begins with a light and luscious seafood stuffed endive. The richness of the seafood filling is beautifully balanced by the refreshing astringency of the endive. This is followed by a wonderful winter salad combining the slightly bitter quality of spinach with the richness of sautéed mushrooms and the color of red cabbage. The entree is an Italian-style lamb stew, flavored with rosemary, pancetta, and leeks with a sauce enriched with egg yolks and flavored with lemon zest. The risotto provides a lovely complement and is a great way to savor every bit of the sauce. This dinner concludes with a moist, homey Apple-Bread Pudding with Brandy Sauce.

Slow simmered dishes with robust flavors evoke feelings of being in a charming European bistro. To capture this atmosphere, a rough textured cloth with over-size paisley napkins works well. Votive candles running down the center of the table help to create intimacy. Instead of a vases, old copper pots filled with unstructured bouquets or primrose plants, surrounded with whole, raw artichokes, heads of garlic, yellow onions, and whole loaves of French bread placed directly on the table. It is a fun look.

MENU

Seafood Stuffed Belgian Endive

Spinach Salad with Sautéed Mushrooms and Cabbage in Sherry Wine Vinaigrette with Garlic-Feta Herb Croutons

Sliced Baguettes and Sweet Butter

Braised Lamb with Pancetta and Leeks

Risotto with Baby Artichokes and Black Fungus

Apple-Bread Pudding with Brandy Sauce

FASTER & FLASHIER MENU

Seafood Stuffed Belgian Endive

Braised Lamb with Pancetta and Onions

Rice

Dessert (purchased)

WINES

Chardonnay or Brut Champagne

Merlot

Late harvest Chenin Blanc

Fast & Fabulous Timetable

Up to 6 Months in Advance and Frozen
Cheese mixture for Garlic-Feta Herb Croutons • Braised Lamb with Pancetta and Leeks through step 8 • Artichokes for risotto • Brandy Sauce

Up to 3 Months in Advance and Frozen
Feta-Herb Croutons

5 Days in Advance and Refrigerated
Sherry Wine Vinaigrette • Cheese mixture for Garlic-Feta Herb Croutons

3 Days in Advance and Refrigerated
Artichokes for risotto • Brandy Sauce

2 Days in Advance and Refrigerated
Braised Lamb with Pancetta and Leeks through step 8 • Thaw frozen prepared-ahead foods

1 Day in Advance and Refrigerated
Seafood Stuffed Belgian Endive filling • Prepare mushroom-cabbage mixture for spinach salad • Garlic-Feta Herb Croutons • Partially bake bread pudding • Set table

Party Day!
Assemble stuffed endive • Finish salad, lamb, and bread pudding • Warm bread • Risotto with Baby Artichokes • Heat Brandy Sauce

SEAFOOD STUFFED BELGIAN ENDIVE

2 ounces cooked bay shrimp

3 ounces cooked crabmeat

1 cup mayonnaise,
homemade or purchased

1/2 cup freshly grated
Parmesan cheese

1/3 cup grated Gruyère
cheese

1/3 cup minced green onions

1 teaspoon Worcestershire
sauce or to taste

1 teaspoon Dijon mustard

1/3 cup minced fresh parsley

2 to 4 tablespoons minced
fresh dill

1/2 cup minced jicama

2 tablespoons capers, rinsed
and drained

Salt and freshly ground white
pepper to taste

Hot pepper sauce to taste

Belgian endive, separated
into leaves (about 4
heads)

Sprigs fresh dill and pansies
for garnish

Yield: about 16 stuffed endive

World class! This hors d'oeuvre is equally well suited to casual or elegant events.

1. Combine all the ingredients, except the endive and garnishes, in a large bowl. Taste and adjust the seasonings.
2. Fill each endive.

Fast: Can prepare filling up to 1 day in advance and refrigerate or fill endive up to 2 hours in advance and refrigerate.

Flashy: Serve on a large platter with sprigs of dill and a pansy or two in the center.

Fabulous: As a cold filling for cooked pasta shells, avocado halves, or cherry tomatoes. As a hot filling in mushroom caps, tartlet shells, omelettes, or crêpes.

Further: Toss leftover filling into hot pasta or a salad.

SPINACH SALAD WITH SAUTÉED MUSHROOMS AND CABBAGE

Herbed Walnut Vinaigrette
  (see page 135)
3 shallots, minced
1/2 cup minced fresh parsley
2 cloves garlic, minced
1 pound domestic mushrooms
  or combination of different
  kinds fresh or rehydrated
  dried mushrooms (shiitake,
  straw, porcini, etc.)
Salt and freshly ground white
  pepper to taste
1 cup shredded finely red
  cabbage
3 bunches spinach, stemmed
  and torn into bite-size
  pieces
Garlic-Feta Croutons (recipe
  follows)

1. Add about 1/4 cup of the vinaigrette to a large skillet and place over high heat.
2. Add the shallots, parsley, garlic, and mushrooms, season with salt and pepper, and sauté over medium-high heat until the mushrooms are just barely tender but still slightly firm, about 5 to 10 minutes.
3. Stir in the cabbage and sauté until tender, about 5 to 10 minutes. Add more vinaigrette if needed.
4. Meanwhile, toss the spinach in a large salad bowl with the desired amount of vinaigrette and place on salad plates.
5. Place some of the mushroom-cabbage mixture in the center of each salad and flank with a crouton on each side.

Fast: Can prepare mushroom-cabbage mixture up to 1 day in advance and refrigerate. Bring to room temperature and reheat in the microwave or sauté before serving.

Fabulous: With radicchio instead of cabbage. With cold or hot seafood, poultry, or pork added to create an entree salad.

GARLIC-FETA HERB CROUTONS

1/2 cup feta cheese

1/4 cup freshly grated
  Parmesan cheese

2 shallots, minced

2 cloves garlic, minced

3/4 teaspoon mixed minced
  fresh herbs (rosemary,
  thyme, dill, basil, and/or
  cilantro)

1/4 cup minced fresh parsley

1 cup extra virgin olive oil

Salt and freshly ground white
  pepper to taste

1 baguette, cut into 1/4-inch
  thick slices

These also make a wonderful hors d'oeuvre.

1. Combine all the ingredients, except the baguette, in a food processor fitted with a metal blade or combine in a bowl with a wooden spoon. Taste and adjust the seasonings.

2. Spread the baguette slices with the olive oil mixture, then place on an ungreased cookie sheet and bake in a preheated 350°F oven until crisp, about 10 to 15 minutes.

Fast: Can prepare up to 1 day in advance and store in an airtight container, or freeze in plastic bag(s) for up to 3 months. Thaw at room temperature for about 2 hours. Reheat in a preheated 350°F oven, or serve at room temperature. Can prepare cheese mixture up to 5 days in advance and refrigerate, or freeze for up to 6 months. Thaw in the refrigerator for 2 days or at room temperature for about 8 hours.

Fabulous: With bleu cheese or chèvre instead of feta.

BRAISED LAMB WITH PANCETTA AND LEEKS

4 to 5 leeks, trimmed and
    washed well
5 tablespoons olive oil
4 ounces pancetta, sliced
    and chopped
3 to 6 cloves garlic, minced
5 tablespoons all-purpose
    flour
3 pounds boneless lamb,
    from the leg, cut into
    1/2-inch pieces
Salt and freshly ground white
    pepper to taste
3/4 cup cream sherry
3 1/2 cups beef broth,
    homemade or canned
Grated zest of 2 lemons
1/2 cup minced fresh parsley
1 bay leaf
1 teaspoon dried rosemary
1/2 teaspoon dried
    marjoram
2 large egg yolks
1 tablespoon Dijon mustard
3 tablespoons fresh lemon
    juice
Grated lemon zest and
    minced fresh parsley for
    garnish

A wonderful Italian-style stew that makes use of Chinese cooking techniques.

1. Cut away any tough portion of the leeks, then slice the white part into thin rings. Save the greens for another use.
2. Add 2 tablespoons of the olive oil to a large skillet over low to medium-low heat and sauté the pancetta until browned. Remove with a slotted spoon and reserve.
3. Add the leeks and garlic to the skillet and sauté over low to medium-low heat until tender. Add more olive oil if needed.
4. Meanwhile, put the flour in a plastic bag. Add the lamb and shake to coat.
5. Heat the remaining olive oil in a wok or large skillet over medium to medium-high and brown the lamb. Season with salt and pepper while cooking, and stir rapidly.
6. Remove the browned lamb, then pour off and discard any fat and add the sherry. Raise the heat to high and deglaze the pan, stirring with a wooden spoon to loosen any clinging brown bits. Cook until the wine is almost evaporated.
7. Stir in the broth, zest, parsley, bay leaf, rosemary, marjoram, leeks, and pancetta. Bring to a boil, cover, and simmer over low heat for about 10 minutes or until the flavors develop. Add more broth and/or wine if needed.
8. Return the lamb to the sauce.
9. Combine the yolks, mustard, and lemon juice in a food processor fitted with a metal blade or whisk together in a small bowl.
10. Remove the wok from the burner and add about 1/4 cup of the sauce to the yolk mixture through the feed tube, while the machine is running, or whisk into the bowl.
11. Slowly stir the yolk mixture back into the lamb. Return to the burner and cook over low heat, stirring for a few minutes until the sauce thickens. *Do not boil* or the yolks will curdle. Taste and adjust the seasonings.

Fast: Can prepare through step 8 (undercook the lamb), up to 2 days in advance and refrigerate, or freeze for up to 6 months. Thaw in the refrigerator for 2 days or at room temperature for about 8 hours. Bring to room temperature before finishing.

Flashy: Garnish with grated lemon zest and minced parsley.

Fabulous: Seasoned with capers. With veal, turkey, chicken, pork, or beef instead of the lamb. With sliced mushrooms, carrots, zucchini, and/or eggplant added.

RISOTTO WITH BABY ARTICHOKES AND BLACK FUNGUS

4 tablespoons (1/2 stick) unsalted butter

4 shallots, minced

4 to 6 pieces black fungus, rehydrated and cut into thin strips

2 1/2 cups uncooked arborio or short grain rice

One 10-ounce package frozen baby artichokes, thawed and at room temperature, or fresh (see below for preparation instructions)

1/2 cup dry or medium dry sherry

5 cups chicken broth, homemade or canned

Salt and freshly ground white pepper to taste

Freshly grated Parmesan cheese to taste

Freshly grated nutmeg to taste

Here we use a classic Italian method for preparing rice with an interesting Chinese ingredient, black fungus. Risotto can best be described as a creamy pilaf.

1. Melt the butter in a large, heavy saucepan over low to medium-low heat and sauté the shallots and black fungus until the shallots are tender.
2. Add the rice and stir until it turns milky white and is coated with the butter.
3. Stir in the artichokes and sherry, and cook until the rice absorbs all the liquid.
4. Stir in a third of the broth and simmer over medium heat until it is absorbed, about 3 to 4 minutes. Repeat this twice, cooking each time until the liquid is almost completely absorbed.
5. Taste and add more liquid if the rice is not tender enough; it should be al dente. This entire process will take about 20 minutes.
6. Stir in the salt, pepper, Parmesan, and nutmeg, taste, and adjust.

Fast: Can prepare through step 3 up to 6 hours in advance and hold at room temperature.

Fabulous: With peas or almost any vegetable instead of baby artichokes.

Further: Add leftovers to soups or stews, or make into patties and fry in olive oil.

TO PREPARE BABY ARTICHOKES:
1. Cut off the tips and stem. Immediately rub the cut portion with half of a lemon to prevent discoloring.
2. Pull off and discard the tough outer leaves. Place in a bowl of acidulated water while preparing the remaining artichokes.
3. Bring a nonaluminum pot of salted water to a boil. Add a generous splash of your favorite vinegar.
4. Drain the artichokes and place in the boiling water until just tender, about 10 minutes.

5. Drain the artichokes and refresh under cold running water to stop the cooking process. They are now ready to be used in the risotto, eaten as is, or used in any other dish.

Fast: Can prepare up to 3 days in advance and refrigerate, or freeze for up to 6 months. Thaw in the refrigerator for 2 days or at room temperature for about 4 hours.

APPLE-BREAD PUDDING WITH BRANDY SAUCE

3 large eggs
1/2 cup packed light or dark brown sugar, plus extra
1 cup sour cream
2 cups milk or buttermilk
1/4 cup brandy
Ground cinnamon and freshly grated nutmeg to taste
2 teaspoons vanilla extract
3 to 4 cups crustless sourdough, egg, or white bread cubes
2 large pippin or Granny Smith apples, cored, peeled, thinly sliced, and squirted with lemon juice
1/2 cup chopped dried apricots
1/2 cup walnuts, toasted (see page 29) and chopped
3 tablespoons unsalted butter, cut into small pieces
Brandy Sauce (recipe follows)

A satisfying, homey dessert that is making a come-back after being forgotten for a long time.

1. Preheat the oven to 350°F.
2. Combine the eggs, sugar, sour cream, milk, brandy, cinnamon, nutmeg, and vanilla in a large bowl.
3. Add the bread cubes, apples, apricots, and walnuts. Let sit for about 15 minutes.
4. Butter a 6- or 8-cup casserole, baking dish, or soufflé dish.
5. Pour the mixture into the buttered casserole and top with the cut-up butter and extra brown sugar if desired.
6. Place the pudding in a larger pan with hot water reaching halfway up the sides of the casserole. Bake until a tester inserted into the middle comes out clean, about 1 hour.

Fast: Can assemble up to 1 day in advance and refrigerate. Bring to room temperature and bake before serving, or bake for half the time up to 1 day in advance and refrigerate. Bring to room temperature and finish baking before serving.

Flashy: Serve Brandy Sauce over the pudding and an optional scoop of vanilla ice cream or a dollop of whipped cream.

Fabulous: With almonds or pecans instead of walnuts, dates instead of dried apricots, or pears instead of apples.

BRANDY SAUCE

1 cup sugar
1/2 pound (2 sticks)
  unsalted butter, cut up
1/2 to 3/4 cup brandy
2 large eggs
Freshly grated nutmeg and
  ground cinnamon to taste

Yield: about 3 cups

1. Dissolve the sugar in a large, heavy saucepan over medium-low heat. Do not stir; rather, hold the pan by the handle and swirl throughout the process. Raise the heat to medium and cook until the sugar turns golden brown, about 3 to 5 minutes.
2. Remove the pan from the heat and stir in the butter, then the brandy.
3. Meanwhile, in a food processor fitted with a metal blade process the eggs until light and lemon-colored, or beat with a mixer in a large bowl.
4. Slowly add the sugar mixture through the feed tube while the machine is running, or stir into the bowl.
5. Return the mixture to the pan and stir for several minutes over low heat. Season with the nutmeg and cinnamon.

Fast: Can prepare up to 3 days in advance and refrigerate, or freeze for up to 6 months. Thaw in the refrigerator for 2 days or at room temperature for about 4–8 hours. Reheat over barely simmering water in a double boiler, stirring until warm.

Flashy: Over anything from poundcake to bananas.

Fabulous: With Scotch, bourbon, or any liqueur instead of the brandy.

Italian Sausage and Mushroom Lasagna Dinner

Is there anything more delicious on a cold winter night than a lasagna dinner? It seems a just reward for enduring the cold weather. This menu is a delight, both to prepare and serve. Everything is done in advance, except for tossing the salad and heating the lasagna and bread. Because of this, it is a great choice for a dinner following an event, such as skiing, the movies, a meeting, or a football game. Conversely, it is also a lifesaver for those times when you need a menu to proceed a major event, such as Christmas Eve. Situations of this nature place the highest demand on advanced and easy preparation. Also, keep this menu in mind for those times when you need to serve large groups.

Our party starts out with an interesting selection of three hors d'oeuvres. Each is delicious and quick to prepare. You need not do all three, but it does add to the spirit of the evening. The salad that follows is composed of beautiful flavors and colors. As for the lasagna, it is fabulous, and anything but typical. So often, this dish is handled poorly and turns out to be a heavy, nondescript mess. The mushrooms and Italian sausages, combined with the ricotta and spinach, come together to create a filling with intriguingly rich flavors and a light texture. The menu concludes with fruit and biscotti. The biscotti are so good that they have become a real addiction for my husband and myself. Hopefully, you will not also succumb!

As you can see, this menu is big and generous in spirit. The tablescape should also reflect this exuberance. A table dressed in a blue-and-white checked cloth works wonderfully. For napkins, red and white handkerchiefs tied with white yarn are fun. Wine glasses should not be delicate. You could use heavy French jelly-jar glasses or Spanish goblets. Use squatty French canning jars, instead of vases, filled with white daisys and cuttings of rosemary. In the very center of the table, create an arrangement in a low basket using breadsticks, baguettes, and rolls. You might even want to spray them with glossy white paint. Intersperse white pillar candles, in terra-cotta saucers, down the table. This is a fresh and fun look of contemporary country.

MENU

Eggplant Caviar and Lentil Hummus with Pita Chips

Cold Scallops Vinaigrette

Romaine and Radicchio Salad

Garlic-Herb Bread (see page 180)

Italian Sausage and Mushroom Lasagna

Chocolate Biscotti and Fresh Fruit

FASTER & FLASHIER MENU

Lentil Hummus with Crackers

Tossed Salad with Oranges and Olives

Italian Sausage and Mushroom Lasagna

Garlic-Herb Bread

Biscotti (purchased) and Fresh Fruit

WINES

Semillon or Sauvignon Blanc

Zinfandel

Port

Fast & Fabulous Timetable

Up to 6 Months in Advance and Frozen
Filling and sauces for lasagna • Chocolate Biscotti

Up to 3 Months in Advance and Frozen
Eggplant Caviar • Pita Chips • Lentil Hummus • Assembled lasagna

1 Week in Advance and Refrigerated
Pita Chips • Balsamic Vinaigrette

5 Days in Advance and Refrigerated
Eggplant Caviar • Chocolate Biscotti

4 Days in Advance and Refrigerated
Sauces for lasagna

3 Days in Advance and Refrigerated
Filling for lasagna

2 Days in Advance and Refrigerated
Cold Scallops Vinaigrette • Lentil Hummus • Thaw frozen prepared-ahead foods

1 Day in Advance and Refrigerated
Prep salad ingredients • Assemble lasagna • Set table

Party Day!
Toss salad • Heat lasagna and bread

EGGPLANT CAVIAR

2 large eggplants

4 red bell peppers, roasted
(see page 28), seeded,
peeled, and minced

1 cup minced fresh parsley

2 cloves garlic or to taste,
minced

1/4 cup pine nuts, toasted
(see page 29)

2 tablespoons olive oil or to
taste

1/2 cup crumbled feta
cheese

1/2 cup calamata olives,
pitted and chopped

Salt and freshly ground black
pepper to taste

Fresh lemon juice to taste

Yield: about 4 cups

My version of peasant caviar.

1. Place the eggplant on an ungreased cookie sheet and pierce with a fork in several places to allow steam to escape. Bake in a preheated 400°F oven until tender, about 40 minutes. Remove and set aside until cool enough to handle.
2. Scoop out the meat and combine with the remaining ingredients in a food processor fitted with a metal blade with several quick on-and-off motions so as not to destroy textures, or in a blender. Taste and adjust the seasonings.

Fast: Can prepare up to 5 days in advance and refrigerate, or freeze up to 3 months. Thaw in the refrigerator for 2 days or at room temperature for about 8 hours.

Flashy: With assorted crackers, melbas, or Pita Chips (see page 277).

Fabulous: Seasoned with minced sun-dried tomatoes, oregano, or fresh basil and served as a cold sauce with roast lamb.

LENTIL HUMMUS

Minced fresh mint leaves to
taste

2 to 4 cloves garlic, minced

1 cup dried lentils, rinsed
well in cold water

1/2 cup olive oil or to taste

1/4 cup tahini or to taste

Fresh lime juice to taste

Salt and hot pepper sauce to
taste

Sprigs fresh mint for garnish

An interesting alternative to the traditional garbanzo beans.

1. In 2-quart saucepan, half full of water, bring the mint and garlic to
    a boil over high heat. Add the lentils and cook until very soft, about
    10 to 15 minutes for pink lentils, 30 to 40 for regular.
2. Remove the lentils, mint, and garlic with a strainer. Transfer to a
    food processor fitted with a metal blade or blender and puree.
    Process in some of the cooking liquid to help thin the mixture.
3. Process in the olive oil and tahini, and season with lime juice, salt,
    and hot pepper sauce.

Fast: Can prepare up to 2 days in advance and refrigerate, or freeze for
up to 3 months. Thaw in the refrigerator for 2 days or at room temperature for about 8 hours.

Flashy: Garnish with sprigs of mint and serve with Pita Chips (recipe
follows) or crackers.

Fabulous: With minced fresh oregano and cilantro added. Without the
tahini.

PITA CHIPS

1 package pita bread, pulled
into halves

1 cup olive oil

OPTIONAL SEASONINGS
Minced garlic
Dried oregano
Minced fresh dill
Salt
Freshly grated Parmesan
cheese

Yield: about 96

1. Preheat the oven to 350°F.
2. Combine the olive oil if you wish with the garlic and/or herb(s) of
    choice in a food processor fitted with a metal blade or whisk to-
    gether in a large bowl.
3. Brush each half with the oil, then stack the pita bread and cut it
    into triangles.
4. Place on an ungreased cookie sheet and sprinkle with salt, extra
    oregano, dill, and/or Parmesan cheese, if desired.
5. Bake for 10 to 20 minutes, or until crisp.

Fast: Can prepare up to 1 week in advance and store in airtight jar(s)
or plastic bags, or freeze for up to 3 months. Thaw at room temperature
for at least 1 hour.

COLD SCALLOPS VINAIGRETTE

1 clove garlic, minced, or to
taste
2 tablespoons minced fresh
parsley
3 to 6 green onions, cut into
1/2-inch lengths
1/2 cup minced sun-dried
tomatoes
2 tablespoons capers, rinsed
and drained
2 tablespoons sesame oil
1 cup olive oil
Salt and freshly ground white
pepper to taste
Fresh lime juice to taste
1 pound baby scallops,
rinsed and soaked in milk
in refrigerator for at least
1 hour to remove
bitterness
1 pound chèvre or
mozzarella cheese, cubed
(optional)
Kale or cabbage leaves for
garnishing

Yield: 4 to 8 servings

1. Bring all the ingredients, except the scallops and cheese, to a boil in a noncorrosive saucepan.
2. Add the scallops and cook until just opaque, about 5 minutes. Pour the entire contents into a bowl and cool to room temperature.
3. Add the cheese and coat well with the marinade.
4. Cover the bowl and chill for 12 hours, or overnight, before serving.

Fast: Can prepare up to 2 days in advance and refrigerate.

Flashy: Served in a bowl lined with kale or cabbage leaves, with thinly sliced baguettes and/or toothpicks.

Fabulous: With shrimp or monkfish, shark, or swordfish cut into bite-size pieces, instead of, or in addition to, the scallops. With feta cheese instead of the chèvre.

ROMAINE AND RADICCHIO SALAD

2 heads romaine lettuce, torn
    into bite-size pieces
1 head radicchio leaves,
    sliced or torn into bite-size
    pieces
2 oranges, peeled, membrane
    removed, and thinly sliced
1/4 cup pine nuts, toasted
    (see page 29), or to taste
1/2 cup pitted calamata
    olives
Balsamic Vinaigrette (recipe
    follows)
Salt and freshly ground black
    pepper to taste

1. Combine the greens, oranges, pine nuts, and olives in a large salad bowl.
2. Toss in the desired amount of dressing. Taste and season with salt and pepper.

Fast: Can prep ingredients up to 1 day in advance and refrigerate, storing the oranges and olives separately.

Fabulous: With spinach instead of romaine.

BALSAMIC VINAIGRETTE

2 to 4 cloves garlic
2 to 4 teaspoons Dijon
    mustard
2/3 cup balsamic vinegar
1/4 cup apple cider vinegar
2 cups olive oil
1 teaspoon salt or to taste
Freshly ground white and
    black pepper to taste

Yield: about 3 cups

1. Combine all the ingredients in a food processor fitted with a metal blade or in a blender.
2. Taste and adjust the seasonings.

Fast: Can prepare up to 1 week in advance and refrigerate.

Flashy: On anything!

Fabulous: With about 2 tablespoons minced fresh ginger and/or green onions.

ITALIAN SAUSAGE AND MUSHROOM LASAGNA

PASTA

6 to 8 quarts water

2 tablespoons olive oil

1 tablespoon salt

3/4 to 1 pound lasagna
noodles

FILLING

1 pound Italian sausages,
casings removed

1/4 cup olive oil

1 to 2 large yellow and/or
white onions, chopped

6 to 8 cloves garlic, minced

2 pounds domestic
mushrooms (or use a
combination of domestic,
shiitake, oyster, and/or
porcini mushrooms, fresh,
or dried and rehydrated),
sliced

Two 10-ounce packages
frozen spinach or chard,
thawed and squeezed to
remove moisture

One 15-ounce container
ricotta cheese

1 cup grated mozzarella
cheese

Two 6-ounce jars marinated
artichoke hearts, drained

1 cup freshly grated
Parmesan cheese

1 bunch fresh parsley,
minced

Salt and freshly ground white
pepper to taste

Yield: 8 to 16 servings

This is the kind of dish that winter dreams are made of.

I have deliberately made this recipe very generous, so it will look inviting when served. Leftovers can be frozen.

1. Bring the water, oil, and salt to a boil in a large pot, then add the pasta and cook according to the package directions, until al dente.
2. Remove the pasta and rinse under cold water. Spread out on clean kitchen towels. Do not stack; the pasta will stick together.
3. For the filling, brown the sausage meat over medium-high to high heat in a heavy cast-iron skillet, breaking it up with a wooden spoon as it cooks. Remove from the skillet, using a slotted spoon, and place on a plate covered with paper towels to remove the extra fat. Set aside.
4. Heat the olive oil in a large skillet over medium-low heat and sauté the onion and garlic until tender.
5. Stir the mushrooms into the onions and cook until all the moisture from the mushrooms cooks away.
6. Meanwhile, combine the cooked sausage, spinach, ricotta, mozzarella, artichoke hearts, Parmesan, and parsley in a food processor fitted with a metal blade with several quick on-and-off motions so as not to destroy the texture, or mix together in a bowl with a wooden spoon. Taste and season with salt, pepper, and nutmeg.
7. For the marinara, heat enough olive oil to cover the bottom of a large, heavy saucepan over medium-low heat. Add the onions, garlic, and parsley and sauté until tender.
8. Stir in the tomatoes, tomato paste, bay leaf, and fennel seeds. Bring to a boil.
9. Reduce the heat to low, season with salt, pepper, and nutmeg, and simmer until the flavors are pleasing, about 15 minutes.
10. For the white wine sauce, melt the butter in a large, heavy saucepan over medium-low heat. Add the shallots and sauté until tender; do not brown.
11. Whisk in the flour and cook over low heat for several minutes.
12. Gradually whisk in the broth, vermouth, and sherry. While continuously whisking, bring to a boil over medium-high to high heat and cook until reduced to a thick sauce, about 10 minutes.

Freshly grated nutmeg to taste

Extra grated Parmesan and
  mozzarella cheese for
  garnish

Extra minced fresh parsley
  for garnish

MARINARA

Olive oil

2 onions, chopped

2 to 6 cloves garlic, minced

1 bunch fresh parsley,
  stemmed and chopped

2 pounds canned
  pear-shaped tomatoes
  chopped

2 tablespoons tomato paste

1 bay leaf

2 teaspoons fennel seeds or
  to taste

Salt and freshly ground white
  pepper to taste

Freshly grated nutmeg to
  taste

WHITE WINE SAUCE

4 tablespoons (1/2 stick)
  unsalted butter

2 to 4 shallots, minced

6 tablespoons all-purpose
  flour

2 cups chicken broth,
  homemade or canned

1 cup dry vermouth

1/4 cup sherry

1 cup heavy cream

Salt and freshly ground white
  pepper to taste

Freshly grated nutmeg to
  taste

13. Whisk in the cream, season with salt, pepper, and nutmeg, and cook for several minutes, continuing to whisk, until the flavors are pleasing. Cool the sauce before using.

14. To assemble, use two 12×9×3-inch baking dishes, one 14×10×3-inch baking dish, or eight individual ovenproof dishes.

15. Place a thin layer of marinara sauce in the bottom of the dish.

16. Layer in the pasta, then add a layer of filling.

17. Top with a layer of both sauces. Repeat until the baking dish is filled. Top with extra grated cheese.

18. Bake in a preheated 350°F oven for 20 to 30 minutes, until hot and bubbly.

Fast: Can assemble up to 1 day in advance and refrigerate or freeze for up to 3 months. Can prepare sauces up to 4 days in advance and refrigerate, or freeze for up to 6 months. Can prepare filling up to 3 days in advance and refrigerate, or freeze for up to 6 months. In each case, thaw in the refrigerator for 3 days.

Flashy: Serve with extra freshly grated Parmesan cheese and a sprinkling of minced fresh parsley.

Fabulous: With ground pork or veal instead of Italian sausages. Without any meat, using extra mushrooms, spinach, and/or cooked eggplant. With feta cheese instead of Parmesan. With cooked seafood instead of sausage.

CHOCOLATE BISCOTTI

4 cups all-purpose flour

3/4 cup packed light or dark
  brown sugar

1 to 2 teaspoons instant
  espresso powder or finely
  ground espresso beans

1/2 teaspoon salt

Freshly grated nutmeg to
  taste

1/4 pound (1 stick) unsalted
  butter, melted

3/4 cup coffee-flavored
  liqueur

1/2 cup buttermilk

1 teaspoon vanilla extract

12 ounces semisweet
  chocolate chips

Grated zest of 2 to 3
  oranges

1 1/2 cups sliced almonds,
  toasted (see page 29)

Yield: about 7 dozen

This is not just another cute little cookie. It is totally adult, not very pretty, but definitely addictive! Dip it in coffee, espresso, or wine, and enjoy!

1. Preheat the oven to 350°F.
2. Combine the flour with the sugar, espresso powder, salt, and nutmeg in a food processor fitted with a metal blade, or a large bowl.
3. Add the butter, liqueur, buttermilk, vanilla, and chocolate. Process or combine until the dough is a smooth consistency and begins to form a ball. Process or stir in more buttermilk if the dough is very dry.
4. Process or stir in the zest and 1 cup of the almonds.
5. Spread the remaining almonds, rather than flour, on the work surface. Place the dough on top and coat with the almonds, as you form it into two cylinders about 3 inches in diameter.
6. Place the dough on an oiled cookie sheet and bake until a tester inserted into the middle comes out clean, about 35 to 45 minutes.
7. Remove from the oven and let cool slightly. Cut diagonally into slices about 1/4 to 1/2 inch thick. Cut each slice in half lengthwise.
8. Reduce the oven temperature to 300°F, return the slices to the baking sheet, and place in the oven. Bake until crisp, about 15 to 20 minutes. Turn the oven off and let sit with the door ajar for another 10 minutes.

Fast: Can prepare up to 5 days in advance and store in an airtight jar(s) or plastic bag(s) or freeze for up to 6 months. Thaw at room temperature for at least 1 hour.

Flashy: Serve with and dunk in coffee, espresso, and/or wine.

INDEX